I0880414

Love in a Cauldron of Misery

Love in a Cauldron of Misery

Perspectives on Christian Prison Ministry

KIRK BLACKARD

WIPF & STOCK · Eugene, Oregon

LOVE IN A CAULDRON OF MISERY
Perspectives on Christian Prison Ministry

Copyright © 2012 Kirk Blackard. All rights reserved. Except for brief quotations in critical publications or reviews, no part of this book may be reproduced in any manner without prior written permission from the publisher. Write: Permissions, Wipf and Stock Publishers, 199 W. 8th Ave., Suite 3, Eugene, OR 97401.

Wipf & Stock
An Imprint of Wipf and Stock Publishers
199 W. 8th Ave., Suite 3
Eugene, OR 97401
www.wipfandstock.com

ISBN 13: 978-1-62032-272-7

Manufactured in the U.S.A.
Scripture taken from the HOLY BIBLE, NEW INTERNATIONAL VERSION ®. Copyright © 1973, 1978, 1984 by International Bible Society. Used by permission of Zondervan. All rights reserved.

To Marcia, my wonderful wife,
who has taught me so much about loving the least of these.

Contents

Acknowledgments

I am deeply grateful to all those who have contributed to this book. Special thanks go to all who willingly gave of their time to visit or correspond with me and share their views on important topics. Most were more than willing to share their identity, but a few were reluctant to do so. Therefore, I have elected not to mention any names of contributors here, although a number are mentioned in the body of the book. All of you know who you are. I greatly appreciate your assistance.

Many inmates or former inmates were among those who assisted me. All were incredibly courteous, helpful, and committed to this effort as one small bit of restitution for what they have done. Thanks to each of you. I hope you will demonstrate the same constructive and helpful attributes in the future that you showed me during this work.

Thanks also to all the many others who assisted me—prison officials, restorative justice and prison ministry practitioners and volunteers, victims of crime, Bible scholars, and others with an interest and expertise in prison ministry. Your input was invaluable.

John Sage, David Balkum, John and Gay Vanosdall, and Sr. Kathie Uhler each read a copy of the manuscript and provided appropriate and much-needed criticism. Thanks.

And finally, thanks to Marcia, Drew, Chris, and Lisa for their continuing support.

Introduction

EVERY PRISON IS A cauldron of misery. Each is miserable in its own way.

Over 2.3 million human beings are locked in jails or prisons at any one time in the United States, and roughly 13.5 million individuals will be incarcerated over the course of a year. Some have committed unconscionable acts of violence and are true threats to society: the drug-crazed burglar who beat a 7-11 clerk senseless for ten dollars, the cold-blooded murderer, the rapist, the gang don. Others are caged because of their drug addiction or their small-time property crime or their mental illness. Prisons house both the worst of the worst and the best of the worst.

Prisons, as well, come in many colors. We read of prison violence and sexual abuse by predatory inmates or prison employees; of pepper spray and mace being used to subdue difficult individuals in spite of the fact that the gas might choke, sicken, or burn inmates in surrounding areas; of vicious attack dogs used to control disturbances; of restraining devices being used on the mentally ill; of total isolation in tiny, solitary cages for twenty-three hours each day; of the essential unfairness and inhumanity of death row.

But there is another perspective. The severe abuses of times past are no longer tolerated. Most correctional professionals are honorable and caring people just trying to do the right thing in very difficult jobs. Many prisons are relatively safe, and some minimum-security, treatment type facilities seem almost pleasant. Rehabilitation efforts help prepare inmates to return to society as law-abiding, productive citizens.

But a skunk of any color still stinks. Think about the day-to-day, common-place misery. Having to deal every waking hour of every day with the guilt, sorrow, and regret of a life gone so badly awry. Dealing with a continuing stream of "what ifs." And doing so while locked up on the Texas Gulf Coast in August without air conditioning, in a sweltering, poorly ventilated cell or dormitory where the air never stirs and the temperature exceeds one hundred degrees, and you finally drop off to sleep each night in a pool of sweat. The tasteless monotony of badly prepared potatoes, beans, corn, and ground meat served day after day on a cardboard or plastic tray and eaten with a plastic spork, and sometimes only peanut butter and jelly on stale rye bread for days on end during lockdowns. The fear of intimidation and possible assault. Having to base your life on falsehood and bluff rather than truth. The depths of loneliness with absolutely no privacy. Hoping against hope for a letter or a visit from a loved one and being disappointed when they don't come through. Having a visit from your children and not being able to show them where you live or adequately explain why you're locked up and can't go home with them. Having a visit from your spouse and returning to your cell frustrated with unmet longings or fears about what's happening on the outside. Having your life controlled by prying correctional officers. The indignity of strip searches or even body cavity searches. The destroyed hope of rejected parole applications. The lack of freedom and hope in a country based on individual freedom and opportunity.

Regardless of how you paint the picture, prisons are cauldrons of misery that warehouse human beings—the really bad and the not-so-bad—all of whom God loves. And Christians are called to respond to all this with radical love. This book will reflect on prisons, prisoners, and biblical principles that guide Christians in demonstrating that love.

My interest in prison ministry began about twelve years ago when I had a chance encounter with John Sage. We had become friends when he was my son's soccer coach. After the kids parted we did also, and we hadn't seen one another for about five years. John, a former Louisiana State University all-American football player and successful businessman, mentioned that he had recently founded and was executive director of a prison ministry called Bridges To Life. He explained that he had started the organization after the brutal murder of his sister, Marilyn, a few years earlier. Two nineteen-year-olds had been cruising a Houston neighborhood looking to steal a car. They spotted Marilyn as she was going back and forth moving clothes from the trunk of her car into her apartment. They crept silently into her home, hid in wait, and attacked her as she returned for another load of clothes. The two stabbed her with at least three different knives, bludgeoned her with a statue from a nearby sofa table, and suffocated her with a plastic bag while she begged for her life.

Marilyn's murderers were arrested within forty-eight hours, convicted, and assessed the death penalty. But John didn't feel that anything had been resolved. He became a prisoner of his own rage and misery and entered into a period of severe depression. John went to a therapist and started taking medication. Most importantly, he threw himself into his spiritual life as he had never done before. After John's depression lifted, he committed to turn his life into a tribute to Marilyn by working to reduce crime and prevent similar tragedies from happening to others. He concluded, perhaps paradoxically, that the best place to do this was in prison. He understood that 67 percent of all inmates who were being discharged from the nation's prisons were arrested again within three years of their release and all too frequently returned to prison. Thus, because of the high rate of recidivism, he could most effectively prevent future crime by influencing the behavior of currently incarcerated people. This logic gave birth to Bridges To Life. John explained that the organization was a faith-based, restorative justice ministry that aimed to help victims of crime deal with their pain and suffering and reduce recidivism among discharged offenders.

This chance discussion piqued my interest. Twelve years later I have volunteered in dozens of prisons, worked with hundreds of incarcerated people, and written *Restoring Peace: Using Lessons from Prison to Mend Broken Relationships*, which has become the centerpiece of the Bridges To Life curriculum.

I am convinced that most well-meaning Christian people are like I was when I began this journey. I had not the foggiest notion of what prison and prisoners were really like. Somewhere, in the deep recesses of my mind, I had this idea that God expected me to love the least of these brothers and sisters and visit them in prison. But I knew nothing of restorative justice or the practical or theological basis of Christian prison ministry.

I've learned a great deal. More importantly, for this book I have obtained direct input from a large number of people who are directly involved in the criminal justice process: inmates in prison, offenders who have been released, victims of crime and their families, prison officials, parole officers, criminal justice professors, theologians, volunteers, and others who have information and views to share. The result is *Love in a Cauldron of Misery: Perspectives on Christian Prison Ministry,* which addresses my initial ignorance and, I suspect, that of many others.

~

Let me be clear about where I stand on matters of prisons and prisoners. I do not believe that prisons as such are unacceptable and all bad. Some people are a threat to civil society and have to be removed. In my work with Bridges To Life I have had the privilege of getting to know a number of victims of very serious crimes: a single mother whose young daughter was stalked and brutally murdered, parents whose four children were murdered by a drunk in a pickup on a lonely country road, a woman who grew up being raped by her grandfather after her grandmother bathed her and "prepared" her for him, and many others. One cannot observe the overwhelming pain, suffering—and dignity—of such victims without, at some level, wanting to see the perpetrators drawn and quartered. While this may be a little extreme, murderers, rapists, pedophiles, serial drunk drivers, and others of that ilk have to be dealt with. I can think of no better way than removing them from society by placing them in prisons, often for a long time. Society requires nothing less.

I also believe that many people who are currently incarcerated should not be behind bars. They are in prison—sometimes for very long terms—for crimes such as minor drug offenses, relatively small property crimes, violation of technical parole provisions, and such. They are locked up for so long, often for so little, that their punishment far exceeds their crime. There are better ways of dealing with them, such as community supervision, drug courts, and short-term intermediate sanctions and treatment facilities

I have a tendency, and I suspect many others may as well, to think of prison ministry as serving those people I don't believe should be in prison. Forget those who deserve to be put away and help the best of the worst. Then I remember that the Bible I read doesn't make this distinction. It speaks of all nations, of the least of these brothers and sisters, and of loving my enemies. The Bible doesn't give me an option to minister just to those whose behavior has been less bad. All inmates are locked away in society's cauldrons of misery. They may be family members, friends, or strangers. Whichever the case, Christians are charged to follow the example of Jesus—to love them all and to minister to them.

Theologians, ethicists, and criminologists since antiquity have spilled enough ink to float a battleship considering questions of criminal justice: What is crime? What is a just response to crime? What is the role of punishment, retribution, and restitution? What is the role of prisons and how should they be run? What is the role of the church in secular criminal justice? And on and on. These and similar questions raise important issues. I believe that society, through its secular leaders, should develop a new theory of corrections and transform the system from top to bottom. The transformation would call on ethical principles derived from the intertwined sources of scripture, moral philosophy, tradition, and empirical data. It would ask society to move in the direction of biblical teaching—in particular the personal and relational values expressed in Jesus' call to forgiveness and love of enemies.

But transformation of the corrections system is not the purpose of this book. This book calls Christians to apply the biblical principles of radical love within the current system. Its focus is on restoring and redeeming prisoners, not on fixing the penal system. It aims to foster personal concepts like fairness, forgiveness, mercy, grace, service, and reconciliation rather than legislation or judicial activism. It does not address biblical teachings on crime, punishment, or justice. Rather, it addresses Jesus' teaching in Matthew 25 to visit those in prison, and to realize that "whatever you did for one of the least of these brothers of mine, you did for me."

Love in a Cauldron of Misery should help Christians fulfill this charge. Part 1 presents a historical and factual context. It briefly summarizes corrections history from colonial times, which emphasized humiliation and corporal punishment of offenders, through the Christian "reform" movements that led to today's prison system, to the explosive growth of the last half century. Part 1 then characterizes the current situation in the United States by providing an overview of who prisoners in general are, what prisons and the prison culture are like, and the aftermath and collateral effects of incarceration. This context should help readers understand that prisons, while probably necessary in our society, negatively affect a broad array of human beings who need the help of Christians—and whom Jesus has charged all Christians to help.

Part 2 discusses prison ministries as a subset of restorative justice. It acknowledges and draws from the many good and effective ministries existing today, while making suggestions for improving them and for doing day-to-day volunteer work. It presents four fundamental biblical principles for a ministry based on the example of Jesus—teaching the gospel by living it, fostering forgiveness, building shalom, and encouraging restoration. These closely related principles form a whole that will help volunteers effectively carry out the biblical charge to demonstrate radical love by ministering to those who are locked away from the society in which most of us live.

~

As noted above, much of what you will read in the following pages is information or opinions from people in a position to know. References are to real people—people I have personally interviewed, corresponded with, or visited in my own prison ministry work. If full names are used, it's the real person. If only first names are used, it's still a real person but the name and a few irrelevant details have been changed to protect the confidentiality of the person involved. And finally, while certain information or quotations may be attributed to a single individual, all references reflect a broad consensus based on my interviews, my personal observations, and additional research.

I have used research data from many sources and in various forms. The fact is, however, that crime statistics are notoriously unreliable. Critics note that many crimes are never reported, and the type and number of reported crimes are often inflated or deflated for political reasons. Dates of studies I have used may differ, and sometimes are older than one would like. Some studies are official and others are not. The standards under which various studies were done may vary. Thus, direct comparison of the details is often difficult. However, the data fairly show trends over time and paint a "30,000 foot landscape," which has been my aim. And I have checked, cross-checked, and verified against anecdotal evidence sufficient to say that the landscape I have pictured is an accurate one.

While essentially all of the hard data is national in scope, a disproportionate number of the interviews and anecdotal information sources are from Texas. There are two reasons for this. The first is that most of my experience has been in Texas and this is where I have developed the most contacts. And second, as Robert Perkinson noted in *Texas Tough*, "Just as New York dominates finance and California the film industry, Texas reigns supreme in the punishment business . . . To a large extent, Texas stands for the country as a whole."[1] Texas is more than a microcosm of the country's prisons. It's a major part of the national system, largely comprised of a wide array of state prisons. As a proud Texan, I take no pride in admitting that my state ranks first among states in size of the prison system, growth, for-profit imprisonment, supermax lockdown, and total number of adults under criminal justice supervision. But those are the facts, and I have used them to tell a broader story.

And finally, a disproportionate number of pronoun gender references are masculine, because a disproportionate number of prisoners are men.

In our prisons we see a human tragedy involving real people who are in many ways like us. In Scripture we see examples of Jesus' radical love for all people. An effective Christian prison ministry combines the two and demonstrates *Love in A Cauldron of Misery*. Enjoy.

1 Perkinson, *Texas Tough*, 45.

PART 1

Prisons

1

Historical Perspective

Crime and corrections in the United States have a long and often sordid history. Our system originated in England and was adapted to meet the myriad needs of the developing colonies and subsequent states. Ultimately, perhaps inevitably, the federal government provided an overlay that made it one system, albeit of many parts.

The role of prisons in the system evolved over time, largely as a result of the efforts of Christian reformers to make colonial practices more humane and effective. That is where our story starts.

COLONIAL AMERICA

Murder, robbery, rape, burglary, and other such crimes were relatively rare in the early colonial period—the 1600s—because of strict social control within the small towns and villages that dotted the Eastern Seaboard. Family, church, and friends were too close for comfort. They generally did whatever was necessary to encourage would-be bad guys to conform to existing cultural standards.

The criminal law that did exist was inherited, for the most part, from Europe, predominantly from the British common law with its roots in medieval Christian religious practices. In the colonies it was typically against the law to swear, be caught in a state of public drunkenness, miss church services, engage in inappropriate behavior on the Sabbath, or engage in unacceptable conduct between members of the opposite sex. Also outlawed were other sins of the flesh such as gambling, illegal liquor, adultery, abortion, prostitution, or other offenses that violated the strict moral code of a religious people. The most common crimes were fornication and drunkenness. For example, many women were pregnant on their wedding day in Essex County, Massachusetts, and authorities prosecuted about 60 percent of them for fornication—with little apparent effect.[1] A typical criminal was not an outcast from society but an ordinary person who had sinned—and gotten caught.

Most petty crimes were dealt with by some form of public punishment involving humiliation before family members, friends, or acquaintances that aimed to shame the wrongdoers into not offending again. A wrongdoer who broke the moral code was required to confess his sins before the church. Adulterers were often forced to wear the letter "A" sewed on their clothes. Public punishment might also include pain and brutality that seems shocking today, such as whipping, confinement to a pillory (head and hands locked while standing) or stocks (ankles locked while sitting against a wall), dunking in water, and dragging through the streets from the back of a wagon. A heretic might have an "H" branded into his forehead, and a woman convicted of sodomy might have a half-inch hole carved into the cartilage of her nose. Fines and restitution were often imposed for property crimes and minor offenses against public decency. Those guilty of other offenses might have their ears clipped or have their head and hands locked in a pillory. In more severe cases, where poor souls were deemed unfit to live in the community, banishment (which could lead to death in that rugged environment) or public executions, regularly attended by thousands of people, including women and children, were sometimes imposed. However, these were avoided where possible, as the colonies needed offenders' labor.

The punishment of Nicholas Stephens and Owen Sullivan in Providence, Rhode Island after their conviction of counterfeiting demonstrates the severity of colonial punishment. In 1752 the local constable used a red-hot branding iron to burn an "R" into each of Stephens' cheeks and also cropped both ears. Sullivan pleaded for and was given mercy. The constable planted the brand above the hairline where it would be less visible, and instead of cutting large pieces off his ears, only severed bloody strips from the edges. Unfortunately, this penalty did not change Sullivan's behavior. He was hanged in 1756 for subsequent

1 Walker, *Popular Justice*, 21.

counterfeiting offenses. And in those days hanging was not by the "long drops" familiar from western movies, but was a slow and painful death by strangulation.[2]

Although prisons have existed since antiquity, for the most part of human history they were not used to punish common criminals. Incarceration was not common, even for convicted felons. People who were locked up typically were being held pending trial or were debtors detained at night while they worked off their debts during the day. This began to change when Massachusetts established a "House of Correction" in 1656, and Pennsylvania passed a law in 1683 directing each county to construct "a sufficient house, at least twenty foot square, for restraint, correction, labour, and punishment of all persons as shall be there-unto committed by law."[3] Historians believe these houses of correction provided the model for the U.S. prisons that appeared in the late 1700s and early 1800s and set the stage for a change in prison function, from a system for detaining people before trial or sentence to a mode of punishment in its own right.

~

The handling of witches—or perhaps more accurately those accused of having magic powers or of practicing sorcery—provides an interesting perspective on colonial times. Their prosecution was an issue in a number of colonies for most of the seventeenth century. The decade of the 1660s saw twenty-five trials, thirty-two people charged, five convictions, and four executions for witchcraft in sixteen different towns in New England.[4] The most famous witch-hunt of all occurred in Salem, Massachusetts in 1692–1693, where as many as two hundred alleged witches were imprisoned, nineteen hanged, and one crushed to death between heavy boulders.[5]

Rebecca Nurse was one of them. She was born in England in 1621 and immigrated to Massachusetts with her parents while still a small girl. Her father became entangled in a number of legal controversies. Her mother was suspected of being a witch—perhaps a factor in Rebecca's vulnerability, as witchcraft was believed to be a heritable

2 Tarnoff, *Money-Makers*, 45, 77.

3 Ibid., 35.

4 Demos, *The Enemy Within*, 111.

5 Oliver and Hilgenberg, *A History of Crime*, 39–41.

condition, passed through families from one generation to another like red hair or blue eyes. Rebecca married Francis Nurse, and they reared eight children. The family prospered and was active in the community, but, like Rebecca's father, became embroiled in controversy with various neighbors. Through it all, Rebecca was a member in good standing of her church.

In March, 1692, twelve-year-old Ann Putnam—one of a little circle of young girls repeatedly driven to "fits"—came upon the apparition of a witch and was "afflicted." She identified the apparition as Rebecca on the basis of where she usually sat at the church meetinghouse. During the weeks that followed, Ann, her friend Abigail Williams, and Ann's mother each claimed that it was as though Rebecca were flying, crying, and throwing firebrands about the room, threatening to tear the souls out of their bodies. They claimed Rebecca was afflicting them with biting, pinching, and pricking and maintained they were almost choked by the apparition. These afflictions by Rebecca Nurse's apparition quickly became the subject of much agitated discussion in the community.

Rebecca, at the lusty age of seventy-one and having been bedridden for some time, was called to the local meetinghouse for an "examination" by two magistrates and the local minister. Onlookers, gawkers, and gossips from the village and beyond were in attendance. Her supposed victims, now numbering around ten, gave evidence against her. Two of them fell into fits and writhed about on the floor in apparent pain. Both claimed that Rebecca's specter, projected out from her person as they alone could see, had directly attacked them. Several others testified similarly against Rebecca.

She denied the allegations. Thirty-nine of Rebecca's friends petitioned on her behalf, but her accusers persisted. Several continued to experience periodic bouts of affliction and claimed to be re-assaulted. They blamed Rebecca's witchcraft for the recent deaths of a pig, a child, and a man in a roadside accident. She was strip-searched by a committee of local women, who found a "supernatural mark" in her genitalia.

The evidence was presented to a jury, which found her not guilty. But the chief judge mentioned a previous comment supposedly made by Rebecca to the effect that other confessed witches were "of our company." When Rebecca was not able to adequately explain her alleged comment—she was elderly, deaf, distraught, confused, and cornered—the jurors reversed their decision and found her guilty. The judges condemned her to death by hanging. She met her maker three weeks later on what came to be called Gallows Hill.

Puritans saw witches as entering into a compact with the devil in exchange for certain powers to do evil. Witchcraft was considered a sin because it denied God's superiority and a crime because the witch could call up the devil in his/her shape to perform cruel acts against others. Many individuals suffered grievously because of these beliefs. In addition to those directly affected, communities were split, and families were set against one another, ripped apart, or had their reputations destroyed at the hands of a system that now seems so misguided. John Hale, a minister directly involved in the trials, explained five years after the fact that God had allowed the devil to orchestrate the "awful tragedy," with all its errors and mistakes.[6]

Historians have speculated over what really happened at Salem: whether it was divine retribution, fraud, class conflict, mental illness, political repression, actual witchcraft, or other possibilities. John Demos, in *The Enemy Within: 2,000 Years of Witch-Hunting in the Western World*, suggests a combination of causes, prominently cultural factionalism, or the interplay of subsistence farmers, more prosperous farmers, tradesmen and artisans, merchants, and other distinct factions; social and economic change, largely involving erosion of self-governing traditions and challenges to the religious establishment; and fear of Indian enemies in the area that created an overwhelming and highly toxic climate of fear.[7] All combined led to irrational behavior by one group against another.

I spend time and ink on this subject now because I sense that what goes around comes around. In later chapters I will question whether, or to what extent, the get tough on crime and war on drugs attitudes of our times are modern-day reincarnations of the witchcraft experience of the colonial period.

~

The community and church continued to be central features of the criminal justice system throughout much of the 1700s. Notwithstanding their influences, the 1700s saw continually escalating crime levels as populations increased and became more mobile. The day's newspapers

6 Demos, *Enemy Within*, 189.

7 Ibid., 111.

reported counterfeiting, thievery, housebreaking, burglary, highway robbery, rape, assault, and murder. Shaming, banishment, and other community activities began to lose much of their force in the increasingly mobile society, so other measures came into more common use. Most involved a continuing adaptation of the exceptionally cruel and barbaric English law. In addition to burning the hand or forehead with a hot iron and cropping of the ears, flagellation with a cat-o-nine tails was not uncommon. English law that imposed the death penalty for over three hundred offenses—including petty treason, burglary, housebreaking, horse-stealing, and stealing to the value of one shilling—was generally in force. While colonial juries were generally reluctant to impose such penalties, hanging for property crimes such as counterfeiting and larceny was not uncommon. Debtor prisons continued to warehouse many of the poor and downtrodden. Prisons were generally intolerable—unbelievably overcrowded; freezing in winter and stiflingly hot in summer; disease ridden; with all ages, sexes, and levels of offense housed together.

The Revolutionary War destabilized what had been a relatively steady economic and social system. This interruption, and an increasing number of male immigrants, caused crime to shoot up after the war ended. At the same time, the American Revolution tended to accentuate the differences between America and England and foster reform of the American judicial system. The Constitution and new criminal codes allowed America to move beyond much of its archaic English heritage and adopt emerging ideas about crime and punishment.

With the Quakers of Pennsylvania in the forefront, more and more people were coming to view corporal and capital punishment as barbaric relics of an unenlightened past. In 1787, the first prisoner relief organization in North America, the Philadelphia Society for Alleviating the Miseries of Public Prisons, came into existence. Its constitution announced the project as religious, based on members' view of the Christian necessity to treat those who commit crimes, including those who are locked in prisons, with kindness. Pennsylvania eliminated many of its forms of corporal punishment, reduced the number of capital offenses, and substituted sentences to hard labor, publicly imposed, in place of death in a number of situations.

CONFINEMENT AS PUNISHMENT

Civic leaders in Pennsylvania began the search for a way of handling lawbreakers that would be more rational and humane and that would rehabilitate rather than merely punish. They studied the House of Correction established in Massachusetts in the mid-1600s and after a long process of experimentation established the Walnut Street jail in Philadelphia in the late 1780s. The first jail in the United States to use confinement as a punishment for offenders rather than as a means of pretrial detention, it was grounded in Quaker idea that solitude would encourage penance and enlightenment from within. Thus, it is fair to say that imprisonment—mainly solitary confinement—was a Christian invention substituted for corporal indignities and hard labor, based on the belief that criminals could change for the better and that prisons would help them do it.

Unfortunately, problems—just like those we see today—began almost immediately. Jailers could not keep inmates isolated because of overcrowding, nor working because not enough work was available. Moreover, whether inmates communed with their consciences or not, they showed an alarming tendency to go mad.

Nevertheless, New York followed Pennsylvania's lead with the construction of its Newgate prison in 1797. This prison was also a result of efforts by social reformers—generally members of the Society of Friends (Quakers) or other Christian churches—to make the criminal justice system more humane. These reformers believed that all humans possessed a capacity for personal redemption and could take responsibility for their wrong conduct, do penance for it (the prison was called a penitentiary), and resolve to sin no more. Therefore, the new system moved toward substituting lengthy prison terms for death sentences or crippling corporal punishment. But Newgate, like the Walnut Street jail before it, developed serious flaws, including gross overcrowding and the use of corporal punishment such as stocks, irons, and flogging to keep prisoners under control.

Both the Pennsylvania and New York systems promised reformation through silence, labor, and solitary confinement. Both emphasized removing offenders from the community and subjecting them to total isolation. A decree of a board of prison inspectors explained the rationale that today seems so spurious: "Cut them off from all intercourse with men; let not the voice or face of a friend ever cheer them; let them walk their gloomy abodes and commune with their corrupt hearts and guilty consciences in silence, and brood over the horrors of their solitude and the enormity of their crimes, without the hope of executive pardon."[8]

The main objective of the two systems was different. In Pennsylvania prisons, inmates generally were not allow to congregate, and labor was performed in individual cells. Reform was the primary objective. The New York system, on the other hand, allowed prisoners to come together to work—but in strict silence. Punishment was its prime objective. Although they were allowed to come together, New York inmates were not allowed to exchange looks, wink, laugh, motion to each other, exchange a word with each other, or communicate in any way. When they were moved from their cells to the work room or mess hall they were marched in silent lockstep, eyes fixed on the inmate in front of them. They sat with their backs to one another during meals. Disobedience was punished by flogging with the "cat," a whip with half a dozen strands of rawhide knotted at the end, or with a bullwhip.

Most prisons established in the early 1800s followed the New York system for two very practical reasons. The total isolation of the Pennsylvania approach drove some inmates insane. And perhaps more importantly, the New York system of group work facilitated prison industries, which soon became a central focus of prison administrations. Unfortunately, both models came to be characterized by overcrowding, corruption, and brutal corporal punishment. The seemingly well-motivated move away from the brutality of individual corporal punishment to imprisonment really just drove the brutality underground, and perhaps exacerbated it.

The Maine State Prison, built in 1824, reflects much about corrections of the time. Dr. Daniel Rose, a colorful man in early Maine politics, designed the prison and was its first warden. Its fifty-six individual cells, actually dug into the ground, reflected Rose's belief that:

> State prisons should be so constructed that even their aspect might be terrible, and appear like what they should be, dark and comfortless abodes of guilt and wretchedness. No mode or degree of punishment which ever has been made or which ever can be adopted is in its nature so well adapted to purposes of preventing crime and reforming a criminal, as close confinement in a silent or solitary cell, in which, cut off from all hope or

8 Damrosch, *Tocqueville's Discovery of America*, 118.

relief during the term for which he shall have been sentenced, the convict shall be furnished with a hammock on which he may sleep, a block of wood on which he may sit, and with such coarse, though wholesome food as may be best suited to a person in a situation designed for grief and penitence . . ."[9]

After only twenty-seven years of operation, New York's Newgate prison was considered irredeemable as a state prison, and Sing Sing was built as a replacement in 1826. When overcrowding became a major problem, two new prisons were constructed in Pennsylvania and an additional large one in New York. By 1830, twenty prisons were in operation in the new nation, mostly in the northeastern part of the country. Solitary cells were the norm, and flogging and caning were common practices for keeping inmates in line. Costs were a continuing problem. To deal with the costs, prison officials often increased prison labor or lowered the already bad living conditions of the inmates.

The move to locking people in jails and prisons as punishment—and perhaps rehabilitation—rather than as a means of pretrial detention or for debts had more than its share of vexations. A contemporary account speaks volumes. In the early 1830s, the French government commissioned Alexis de Tocqueville to compile a report on American prisons. He toured the U.S. for nine months and wrote his famed volumes, *Democracy in America*. After returning to France, he submitted a report that described the following prison conditions in fifteen of the twenty-four American states:

> Crowding of prisoners; confusion of different crimes, ages, and sometime sexes; mingling of indicted and condemned prisoners, criminals, debtors, guilty people, and witnesses; frequent escapes; absence of all discipline; never any silence that might lead criminals to reflect; never any work that might accustom them to earn an honest living; insalubriousness of living quarters that ruins their health; cynical conversations that corrupt them; idleness that depraves; and, in a word, collecting together every vice and every immorality . . . Absolute solitude, with nothing to distract or interrupt it, was beyond the strength of man; it consumes the criminal relentlessly and pitilessly, and it doesn't reform, it kills.[10]

9 Oliver and Hilgenberg, *A History of Crime*, 100.

10 Quoted in Damrosch, *Tocqueville's Discovery of America*, 37.

The Jacksonian era, roughly from the 1830s through the 1850s, saw a severe increase in both property and violent crime—variously attributed to increases in urbanization, immigration, availability of firearms, and poverty. This increase in crime fostered a continued growth in the penitentiary system, as prisons became alternatives of first resort rather than last. A number of new facilities were opened during this era—in Maryland, Massachusetts, Tennessee, Vermont, Georgia, New Hampshire, Louisiana, Missouri, Ohio, New Jersey, Mississippi, Alabama, Michigan, Indiana, and Illinois. They came to be called "Jacksonian prisons."

Work became an even more significant component of prison discipline. Some claimed its purpose was to instill habits that would lead to a productive, law-abiding life, but, without question, its most important function was its potential to reduce the cost of imprisonment. Prison labor took several forms: a contract system under which contractors paid a set fee for inmate labor, a lease system whereby states leased prisoners to businesses for a fixed annual fee, and a state-account system through which prisoners produced goods for state agencies or for sale. Each form led to outrageous abuses, as the profit motive superseded all concern for rehabilitation or simple human decency.

In the Civil War era, use of prisons continued to escalate as the quality of the system declined. While some reform efforts were made, they were limited by the social, political, and economic climate of the war. Penitentiaries deteriorated at a rapid pace as attention and resources were focused on other things and many were converted to house prisoners of war.

Robert Perkinson maintains, in *Texas Tough: The Rise of America's Prison Empire*, that corrections historians have for the most part focused on prisons in the North, while in fact a parallel system developed in the South. The northern branch, which can be traced back to Pennsylvania, tended to be more reformative, integrative, and conceived by churches, while the southern branch, which can be traced to slave plantations, was more retributive, exclusionary, and conceived on southern work farms. Perkinson writes, "The evolution of the prison has had surprisingly little to do with crime and a great deal to do with America's troubled history of racial conflict and social stratification."[11]

When prisons were reopened in the South after the Civil War, they were used primarily to house black inmates as part of the white supremacy movement and Jim Crow segregation. The postwar years saw the extensive use and abuse of leasing programs, in which convicts were leased for profit to private companies to perform various forms of labor, such as agricultural, construction, road and railroad building, sugar milling, and mining. These years also saw equally brutal state-managed convict farming, in which inmate farm laborers raised crops for inmate food and for sale at a profit.

Convict leasing and prison farms were profitable for the prisons but devastating to the inmates. Under both systems inmates nearly always worked from daylight to dark under brutal overseers, were fed poorly, and received little or no medical care. They often were housed in mobile cages and chained together—in the proverbial chain gangs—while they worked, ate, and slept. It has been estimated that this practice caused over thirty thousand inmate deaths over the fifty plus years it was in vogue.

A decision of the Supreme Court of Virginia sheds light on the prevailing attitudes and practices of the time. Woody Ruffin, a convict in the Virginia penitentiary, was hired out with other convicts to work on the Chesapeake and Ohio Railroad. He killed a guard in an escape attempt. Ruffin was tried in 1871 in the circuit court of the city of Richmond, found guilty of murder in the first degree, and sentenced to be hanged. On appeal, the only question presented was whether the court below was in error in holding the trial in Richmond rather than in the county of Bath, where the offense was committed. Not surprisingly, the judgment of the lower court was affirmed. The real issue turned on whether Ruffin would be afforded the protection of the Bill of Rights. The court's discussion of this issue is an interesting commentary on several aspects of corrections of the day:

> We have said that a reasonable and not a literal construction must be given to the clause under consideration, and a construction that is consistent with the other declarations of general principles in the same instrument. One of these declarations is, "that government is instituted for the common benefit, protec-

11 Perkinson, *Texas Tough*, 2.

> tion and security of the people," &c. Now one of the most effectual means of promoting the common benefit and ensuring the protection and security of the people, is the certain punishment and prevention of crime. It is essential to the safety of society, that those who violate its criminal laws should suffer punishment. A convicted felon, whom the law in its humanity punishes by confinement in the penitentiary instead of with death, is subject while undergoing that punishment, to all the laws which the Legislature in its wisdom may enact for the government of that institution and the control of its inmates. For the time being, during his term of service in the penitentiary, he is in a state of penal servitude to the State. He has, as a consequence of his crime, not only forfeited his liberty, but all his personal rights except those which the law in its humanity accords to him. He is for the time being the slave of the State. He is civiliter mortuus; and his estate, if he has any, is administered like that of a dead man.
>
> The bill of rights is a declaration of general principles to govern a society of freemen, and not of convicted felons and men civilly dead. Such men have some rights it is true, such as the law in its benignity accords to them, but not the rights of freemen. They are the slaves of the State undergoing punishment for heinous crimes committed against the laws of the land. While in this state of penal servitude, they must be subject to the regulations of the institution of which they are inmates, and the laws of the State to whom their service is due in expiation of their crimes.
>
> When a convict in the penitentiary, while undergoing punishment for the crime of which he stands convicted, commits other offenses, it is unquestionably in the power of the State, to which his penal servitude is due, to prescribe, through its Legislature, the mode of punishment as well as the manner of his trial. If he commits an offense not amounting to a felony, the superintendent is vested by law with authority, to punish him by stripes, or the iron mask, or the gag, or the dungeon. If he commits an offense which in law amounts to a felony, he has the privilege of a trial by jury . . .[12]

The 1800s saw some attempts at prison reform. Early in the century, several groups of women began efforts to improve conditions for female prisoners. Women had been incarcerated primarily in local jails or isolated areas in men's prisons. They often were confined in crowded spaces and abused by starvation, beatings, limited removal of waste,

12 *Ruffin v. The Commonwealth.*

rape, forced prostitution, and such conditions. Although early efforts did not result in systemic reforms, they did lay the groundwork for improvements that would come decades later.

A second wave of prison reform began with the 1870 National Congress on Penitentiary and Reformatory Discipline that led to the founding of the American Correctional Association (known then as the National Prison Association). Improvements included efforts to classify and segregate types of prisoners, provide individual treatment such as vocational training and rewards for good behavior, and move to indeterminate sentences. The focus generally shifted from penitence and punishment toward individual treatment.

In the 1880s many states began to restrict prison industries, primarily the inmate leasing practices. The impetus for this move came less from humanitarian forces than from organized labor and small businesses, who objected that convict labor was unfair competition. Abolished leasing programs often were replaced with the equally brutal state-managed convict farming, which lasted until well into the twentieth century.

The brutality of the prison farm system of labor in the South is demonstrated by the story of Clyde Barrow, the male half of the iconic Bonnie and Clyde outlaw team of the early 1900s. Clyde was locked up at the notorious Eastham unit in deep South Texas. But even worse, from Clyde's point of view, he was assigned to the work farm. Conditions were so brutal that inmates were known to do almost anything to escape—to another prison. They were known to shoot kerosene into their veins, pour contaminants into their eyes, break their feet in commodes, and sever their Achilles tendons in efforts to be reassigned. But mostly inmates had "accidents" with axes. One report was that fourteen men cut their hands and feet off in one week. And poor Clyde Barrow. He put his foot on a stump and had a buddy chop off his big toe and some of the next one—two weeks before his mother arranged a parole from Governor Ross Sterling. He got out, but was on crutches.

The late nineteenth century saw isolated experiments involving academic and industrial education, where prisoners were taught a specific trade best suited to their talents and were offered physical fitness and sports programs. A number of women-only prisons were constructed. But overcrowding, poor conditions, and brutality continued to be major problems, as the emphasis was generally on retribution, deterrence, and production rather than reclamation or reformation.

A "new penology" that introduced social workers, psychologists, and psychiatrists into the corrections mix began to develop in the early decades of the twentieth century. Many prisons began to move away from inmate silence and isolation from the outside world, and visits from family and friends began to be allowed. Systems of probation and supervised parole were developed, and the system of convict leasing was abolished in more and more states.

Crime was thought to have increased in the 1920s and 1930s, although historians disagree as to whether there was a real increase or only a crime wave scare resulting from the publicity machine of FBI director J. Edgar Hoover. During these decades the "noble experiment" of prohibition turned millions of otherwise law-abiding citizens into lawbreakers, created disrespect for the law that had incalculable results, and often taxed law enforcement resources. However, it had little effect on prisons because enforcement generally was so lax that relatively few were ever locked up.

Nevertheless, the mood of the day gave rise to a spurt of prison construction, including creation of large prisons often referred to as the "big house." These frequently were built with the expectation of industrial labor by inmates, but the Great Depression and a backlash by the public who could not find work brought the move toward prison industries largely to a halt. Prisons returned to their old ways of simply warehousing people. They typically were characterized by crowding and idleness.

One of the most famous of all U.S. prisons—Alcatraz—was opened in 1934 as a special federal prison to house kidnappers, racketeers, and individuals guilty of predatory crimes. Located on a rock island in San Francisco Bay, it was considered a super-prison of its time, where difficult-to-manage prisoners from other institutions were warehoused under one roof. It had no concept of rehabilitation. Al Capone and Robert Stroud, the Birdman of Alcatraz, were among its most famous visitors. Thirty-six prisoners tried to escape during its tenure. Seven were shot and killed, two drowned, five were unaccounted for, and the remainder were recaptured. With no facility for rehabilitation, a deteriorating physical plant, and continually increasing costs, the prison was closed in 1963.

The economy returned to life after the Great Depression and many potential criminals joined the war effort. These factors apparently caused crime rates to fall during the 1940s, and there was a commensurate decline in prison population. Both bottomed out during World War II, remained flat into the 1950s, and began a steady rise late in the decade.

Prison reforms that had been curtailed during the Great Depression and World War II began to appear again with expanded efforts to achieve rehabilitation. And many inmates began to assert their rights. This led to an increase in the number of prison riots in the early 1950s. They generally were aimed at poor living conditions, inadequate food, limited health care, and abusive guards.

Studies done in the 1940s and 1950s revealed a complex web of relationships shaping day-to-day prison life. Based on these studies, Samuel Walker described prison life of the day: "Inmates exercised considerable de facto power, and guards overlooked violations of prison rules as long as inmates did not directly challenge their authority. As a result, contraband money, bootleg alcohol, drugs, and sexual assault flourished. Prison violence was frighteningly routine. Staff 'goon squads' brutalized inmates, while inmates raped fellow prisoners."[13]

In summary, crime, corrections, and attempted reforms evolved in fits and starts from colonial times to the 1950s. Crime rates fluctuated over the years but were relatively stable from the 1930s until the 1960s. Incarceration rates remained relatively stable as well, at about 10 percent of the crime rate. While corporal punishment and severe, sanctioned abuse were abolished, overcrowding, poor conditions, brutality, and lack of rehabilitative services were continuing issues. Like crime itself, attempts at prison reform came and went and came again over the years. Prison reform efforts that had been shelved during WWII began to appear again in the late 1950s.

And then our country decided to get tough on crime.

13 Walker, *Popular Justice*, 176.

2

Prison Growth

THE DECADE OF THE 1960s was a time of extremes, transformational change, and bizarre contrasts. A Monday morning quarterback can see a positive social revolution that fostered new ways of thinking and real change in the cultural fabric of American life—or an era of irresponsible excess and flamboyance. It was a time of flower children and assassins, idealism and alienation, rebellion and backlash. The middle of the decade saw the beginnings of racial reforms and increasingly unruly forms of political protest. The second half was dominated by the counterculture movement, with its Summer of Love in San Francisco and Woodstock Festival in upstate New York. Psychedelic drugs, especially LSD, became widely used medicinally, spiritually, and recreationally. Seventy million children from the postwar baby boom became teenagers and young adults. The changes affected education, values, lifestyles, laws, entertainment, and—ultimately—crime and corrections.

As America entered the 1960s, crime had been relatively stable for several decades. Rehabilitation, aimed at correcting the behavior of inmates, was the country's predominant correctional philosophy. This philosophy soon came to include reintegration, which advocated returning offenders to full membership in society. Use of probation and parole was increased in an effort to keep less serious offenders in their communities. Efforts were also made to keep the mentally ill in their family environment and, it was thought, make them more stable. Many mental health facilities were closed. Notwithstanding the rehabilitation, reintegration, and reform efforts, crime rates skyrocketed during the sixties and seventies as children of the postwar baby boom reached young adulthood and their crime-prone years during this period of vast social change, declining family stability, and economic insecurity.

Society's response to the social turmoil and skyrocketing crime was to send more people to prison. This involved a national attitude that encompassed a network of punitive practices: the get tough on crime movement; the war on drugs; sentencing reform, which included policies such as mandatory sentencing, "three strikes and you're out," and "truth-in-sentencing"; and the prison-industrial complex.

THE "TOUGH ON CRIME" MOVEMENT

The modern "tough on crime" movement can be traced to the late 1960s and early 1970s. Republican presidential candidate Barry Goldwater made law and order an issue in his 1964 campaign, and his tough anticrime rhetoric struck a chord among many voters. President Lyndon Johnson, who won the election, publically declared war on crime, and the popular press blew wind into the sails of the emerging get tough policies. Newspapers, radio, and television began giving more publicity to the dramatically increasing crime rates and making crime a more important part of each news cycle. They often characterized juvenile delinquents as evil and beyond rehabilitation, all lawbreakers as brutal, hardened criminals, and all inmates as stereotypically subhuman.

Inmates fed the storm. Despite the emphasis on rehabilitation and reintegration of the 1960s, prisons across the country saw a rise in violence and riots. The worst occurred in September 1971, when 1300 prisoners rioted and seized control of the Attica Correctional Facility, a maximum security prison in western New York. They held thirty-nine prison guards and employees hostage for four days and demanded negotiations with state officials. Early in the process the inmates issued a list of demands, including calls for improvements in living conditions, education, and training. After negotiations stalled and an ultimatum was rejected, helicopters flew over the yard dropping tear gas. State police and corrections officers stormed in with guns blazing and seized the prison. Thirty-nine people were killed, including twenty-nine prisoners and ten prison guards and employees held hostage since the onset of the ordeal.

Citizens watching this spectacle on national television and experiencing the continuing rise in crime became less inclined to have criminals back in the community. Prisons generally moved toward simply warehousing inmates rather than providing rehabilitation and treatment programs. In less than a decade, the predominant philosophy changed from reintegration to punishment or retribution.

Crime rates leveled off in the 1980s, but public opinion did not reflect the stabilization. Most people believed crime was still rising. Measures emphasizing punishment came to overshadow considerations of crime prevention in the 1990s, as both conservatives and liberals attempted to outdo each other in their posturing and proposals to punish criminals. In 1994 President Clinton signed the largest crime bill in the history of the U.S., providing for 100,000 new police officers, $9.7 billion for prisons, and $6.1 billion for prevention programs.[1] The law banned assault weapons, made it illegal for certain groups to possess any firearms, and greatly expanded the federal death penalty. It also created a variety of new crimes relating to immigration, hate offenses, sex offenses, and gang-related activities, and implemented a "three strikes" provision for violent offenders.

The "three strikes and you're out" metaphor captured much of the public discourse on crime during the 1990s. The basic idea was to have mandatory life sentences without the possibility of parole for offenders convicted in a series of crimes. The idea quickly gained widespread popularity, and President Clinton endorsed a version of it. The first true "three strikes" law, with virtually no exceptions, was passed in Washington state in 1993. California passed one in 1994. By 2004, twenty-six states and the federal government had some form of "three strikes" statute—typically specifying that a third felony conviction brings a sentence of life in prison, with no parole possible until a long period of time, most commonly twenty-five years, has been served.

Federal and state lawmakers also enacted a number of other, mostly incremental crime-fighting programs throughout the period. Many were aimed at the continuing drug problem, and the war on drugs became an indistinguishable part of the get tough policies.

1. U.S. Department of Justice, "Violent Crime Control," 1.

THE WAR ON DRUGS

Drugs were simply a commodity until one hundred years ago. Since then, cultural shifts, largely lead by religious movements, have made them immoral and deviant, synonymous with evil. For example, in 1904, an Episcopal bishop returning from the Far East argued for banning opium based on his observation of "the natives' moral degeneration." And in 1914 the *New York Times* reported that cocaine caused blacks to commit violent crimes and made them resistant to police bullets.[2] In the 1930s a national panic over marijuana broke out, and drugs began to be considered a criminal rather than a social problem, with harsh penalties established for possession and sale of the drug.

The Boggs Act of 1951 established mandatory minimum federal sentences for possession of marijuana, cocaine, and opiates as part of a governmental effort to stamp out narcotic addiction. Then policymakers came to see drug abuse as primarily a social disease that could be addressed with treatment, and by 1970 federal mandatory drug sentences had been largely repealed. A focus on rehabilitation and reintegration, as opposed to retribution and punishment, led to broad adoption of indeterminate sentencing involving probation rather than incarceration, time off for good behavior, and parole. The federal sentencing scheme included a penalty range within which judges imposed sentences. Typically, after one third of a sentence was served, a parole board would determine if the offender could be released from prison. Most states adopted similar systems. And then the war on drugs exploded on the scene.

The passage of the Comprehensive Drug Abuse Prevention and Control Act of 1970 gave the federal government a more active role in drug enforcement and drug abuse prevention. President Nixon called drug abuse public enemy number one. Although he emphasized treatment of drug addicts, he moved early in his administration to use his political power to foster law and order through policing, prosecution, and imprisonment.

In 1973, New York, under the leadership of Governor Nelson Rockefeller, passed drug laws that imposed penalties comparable to those for kidnapping, arson, murder, or other such brutal crimes. In a State of the State address Rockefeller demanded that every illegal-drug

2. Williams, "Negro Cocaine."

dealer be punished with a mandatory prison sentence of life without parole, that plea bargaining be forbidden in such cases, and that even juvenile offenders receive life sentences. Rockefeller had demonstrated his newfound commitment to law and order in 1971 when he crushed the Attica prison uprising. When he doubled down by proposing the harshest drug laws in the United States, he took the lead on an issue that would soon dominate the nation's political agenda. The Rockefeller drug laws, enacted a few months later, were somewhat less draconian than his proposal but nevertheless were very severe: the penalty for possessing four ounces of an illegal drug, or for selling two ounces, was a mandatory prison term of fifteen years to life. The legislation also established a mandatory prison sentence for many second felony convictions, regardless of the crime or its circumstances. Rockefeller proudly declared that his state had enacted the toughest antidrug program in the country.

The misery created by the Rockefeller policy was illustrated in Jennifer Gonnerman's 2004 book, *Life on the Outside*, which tracked the odyssey of Elaine Bartlett, a mother of four living in a decrepit housing project on the Lower East Side of Manhattan. She spent sixteen years in prison for a single sale of cocaine, and at age forty-two, having spent most of her adult life behind bars, was released to no money, no job, no real home, and a large and troubled family. But Nelson Rockefeller had set in motion a profound shift in American drug policy.

The term "war on drugs" began to be used after President Nixon merged several existing agencies to create the Drug Enforcement Administration (DEA) in 1973 and declared an all-out global war on the "drug menace." This was a significant step toward a criminal justice approach to drug enforcement, and by the early eighties most policymakers came to view drug abuse as a law enforcement problem that should be addressed with aggressive criminal justice measures. This policy continued into the Reagan years. President Reagan's administration beefed up the enforcement effort by enlisting the FBI in the fight, adding five hundred DEA agents, and establishing thirteen regional antidrug task forces. It also scored record numbers of drug seizures and convictions.

Drug use among children erupted as a national issue, and in 1984 First Lady Nancy Reagan toured elementary schools, warning students about the danger of illegal drug use. When a fourth-grader asked Mrs. Reagan what she should do if approached by someone offering drugs, Mrs. Reagan responded, "Just say no." This slogan, and Nancy Reagan's activism on the issue, became central to her husband's antidrug message. Within a year, five thousand "Just Say No" clubs had formed around the country. The Los Angeles Police Department's 1983 Drug Abuse Resistance Education (D.A.R.E.) school lecture program grew into a national phenomenon that, by 2003, cost $230 million and involved 50,000 police officers. Partnership for a Drug-Free America launched a similarly memorable campaign in 1987 with a television ad featuring a hot skillet, a raw egg, and the phrase, "This is your brain on drugs." By portraying drugs as a threat to children, the administration was able to pursue more aggressive federal antidrug legislation.

Subsequent administrations continued to escalate the war. The George H. W. Bush administration substantially increased spending and focused on attacking and arresting drug users, rather than on prevention, education, treatment, or interdiction. It penalized states that did not comply with its plan by imposing a reduction in federal funding. Federal drug spending increased every year of the Clinton presidency, though more slowly than under Bush and Reagan. The George W. Bush administration basically continued existing policies, although it did provide $1.4 billion to Mexico and other countries over three years to help combat drug smuggling and violence. The Obama administration has increased spending on interdiction and law enforcement to record levels both in dollars and in percentage terms. It promised a new national policy to treat drugs as a public health issue and focus on prevention and treatment, but no programs have as yet evolved.

~

So what do we have? The battle has been waged through seven White House administrations. Experts estimate the costs of drug programs currently run close to $40 billion dollars annually. The federal Drug Enforcement Administration alone has a budget of over $2.6 billion, employs 11,000 people, and operates eighty-six offices in sixty-three countries. Just over 400,000 people were arrested for drug abuse in 1970. By 1992, the number had exploded to just over one million, and more people were in federal jails for drug charges than had been for all crimes in 1980. In 2007 over 1.8 million people were arrested on drug charges. And nearly a half million drug offenders were locked up in the nation's prisons.[3]

SENTENCING REFORM

Indeterminate sentencing is a process in which offenders are sentenced to prison for a minimum and maximum amount of time, such as five to twenty years. After the minimum period is served, a parole board releases them under continuing supervision if it believes they have been rehabilitated. Indeterminate sentencing, which had been used for years, began to come under attack in the late 1970s. Critics contended that the system was not rehabilitating criminals and instead simply led to uncertainty of punishment and unwarranted disparity in sentences. These issues, coupled with renewed concern about rising crime rates in the mid-1970s, led to experimentation with new sentencing systems at both the federal and state levels. The 1984 Sentencing Reform Act, the 1986 Anti-Drug Abuse Act, and the sentencing guidelines they spawned were the result: a witches' brew of government action that represented perhaps the most dramatic change in sentencing law and practice in our nation's history.

The Sentencing Reform Act of 1984 eliminated indeterminate sentencing at the federal level and set out a uniform policy for those convicted in federal courts of felonies and serious misdemeanors. It essentially abandoned rehabilitation as a penal goal and substituted retribution, deterrence, and incapacitation. The act established the U.S. Sentencing Commission, charged with establishing guidelines that in effect made all federal sentences determinate and authorized appellate review of sentences in which the judge departed from the guidelines. The result was an increased likelihood that convicted offenders, particularly those with a history of violent criminal activity, sex offenses, drunk driving, or drug offenses, would serve longer prison terms for their offenses.

The vast majority of criminal sentencing in the United States is done at the state level, and most states followed suit with similar laws. The policies that unfolded included requirements such as mandatory

3. Harrop, "Waging War."

minimum terms of imprisonment, "three strikes" provisions that often required a life sentence after a third offense, and "truth in sentencing" measures that required offenders to serve a large percentage of their sentence. Forty states passed mandatory minimum penalties for offenders with long criminal histories and over thirty passed mandatory penalties for various drug offenses.

The 1986 federal Anti-Drug Abuse Act strengthened federal efforts against drugs and reinstated mandatory prison sentences for drug possession. Among other things, Congress defined the amounts of various drugs that it believed likely to be in the hands of drug "kingpins," or high-level dealers, and established penalties accordingly. The law provided for a five-year minimum sentence for possession of crack cocaine but no mandatory minimum sentence for possession of powder cocaine. It set a five-year minimum prison penalty for a first-time trafficking offense involving five grams or more of crack cocaine or five hundred grams or more of powder cocaine, and a ten-year mandatory minimum penalty for a first-time trafficking offense involving fifty grams or more of crack cocaine or five thousand grams or more of powder cocaine—a 100:1 ratio between the two forms.

Cocaine is a powerfully addictive stimulant drug. The powdered form, which can be snorted or dissolved in water and injected, came to be associated with white yuppies. Crack cocaine—the form of cocaine that has been processed to make a rock crystal, which, when heated, produces a crackling sound along with vapors that are smoked—was more common in inner-city black communities and has been associated with violent street crime. It is no surprise that many made the case that the disparity of treatment between powder and crack cocaine amounted to institutional racism By the 2000s the country saw a national trend toward setting aside federal sentencing guidelines and equalization of the penalty associated with the two forms of the same drug. In its 2005 *United States v. Booker* decision,[4] the U.S. Supreme Court held that the system of federal mandatory guidelines violated the Sixth Amendment right to trial by jury. In the aftermath of Booker and other Supreme Court cases, guidelines are now considered advisory only, on both the federal and the state levels. Judges must consider the guidelines when

4. *United States v. Booker*.

determining a sentence but are not required to issue sentences within them. Their sentences are still, however, subject to appellate review. The Supreme Court ruled more specifically in 2007 in *Kimbrough v. United States*[5] that the guidelines for cocaine are advisory only and that a judge may consider the disparity between their treatment of crack and powder cocaine offenses when sentencing a defendant.

Given all the above, the time convicted offenders spent in prison rose substantially throughout the nineties. In 1990 offenders sentenced to state prisons served 38 percent of their sentences, while in 1999 they served almost 49 percent. During this period, the average time served in state prisons for all offenses rose from twenty-two months to twenty-nine months.[6]

THE PRISON-INDUSTRIAL COMPLEX

Crime rates in the United States have declined over the last couple of decades. But the prison system has been "on steroids." The number of people sentenced to prison or jail has grown like wildfire and sentences have gotten longer, creating a prison boom with its own apparently inexorable logic. When crime goes up, we build more prisons to control it. When crime goes down, we give prisons the credit, and building even more prisons seems like a good idea.

The dollar cost of prisons and jails in the U.S. grew from just over nine billion dollars per year in 1982 to almost seventy billion dollars in 2006. That's an increase of roughly 650 percent, or 26 percent per year over the twenty-five years.[7] The cost of corrections in 2006 exceeded the gross domestic product of thirteen U.S. states and the gross national product of 224 countries. Expenditures exceeded the annual revenues of all but approximately one hundred of the world's largest companies. Quite an industry.

We have seen that the war on drugs and sentencing changes were responsible for much of the growth of this gigantic industry. But if these factors planted and cultivated the seeds of growth, they found fertile soil in the country's prison-industrial complex—a set of bureaucratic,

5. Kimbrough v. United States.
6. Pastor and Maguire, *Sourcebook*, sect. 6.
7. Bureau of Justice Statistics, "Direct Expenditures," 1.

political, and economic interests that many believe encourages increased spending on imprisonment, regardless of the actual need. It is a confluence of special interests that has given prison construction and operation a seemingly unstoppable momentum, at least until the budget crises of recent years. The special interests include politicians who have used the fear of crime to gain votes, poor rural areas that view prisons as a key to economic development, private companies that see corrections as a lucrative market, corrections officials whose fiefdoms have expanded along with the inmate population, and labor unions that benefit from representing more corrections employees.

~

Russian novelist Fyodor Dostoyevsky has said that the degree of civilization in a society can be judged by the state of its prisons. And prisons, along with the broader criminal justice system, each subject to a high degree of public control, reflect both the best and the worst of our democratic society. The good news is that politicians and their gargantuan bureaucracies tend—most of the time—to respond to the will of the people who elect them. The bad news is that usually they respond to the will of the majority at the expense of unpopular, underfunded minorities. Politicians don't do election polls in prisons, and a majority of the electorate apparently agrees with—or at least goes along with—a get tough on crime philosophy. And politicians have not hesitated to take advantage of the situation. While most of the influence is insidious, under the radar, some situations are more blatant.

The 1974 Willie Horton incident involving George H. W. Bush was an early example. Horton and two accomplices robbed a seventeen-year-old gas station attendant, stabbed him nineteen times, and dumped his body in a trash can, where he died from blood loss. Horton was convicted of murder, sentenced to life imprisonment without the possibility of parole, and incarcerated at the Concord Correctional Facility in Massachusetts. After he was allowed outside the prison as part of a weekend furlough program, Horton twice raped a local woman after pistol-whipping, knifing, binding, and gagging her fiancé. He was later captured by police and sentenced to two consecutive life terms plus eighty-five years.

Democratic Presidential candidate Michael Dukakis was the governor of Massachusetts at the time of Horton's furlough. While

Dukakis did not start the program, he had supported it as a method of criminal rehabilitation and had vetoed a bill that would have prevented convicted first-degree murderers from receiving furloughs. The 1988 Bush presidential campaign ran TV ads attacking Dukakis, by then the Democratic party's nominee for president, over the program. Bush brought it up repeatedly in campaign speeches, claiming that Dukakis had let Horton loose to terrorize innocent people, and declared himself in favor of life without parole for convicted murderers.

A Monday morning quarterback can clearly see that Willie Horton should not have been furloughed. He caused great and regrettable harm while he was out. But the incident is what author Nassim Nicholas Taleb has described as a black swan event.[8] Such events are a surprise to the observer, have a major impact, and after the fact are rationalized by hindsight, as if they had been expected. One single event can, and often does, invalidate a general proposition that may be based on extensive data. In this case, Willie Horton's behavior persuaded millions of voters that more incarceration of more offenders was the best policy. They reached this conclusion without any data one way or the other on whether, on balance, a furlough policy would be best for society.

In a similar example, *NYDailyNews.com* noted, "Former Arkansas governor Mike Huckabee's future presidential aspirations took a serious hit in the hail of bullets that killed four police officers in a suburban Seattle coffee shop Sunday morning. The once-and-future Republican presidential hopeful has been forced to defend his decision as governor in 2000 to commute the sentence of Maurice Clemmons, the now 37-year-old suspect in the Lakewood, Wash., murders. Clemmons was shot and killed by Seattle police Tuesday."[9] Conservative bloggers broadly condemned Huckabee for his "bad judgment" in going along with the commutation.

More recently, State Representative Todd Smith of Texas persuaded his colleagues in the Legislature to pass a bill—by 131-12 in the House and 30-0 in the Senate—that would allow a judge to remove from the sex offender list persons convicted of having consensual sex with a minor at least fourteen years old who was less than four years younger than they were. Smith had heard testimony of men who wanted to provide for children who were born of these youthful crimes

8. Taleb, *The Black Swan*.

9. Sacks, "Mike Huckabee's."

but couldn't earn a decent living because they were on the sex offender registry. The bill was vetoed by Governor Rick Perry, who—perhaps not coincidently—said he was not running for president in the next election but ultimately did. And Jeff Cason, Smith's challenger in Smith's 2010 re-election campaign, charged in mailings and robo-calls that Smith was coddling sexual predators. While this did not lead to Smith's defeat, the publicity was clearly untruthful and another example of a politician trying to gain personal benefit from the prevailing get-tough mood of the country.[10]

~

The consequence, of course, is obvious. Politicians espouse get tough, lock 'em up policies to get elected. They build prisons to deliver on their promises and keep their jobs. And society fills the prisons. Not surprisingly, this scenario has led to an elephantine prison bureaucracy. Over 750,000 people are employed by prisons and jails in the United States. Over 450,000 correctional officers and jailers are at work at the federal, state, and local level. Their mean annual wage exceeds $42,000, and some are paid as much as $65,000 per year. They have almost fifty thousand immediate bosses, with average pay of almost $58,000, and some are paid in excess of $90,000.[11] The secretary of California's Department of Corrections and Rehabilitation is paid over $203,000, and numerous wardens and other staff, primarily medical professionals, are paid from the high $200,000s to the $600,000s.[12] The executive director of the Texas Department of Criminal Justice receives an annual salary in excess of $186,000. Corrections superintendents in New York receive annual pay in the $150,000 range.[13] All are dependent on prisons for their livelihood—and prisoners are the raw material of prisons.

This bureaucracy often feeds on itself, fostering its own growth. Those who most ardently want to lock people up and keep them there are the corrections system apparatchiks doing the locking up. Cal Biggins, who was sentenced to two life sentences for double murder and served thirty-five years in the Texas prison system, presented his view of the situation this way: "The system is set for failure. The officials want

10. Casey, "Predicted."

11. Bureau of Labor Statistics, "Occupational."

12. California Department of Corrections and Rehabilitation, "California."

13. Salary Expert, "Prison Warden."

everything to be done wrong, because you got people who want jobs. If everybody's right, you got people start losing jobs. To me, it's about a job thing. Make more rules, create another job for somebody. You got some good, sincere people who really try to help inmates improve their lives. But most don't want you to improve. One less inmate that learns, one more coming back through that door—and creating more jobs." And Jens Soering, an inmate with a very long sentence, writes, "What the attempted closure of correctional centers in Virginia and New York shows is that America cannot conquer its addiction to prisons without a major retraining and job placement initiative for guards. Focusing only on the rehabilitation, education, and reentry of inmates is not enough. Unless correctional officers are given significant help in transitioning to a different line of work, they will fight to keep 'their' penitentiaries open."[14]

Most prison officials and employees deny the claims of Biggins, Soering, and others with similar views. The truth, no doubt, is somewhere in the middle. Many prison administrators, chaplains, correctional officers and others are devoted to doing the right thing, rehabilitating offenders, and reducing prison populations. But it is naive to think that all are so altruistic. The issue is much clearer in the case of private prisons.

Increased incarceration rates led to overcrowding and rapidly escalating capital and operating costs, followed, not surprisingly, by taxpayer resistance to paying those costs. Society wanted more law-breakers locked up, but it didn't want to pay the piper. A partial answer to the growing dilemma was seen as "privatization." Privatization may take a number of forms, including contracting out prison labor, contracting out services or prison management to national corporations, or private ownership and operation of prisons.

Privatization of one sort or another is not a new phenomenon. Although prisons were the property of the king in eighteenth-century England, many were in effect under the private control of a lord, bishop, or other person of privilege. Operating one was a significant economic opportunity, as prisoners were often required to pay their board as well as an assortment of fees and taxes. In colonial Australia, one bishop turned a profit, as follows: "On entering the Bishop of Ely's lockup, a

14. Soering, *The Church of the Second Chance*, 160.

prisoner was chained down to the floor with a spiked collar riveted round his neck until he disgorged a fee for 'easement of irons.' Any jailer could load any prisoner with as many fetters as he pleased and charge for their removal one at a time. The 'trade of chains,' though often denounced as a national disgrace, survived well into the 1790s."[15]

The birth of the contemporary American private prison industry can be traced to 1984, when the United States Immigration and Naturalization Service became the first federal agency to contract for private correctional services. This initial movement was quickly followed by contracts for outsourcing developed by the U.S. Marshals Service and the U.S. Bureau of Prisons in 1986. The first county-level private prison contract was signed in 1984, and in 1985 the first state-level contract was signed.

Nearly all the growth in prisons since 1995 has been in facilities owned or operated by private companies. By 2005, over 100,000 inmates were held under federal or state authority in 415 private prisons.[16] Thus, the presence of private prisons, owned and/or run for a profit by private companies as part of the free enterprise system, is a major factor in the prison/industrial complex. They aim to reduce costs and maximize profit by, among other things, incarcerating more inmates at lower unit costs.

Two corporations are leaders in the private prison business in the U.S. Corrections Corporation of America operates sixty-five facilities, and in 2010 generated operating income of $323 million while housing an average daily inmate population of over eighty thousand.[17] The GEO Group, Inc. managed 81,000 correctional and detention beds and reported $132 million operating income.[18]

Much debate has occurred over the privatization of prisons. The arguments for privatization stress cost reduction and flexibility, including the ability to terminate a contract more easily and cost-effectively than to close down a government prison and lay off civil servants in the event of a decline in prison population. Arguments against it start with the philosophical, maintaining that privatization is merely a ruse that takes taxpayer money and gives it to a private corporation to do a

15. Hughes, *The Fatal Shore*, 37.

16. Kirchoff, "Economic Impacts," 20.

17. Corrections Corporation of America, "Corrections," 32.

18. GEO Group, Inc., "2010 Annual Report," 33.

mandated public service without actually shrinking government. This approach, the argument goes, is a form of cronyism that gives monopoly rent to a private contractor who then goes about the same business the state would have provided. The con arguments also focus on standards of care, and the question of whether a market economy for prisons leads to a market demand for prisoners that fosters tougher sentencing in order to get cheap labor and economies of scale for the industry.

Studies on the subject, too numerous to list, go both ways. A recent one published by CCA—not exactly an unbiased source—claims that California's soaring prison costs of $47,000 per year per inmate could be curbed by $120 million a year for each 5,000 inmates it sends to private prisons in other states. The report details a five-year prison privatization plan that, it says, would save California taxpayers $1.8 billion over that span by gradually transferring 25,000 inmates out of state.[19] In a contrary example, the Colorado Criminal Justice Reform Coalition has published a study detailing troubled performance of private prisons—poor inmate programs, security problems, and fiscal woes—and stating that studies of fiscal performance "have yet to show any conclusive cost savings through contracting."[20] While the truth seems to be in the eye of the beholder, the recent growth in the industry suggests that, from a practical viewpoint, privatization is winning the debate. The free enterprise system, which demands more prisoners as the raw material for the industry, may well be foisting a Faustian bargain on society.

Many communities want, even feel they need, prisons for economic reasons. Throughout the 1960s and '70s, an average of four prisons were built each year in rural America. The rate quadrupled in the 1980s and reached twenty-four a year in the 1990s.[21] Examples abound of communities trying to hold on to prisons regardless of their need from a corrections' viewpoint. Residents of Pontiac, Illinois mobilized for a fight when they heard that the governor wanted to close the 137-year-old Pontiac Correctional Center to save money for the state. The prison

19. Corrections Corporation of America, "Weathering the Economic Downturn," para. 1.

20. Colorado Criminal Justice Reform Coalition, "Private Prisons and Public Money," 2.

21. Santos, "Plan to Close."

was the town's second largest employer, and its closure would take an estimated 750 jobs and fifty million dollars a year from the area. They held rallies and a parade, carried blue and white "Save Our Prison" signs, wore matching T-shirts, and appealed to prison officials, the governor, and other politicians. Plans by the Spitzer administration in New York to close three facilities, all of which were operating below capacity, caused similar problems in Franklin County, a rural area at the northern end of Adirondack Park.[22] And when Governor Rick Scott and the Florida legislature announced closure of seven prisons in addition to four that had already been slated for closure, there was plenty of disappointment in the host communities. The president of a local chamber of commerce noted in early 2012 that the closing of only one institution in a small community would cause the loss of over 4.4 million dollars in salaries, with major negative implications for local businesses.

The fact is, however, that the pursuit of economic gain seems illusory at best. Building booms provide employment but also foster a cycle of dependency. Depressed rural communities come to rely on the prisons as a source of jobs, economic sustenance, and services, while little effort is devoted to attracting businesses that will grow the economy over the long term. The few studies on the local economic impacts of prisons to date have not found significant positive impacts. They have instead found no significant difference or discernible pattern of economic trends between counties that were home to a prison and counties that were not.[23] Another analysis in Texas found no impacts as measured by consumer spending in nearly three fourths of the areas examined.[24]

And the consequences can be worse. By spring 2011, at least thirteen Texas public-private jails or prisons were sitting empty or partially empty.[25] The *Waco Herald-Tribune* reported in April, 2010 that a private prison that two years previously was touted as a multi-million dollar moneymaker for a central Texas county appeared to be headed into a financial death spiral. It had no inmates to fill it, and the New Jersey-based detention company under contract to manage and operate the

22. Ibid.

23. Tootle, "Role of Prisons," 2.

24. King, Mauer, and Huling, "Big Prisons," 2.

25. Grits for Breakfast, "Private Prison?"

jail wanted the county to bail them out.[26] In another case, a prison management company exercised an escape clause in early 2010 to pull out of managing Johnson County, Texas jails even though it had one more year to go on a three-year contract. And Littlefield, Texas had its bond rating lowered and had to reduce spending in other areas to pay a debt service on an empty jail.[27] Similar situations are occurring elsewhere, as the market "bubble" that private prisons enjoyed over the last several years appears to be bursting.

Labor unions are the final spoke in the prison-industrial-complex wheel. Unions claim to protect their member's interests, and this usually is the case. But labor unions also protect the interests of labor unions—of the institution itself along with its employees and officers. Regardless of who the beneficiary is, unions want more jobs—within the correctional system for corrections officers and others represented by the unions, and within the union hierarchies for people who represent employees of the correctional system. The number of jobs is greater when more people are incarcerated. So unions have a substantial interest in assuring that as many people as possible are locked up and that more prisons are built or expanded. Unions also want higher—sometimes disproportionately higher—pay for the people they represent. Tales from two of the country's largest prison systems make the point.

The California prison system is the third largest penal system in the country. The California Correctional Peace Officers Association (CCPOA) is the California prison guards' union. It has represented its members well, winning them by far the most generous wages and benefits of prison officers anywhere in the country. Under a deal that expired in 2006, the average member of the CCPOA earned around $100,000 a year with overtime. (Since then, wages have gone up again.) And they earn pensions of up to 90 percent of salary starting as early as age fifty—more than teachers, nurses, or firefighters and matched only by the state's highway patrol.

In recent years the CCPOA has become a major player in California politics, and it is widely considered to be one of the most powerful political forces in the state. The union has traditionally supported tough

26. *Waco Herald-Tribune*, "New Jail."

27. Hudson, "For-Profit Lock-Up."

anticrime initiatives such as the state's "three strikes you're out" law and has pushed California politicians to maintain hard-line attitudes towards corrections. Its lobbying efforts and campaign contributions have greatly facilitated the passage of legislation favorable to union members and have prevented reforms that could have reduced incarceration.

In January 2005, Governor Arnold Schwarzenegger proposed restructuring the California prison system. Part of the plan involved sending parole violators to halfway houses or community-based drug abuse programs instead of returning them to prison. California prisons were dangerously overcrowded, and rehabilitation was expected to clear more space, keep prison costs down, and reform convicts more adequately than imprisonment. The Department of Corrections began allowing some parolees to enter halfway houses and substance abuse facilities, and the program was on its way to full implementation. But the union objected, maintaining that the governor's new stance was soft on crime. The CCPOA, along with other groups, launched a television ad campaign against the proposal. They appear to have been successful, as Schwarzenegger abandoned the parole program.

The American Federation of State County and Municipal Employees (AFSCME) represents correctional officers and staff in disciplinary hearings, grievances and mediations in Texas. It regularly meets with Texas Department of Criminal Justice officials to discuss pay, training, the grievance process and other key issues. In April 2009, AFSCME organized a "lobby day" in Austin, and dozens of corrections officers visited their representatives and senators to push their agenda. The union states that employees it represents received larger pay raises than any other state employee group, and that it waged successful efforts to create a new corrections officer position. AFSCME is pushing the U.S. Congress to pass a law to require most U.S. employers of public safety officers to enter into collective bargaining agreements with their employees.

THE RESULTS

Numbers capture the grand magnitude of the get tough policies, the war on drugs, the changes in sentencing, and the influence of the prison-industrial complex. Direct expenditures for the three key criminal justice functions—police, judicial, and corrections—grew from roughly 36 billion dollars in 1982 to approximately 214 billion dollars in 2006.[28] In spite of—or perhaps because of, depending largely on one's worldview—all the get tough efforts, crime rates rose dramatically from the 1960s to the late 1980s. Then they generally leveled out for a decade or so before beginning a steady decline in the early 1990s that continues to today.[29] The estimated number of violent crimes was 288,000 in 1960.[30] The number peaked in 1993 at 1,926,017 and then declined to 1,318,398 in 2009.[31] However, drug use continued at an alarming rate.

Correctional populations were a very different story. Prior to 1972, the rate of growth in the number of people being put in prison was about the same as growth in the general population. In 1973, however, incarceration rates and the prison population began to grow precipitously along with the crime rate, increasing by over 700 percent in just four decades.[32] The 1973 population of federal and state prisons was just over 200,000 people. By year-end 2009, over 1.5 million human beings were behind bars in state and federal prisons, and another 760,000 were in state and local jails. Incredibly, over seven million people were under correctional supervision—in jail or prison, or on probation or parole.[33]

The number of people under correctional supervision in the United States began a modest but significant decline in 2009. As of January 2010 the number of persons under the jurisdiction of state prison authorities had declined by 5,739, or 0.4 percent, since December 2008. This decline, the first in nearly forty years, occurred in twenty-seven states, as a number of jurisdictions adopted policies designed to reduce their prison populations, such as increases in residential and community-based treatment and diversion programs, shortened probation terms, and increased parole rates. Notwithstanding all the changes, while there was a modest decline in the number of people under correctional supervision, prison populations actually continued their increase through 2009. Decreases in the probation, parole, and jail populations contributed to the decline in total correctional population.[34]

28. Bureau of Justice Statistics, "Direct Expenditures."

29. The Disaster Center, "United States."

30. Federal Bureau of Investigation, "Crime and Crime Rates."

31. Ibid., "Crime in the United States."

32. Pew Center on the States, "Prison Count 2010."

33. Bureau of Justice Statistics, "Correctional Populations."

34. Ibid.

The number of offenders under adult correctional supervision in the U.S. declined 1.3 percent and the total U.S. prison population fell 0.6 percent in 2010, the first decline in the total prison population in nearly four decades. While these are the most recent data available, anecdotal information indicates the trend of slight reductions in numbers incarcerated continued into 2012, as governments at all levels attempted to cut costs in efforts to balance budgets.

All of this raises questions as to the relationship between crime and imprisonment, or between imprisonment and crime. Alexis de Tocqueville gave us something to think about. When he was touring the United States in the 1830s, military rank in Europe was a privilege of nobility, and lower officers had little opportunity to gain promotion. He noted the difference in the States, with their more democratic approach: "In a democratic army all the ambitious men eagerly hope for war, because war opens up vacancies and permits the right of seniority, which is the sole privilege natural to democracy, to be violated. We thus arrive at the remarkable conclusion that of all armies, the ones that desire war most ardently are the democratic ones, even though the peoples who love peace best are the democratic ones."[35]

Similarly, free people, exercising the rights of the majority and the free enterprise system in their own self-interest, can easily trample on the rights of the minority. The powerful can subdue the weak. Locking people in prisons can get votes for politicians, jobs for prison employees and unions, profits for private prison companies, and economic development for rural communities. But at what cost? And who are the people being affected by the system?

35. Quoted in Damrosch, *Tocqueville's Discovery of America*, 214.

3

The People

THE MAY 14, 2010 *Houston Chronicle* detailed the criminal exploits of Billy Galloway and Kevin Varga. The two met in a South Dakota prison in 1998. Both were paroled, Galloway after serving time for theft and attempted robbery and Varga for grand theft. They agreed to make a road trip to Mexico, to be financed by a scam in which each had his girlfriend offer sex to men along the way. The two criminals would then ambush and rob the men. The body of their first victim was found in Wichita, Kansas, wrapped in sheets in Galloway's abandoned SUV. Their second victim was found in Greenville, Texas. According to the *Chronicle*, "Police said a hammer and bloody tree limb were found near [the] battered body, which the four dragged into some woods and set on fire."[1]

The prosecutor in their capital murder case said of Galloway, "A pretty violent son of a gun, a nasty dude. These were brutal, horrible murders, just absolutely disgusting."[2]

They were, without doubt, brutal, horrible, disgusting—"nasty dudes." I'd as soon share a cell with Hannibal Lecter as with one of them. They deserved to be removed from society. And others like them—the malicious murderers, the rapists, the pedophiles, the armed robbers—have to be prevented from preying on other human beings.

But news headlines and society's conventional wisdom often overstate the case and demonize all people who are or have been behind bars. And society all but ignores their families, who often suffer as much as those imprisoned. Just who are these people, anyway?

1. Graczyk, "Day After."
2. Ibid.

THE INMATES

Over 7.3 million people are under criminal justice jurisdiction—in jail, prison, on probation, or on parole—and over 2.3 million are actually incarcerated in jails or prisons at any one time in the U.S. An estimated 13.5 million Americans are in a prison or jail over the course of a year.[3] Most have a great deal in common. As Samuel Walker, emeritus professor of criminal justice at the University of Nebraska, Omaha, has noted in *Popular Justice*, in spite of all the changes over the years, "There is one overriding continuity in the history of American criminal justice. The 'clients' of the justice system today bear a striking resemblance to their counterparts in earlier times. At every point in the history of criminal justice, the people arrested, prosecuted, and punished have been mainly the poor and the powerless. The major changes within that group have been shifts in the ethnic and racial balance."[4] Or in the words of Ecclesiastes 1:9, "there is nothing new under the sun."

Almost all American inmates are U.S. citizens, male, poor, poorly educated, young, nonwhite, irresponsible, angry, and in pain. Most often they are innocent of any crime of violence. They nearly always have drug use in their past and, as often as not, have been to a previous rodeo—or several. Meet John Doe, an archetype of people behind bars. John is male, twenty-four years old, and his skin is not white and his hair is not blond. His mother was seventeen when he was born, and he has never met his father. John stayed mostly with his grandmother when growing up, although for periods he stayed with an auntie and on one occasion in a foster home for a short time. Life was a series of chaotic events. He always resided in "the hood," a poor section of a large city, and John began to learn the streets at an early age: smoking stolen cigarettes from early childhood, marijuana at age twelve (sometimes with his stepfather), doing and dealing hard drugs at fourteen, shoplifting and other property crimes along the way to support his habit—and sometimes his family, as it was. In eighth grade he got into trouble at school and was transferred to an alternative school. He dropped out during the fall of his tenth grade year. John has never been married, but he has two children—a daughter who is three and a one-year-old son whom he has never seen. John spent five months in a juvenile facility and this is his second time in the big house. He was incarcerated first

3. Gibbons and Katzenbach, "Confronting Confinement," 11.

4. Walker, *Popular Justice*, 8.

for aggravated robbery, was paroled, and was sent back after he had a dirty drug test. His younger brother and a favorite uncle are also in prison. John is making some effort to get his GED, but he is worried about what life will be like when he is released, how he will make a living, how he will pay his back child-support payments, how he will stay away from drugs. Drugs are like quicksand. The more he struggles, the faster he sinks. John likes drugs and the excitement of the drug lifestyle, and is not sure there is anything wrong with them—particularly with marijuana. It all seems hopeless.

More than 90 percent of inmates are men. Thirty-nine percent are black, 33 percent are white, 21 percent are Hispanic, and 7 percent are of other races. At the start of the 1990s, the U.S. had more black men between the ages of twenty and twenty-nine under the control of the nation's criminal justice system than the total number in college. Black men had an incarceration rate of 4,618 per 100,000 U.S. residents while white men had a rate of 773 per 100,000 U.S. residents. Approximately 6 percent are non-citizens.

Thirty-three percent of all inmates are under age thirty, and 60 percent are under age forty.[5] But this is changing, as aging inmates are the most rapidly growing group in U.S. prisons. A January 2012 study by Human Rights Watch found that the number of state and federal prisoners age sixty-five or older grew at ninety-four times the rate of the overall prison population between 2007 and 2010. The number age fifty-five or older grew at six times the rate of the overall prison population between 1995 and 2010. The study noted that many current prisoners will not leave prison until they become extremely old, if at all, as one in ten state prisoners is serving a life sentence and 11.2 percent have sentences longer than twenty years.[6]

Twenty-six percent of state prison admissions are for violent offenses such as homicide, kidnapping, rape, robbery or assault. Approximately 30 percent are for property crimes and another 31 percent for drug offenses, with the remainder for miscellaneous public order violations.[7]

5. Sabol and Couture, "Prison Inmates," 7.
6. Human Rights Watch, "Old Behind Bars," 18.
7. Bureau of Justice Statistics, "Survey," 4–5.

Almost 200,000 women are in U.S. correctional facilities.[8] The female prison population has grown by over 800 percent during the past three decades, as compared to a growth of just over 400 percent for men. About half of the women in prison are white, 30 percent are black, and 20 percent are Hispanic.[9]

Most women are incarcerated for low-level crimes, such as prostitution, various drug offenses, forgery, writing bad checks, and other property offenses. Their crimes are often committed while assisting their boyfriends or husbands with duties such as making the drops, holding and carrying stuff, or driving the car. Before the new sentencing laws of recent decades, judges were often inclined to sympathize with women who may have played a secondary role in a crime and sentence them less aggressively. But with the stricter sentencing laws and the move toward gender equality, more women are being incarcerated and for longer terms.

Roberta Rogers had never had any problems with the law for most of her life, and then she became a statistic and an archetype of women inmates: abused, single parent, doing alcohol and drugs, committing theft to cover the habit. She received a six-year sentence, and served three, for a theft of over $100,000. She explains,

> As a single parent I felt like my life had been pretty good. But when I got the call that my dad had molested my brother's girls, it totally sent my life into a whirlwind. Immediately I felt like I had not told enough people. The only person that believed me when it happened to me was my mom. My dad denied all of it for the next thirty years. I think I had actually started second guessing my own memories. The feelings I felt while realizing the feelings and pain that my nieces were going to feel the rest of their lives was horrible. It was that very night that I went to a nearby town. I went to get drunk. Even though I am not a drinker and never drank, I wanted to be drunk. What I found at that bar was so much worse than I thought I was looking for. I met some people that "shared" some of their dope with me, and I never turned back. The dope turned into an every minute habit for me. And while I was high, gambling was my way of escape. I would lock myself in my room and turn to the hundreds of gambling

8. Ibid., "Correctional Populations," 3.

9. Institute on Women and Criminal Justice, "Quick Facts," 1–3.

> websites on the Internet. That was how my theft started. I was so sure that I could pay it back the next day because I would win that night. I was so sure! I was the bookkeeper for the office so I just wrote my own checks and figured I could pay it back when I won online. Of course that usually didn't happen, and so it went on. But it did the purpose I meant it for. I didn't have to interact with many people when I was home and I didn't have to think about anything except the gambling that was taking place.

Roughly 65,000 women in federal and state custody are mothers of approximately 147,000 minor children. Over 75 percent of these mothers provided most of the daily care for their children before they were sent away.[10]

Although offenses of record vary, drugs are the albatross around the neck of prison inmates. Many are convicted of drug violations per se—use, possession, manufacture, or distribution of illegal drugs such as cocaine, heroin, marijuana, and amphetamines or inappropriate activities with legal drugs. And of course drugs, including alcohol, affect the user's behavior, often fostering violence and other illegal activity. Most users are also engaged in a lifestyle where they do not participate in the legitimate economy and have frequent contact with criminals and illegal markets. Like the biblical Adam himself, they get swept up in the temptation to do wrong. All told, drugs and crime work hand in glove to fill the country's prisons.

The data is staggering. Drug and alcohol abuse and addiction are implicated in 78 percent of violent crimes and 83 percent of property crimes. Over 30 percent of inmates assigned to state prisons and over 50 percent of those assigned to federal prisons are sent there for drug offenses.[11] Sixty-five percent of the 2.3 million inmates in American prisons meet the standard medical criteria for drug and alcohol addiction and abuse. Roughly a third of all inmates were under the influence of alcohol or drugs when they committed their offense—committed acts of violence, stole money to buy drugs, abused drugs, violated drug laws, or some combination of the above.[12] Over half used drugs during

10. Ibid.
11. Bureau of Justice Statistics, "Drug Use," 4.
12. Califano, "Criminally Unjust," 1.

the month of their offense, and roughly two-thirds had used drugs regularly at some time in their lives.[13] Drugs of choice vary, including alcohol, marijuana, cocaine, heroin, methamphetamines, various stimulants or depressants, and others.

Shawn is a poster boy for the human juggernaut that drugs have become. He explained,

> My name is Shawn. That's what they call me. At eight years old I started smoking weed. My brother gave me my first joint. He just passed it to me. Told me "hit it." I started choking. He told me, "Just swallow it. Swallow the smoke." After about five or ten minutes I started laughing. Then after about thirty, forty-five minutes, I was in a refrigerator. I had found a new passion. I loved smoking weed. But smoking this weed cost money, so I had to start doing criminal things. My brother introduced me to stealing. But really, he wanted me to support his weed habit. Now we all stealing for my brother, just to get high.

Shawn was sentenced to juvenile detention, got out, and got a job as a busboy but soon remembered how much more money he thought he could make selling drugs.

> I fell in love with the drug game. My mother never knew where I was when I was selling drugs. By the time she found me, I had my own apartment, had my car, my truck, I had my girl friends. It was a beautiful thing. When I made that first forty dollars in less than thirty seconds, I was hooked. And that's when my journey began. I became a hustler, and I'm gonna sell this dope regardless. I'm gonna do what I have to do. If it's hard or if its soft, I'm gonna sell it. I loved to sell drugs. I loved the life of selling drugs. I loved the attention I got from the females. The respect from the streets. I loved the clothes I was wearing. I loved the jewelry I was wearing. I loved smoking weed and getting high. I used to say, "I can't face the day sober. I got to blow me a joint." The dope game took me to another level. When people started seeing my money and power, I had to start packing that thing. I started getting reckless with it. That's what the streets taught me. You respond with violence to protect your reputation. The game flipped.

Shawn is now thirty-seven years old and has been in prison for over fifteen years on a murder conviction.

13. Bureau of Justice Statistics, "Drug Use," 4.

One study concluded that blacks comprise over 62 percent of all drug offenders admitted to state prison, even though this racial disparity bears scant relation to racial differences in drug offending. There were, for example, five times more white drug users than black, but relative to population, black men were admitted to state prison on drug charges at a rate thirteen times greater than that of white men. In large part because of the extraordinary racial disparities in incarceration for drug offenses, blacks were locked up for all offenses at over eight times the rate of whites.[14] Of the country's 253,300 state prison inmates serving time for drug offenses at year end 2005, 45 percent were black, 28 percent were white, and 20 percent were Hispanic.[15]

~

Most offenders have had dreadful home lives, where their closest companions were poverty, chaos, abuse, and crime. Significantly fewer than one-half lived with both parents while growing up, and one in six were abused during that period. Roughly 20 percent of offenders' parents abused alcohol or drugs, while approaching 50 percent have at least one family member who is also incarcerated—most likely their father or a brother. They often are the latest in generations of miscreants.[16]

Carol Vance, who formerly ran the Texas prison system, told me, "Most people are in prison due to lack of effective fathers in their lives—they have holes in their lives that they try to fill with drugs and alcohol."

Consider Mario, age 27, convicted of aggravated robbery at age twelve, in and out of the system, locked behind bars for all but eight months of the last fifteen years, currently incarcerated for three counts of armed robbery and two counts of attempted murder. He never knew his father. Mario explained,

> I'm from the projects, where I growed up around my mama smoking crack. My grandmother raised me most of the time. By the age of ten my mama came back into my life. She had been in rehab. She tried to change her life, but at the time I was already rebelling, because I didn't really feel like my mother loved me. I felt like she put crack over me and my brothers and sisters. At the time I didn't understand the addiction you can have to

14. Human Rights Watch, "Punishment and Prejudice," para. 18.
15. Sabol and Couture, "Prison Inmates," 21.
16. Bureau of Justice Statistics, "Drug Use," 8.

> drugs. My big brother is who I looked up to—my role model. I considered my big brother a gangster. Growing up, that's what I wanted to be. My big brother showed me how to cut crack—how to sell it. Since I've been in prison, I've had people show me more love than my family did.

Poverty is as pervasive among inmates as cell phones among teenagers. A relatively old (1991—but there is no reason to believe things have improved) study concluded that more than half of all state prisoners reported an annual income of less than $10,000 prior to their arrest, and only 15 percent reported more than $25,000. Only 55 percent were working full time when they were arrested.[17] And, notwithstanding the conventional wisdom, there is considerable evidence that most of those involved in the drug trade are also poor. In the 1990s Steven Levitt and Stephen Dubner did a case study of drug traffickers for their book, *Freakonomics*. In a chapter entitled "Why Do Drug Dealers Still Live with Their Moms?" they concluded that the answer is that "except for the top cats, they don't make much money. They had no choice but to live with their mothers. For every big earner, there were hundreds more just scraping along."[18]

Jake is a model of the disastrous family life that is so common among prison inmates, as well as the generational effect of poverty and crime. By nineteen Jake was burglarizing businesses, and he celebrated his twentieth birthday in prison, convicted of burglary and criminal mischief. He has been out, and back in, on two occasions for similar offenses. He is now serving his third hitch in the Texas prison system. Jake understands that he must assume responsibility for his own actions, but he also says that "Five generations down we're still trying to heal from the wounds that began decades ago."

Jake's mother remembers, "When I was two we lived in a barn, we had nothing. It was winter, very cold and I stopped wetting the bed, because if I did it would wet my socks and freeze my feet."

When Jake was a toddler, his parents were often smoking pot, cooking meth, and speeding on "prelude," a type of drug that was in a sugarcoated pill capsule. After they broke the pills open and took the powder, they put the shells in an ashtray, where Jake would find and eat them and get high on the residue. When Jake was nine, his mother

17. Political Research Associates, "Defending Justice," para. 2.

18. Levitt and Dubner, *Freakonomics*, 103.

robbed a gas station. She was drunk and had nothing to give her children for Christmas. By age fifteen he was hooked on weed and had quit school. His dad had an insatiable drug addiction. His parents divorced when he was seventeen. His mother went to rehab for a probation violation, and his dad left town. Jake lived with his sister in a motel room, where he became so depressed and malnourished that his hair began falling out.

Jake's uncle Hugo has been busted twice for drug trafficking, his uncle Otis was imprisoned twice and is now a functioning marijuana addict, and his aunt Sandra is addicted to crack and is in and out of prisons in another state. Jake's aunt Alice was on crack for twenty years and in prison twice before she died in a collision with a train that looked suspiciously like suicide. Two male cousins have been murdered. One female cousin is a recovering heroin addict, a second has been to prison, and a third is into crack cocaine and prostitution.

Jake's grandmother was picked up for selling drugs six months before her death. His grandfather was extorting local businessmen by age sixteen and later made a living growing and selling weed. He had a bad temper, beat and abused his wife, and molested a daughter. He served one term in prison. When he died most in the family were relieved that the "monster" was gone.

Most inmates make several trips through the revolving prison door. More than two-thirds of state and federal prisoners have received prior sentences and served probation or prison time before their current term of incarceration. More than half of these had received two or more prior sentences. Of nonviolent offenders expecting release from state prison, 80 percent previously had been incarcerated or on probation, many on four or five previous occasions.[19]

As many as one in five of the Americans in jail and prison are seriously mentally ill, far outnumbering the number in mental hospitals.[20] More than half of all prison and jail inmates have some sort of mental health problems. On any given day, it is estimated that about 70,000 inmates

19. Bureau of Justice Statistics, "Profile," 3.

20. Fellner, "Ill-Equipped,"15.

in U.S. prisons are psychotic and from 200,000 to 300,000 suffer from mental disorders such as schizophrenia, bipolar disorder, and major depression.[21]

As more state hospitals have closed, jails and prisons have become the nation's default mental health system. The majority of those with mental illness in the criminal justice system are people on the margins of society, locked away for misdemeanors and crimes of survival or because of their behavioral disorders. They are often minorities, are almost always impoverished and disabled by their illnesses, and most likely have used and abused drugs.

Prison compounds the problems of the mentally ill. They often have trouble following the everyday discipline of prison life, and many become involved in disruptive behavior, belligerence, aggression, and violence. Such behavior may lead to them being placed in solitary confinement, where medical care may be even more limited, and the isolation and idleness can be psychologically destructive.

~

Regardless of their crime, their family, their prior life, their mental health, or any other characteristic—or even how tough they appear on the surface—essentially all inmates are lonely, hopeless, and fearful. Many describe the experience as like being buried alive. Richard Callahan, who has been behind bars for fifteen years, had a similar description: "We're all just a bunch of walking dead." I asked him to explain. His response was intriguing—sad. Richard said that probably 80 percent of inmates would tell you they feel dead, and the walking dead feeling boils down to hopelessness, anger, and frustration. Richard continued, "There's a guilt and shame that manifests from all the bad choices I've made. At one point in my life I allowed the guilt and shame to consume me. Today it's a constant battle because that type of guilt and shame works to steal a person's hope. When I was overcome with guilt and shame I felt defeated to the point of giving up on things positive. All of this leads to a dead hopelessness—a perspective of total and constant discouragement."

Upon reflection, Richard explained inmates' "deadness" another way. He noted that men are raised to be heads of their households, the

21. Kanapaux, "Guilty."

family leaders and protectors. But all this changes when one goes to prison. When a man goes to prison,

> He feels powerless where he used to be in control and it's almost like everything he was trained to be, his duties as a man, are ripped away from him. This type of man feels dead because he has no control in areas where he used to. Wives leave and take their children, girlfriends cheat and move on. Mothers and parents grow older and have a harder time at normal activities. Girlfriends and wives who stay face struggles. The circumstances are endless, but not being able to handle the situation like a man thinks he should makes a man feel out of control, powerless, and leads to feeling dead. Incarcerated women feel the same pains but it's increased when it affects their parents and their children. Richard concluded, "We entertain the concept that our lives have no significance while we're locked up."

Richard Halliburton is fifty years old and has been locked up for over eighteen years—on and off since he was incarcerated by the Texas Youth Commission as a fifteen-year-old. Most recently he was convicted of forgery of a stolen check for $73.00 and sentenced to forty-five years as a habitual criminal. He received another five years "stacked" for an aggravated assault while in prison. Richard explained the same concept in different words: "Life in here is very lonely and most people just can't see anything good happening in the future because the past they have chose has brought nothing but pain and heartache."

Danny Sneed used different words: "You can easily lose the sense of reality. I base this on the shame, the guilt, the remorse. I sense a huge dark cloud of failure that looms over me constantly. Alienation from family and friends. On one sentence I spent ten years and I only had two visits from my family during those ten years. That for sure was a problem."

Roberta Rogers, on drugs and incarcerated for theft, explained the feeling of deadness as follows: "I guess the biggest problems I faced in prison were the feelings of worthlessness. I had been a upstanding member of my community and had raised two sons as a single parent. Then to let my life spiral out of control as I had was almost more than I could handle. Most of my family had decided they did not want me in their lives any longer and so the feeling of loneliness was also tremendous."

A yearning for relationships in prison is more obvious among women than among men, who tend to cover their feelings with a thick blanket of "machismo." Women, who typically have fewer visits from the outside than men, often close the gap by fantasizing and inventing make-believe relationships. They often band together as "families," with individuals recognized for specific roles such as mother, father, children, or grandparents.

Jerry Bryan, a former pastor and televangelist, worked for several years as a chaplain at Texas' Darrington unit, a large, tough, high-security, eighty-five-year-old facility on approximately 6,500 acres of agricultural land in south Texas. He is currently the chaplain at the Carol Vance unit, a smaller, newer, faith-based pre-release operation. I asked him about how inmates felt about themselves and their lives. Not surprisingly, he said, "It depends." Then he explained, "It's different in different units. In the Darrington unit, almost no one could see their freedom on the horizon, so they just had to make the most out of what they had there. There was an overwhelming feeling of despair. They tried to maintain family contacts and so on and saw those relationships eroding. Dear John letters, and things like that. It is different in the Vance unit. They are all short-timers, who will be getting out soon. Their biggest concern is fear—fear of re-entry. Many of them are two, three, four, or five time losers. They almost assume they will come back. They look forward to being released, but they also are fearful of it."

Jack Brady, assistant professor of criminal justice at Indiana Wesleyan University, suggested a major implication of all this during our long visit over a lunch of barbeque and iced tea. Jack is involved in a number of restorative justice programs in Indiana prisons and previously worked as a police officer, probation officer, county coroner, and sheriff's chaplain. Time and again he mentioned "criminal thinking." I asked him to explain. Jack characterized criminal thinking as a victim orientation, where an inmate continually blames others for his own situation, claims he is the one who was really wronged, and believes no one in the world has experienced what he has experienced. He refuses to take responsibility for what he has done and assumes that others are out to get him. Not surprisingly, he spends a lot of time trying to figure out other peoples' angles. Those involved in criminal thinking typically make choices based on what they wish were true rather than what is true, and try to act fearless but in fact live in fear. Jack believes various aspects of criminal thinking are common among nearly all inmates.

A generalized picture of today's inmates and why they are locked up is not a pretty scene. Compare it with the witchcraft events of the 1600s, discussed in chapter 1. There are stark differences. Mainly, there is no evidence that alleged witches violated any laws, committed any crimes, or even did anything wrong, while nearly all inmates have violated criminal laws and hurt other individuals or society. But there are startling parallels. As previously discussed, the punishment of alleged witches was thought to have been driven by factors such as cultural factionalism: the interplay of more prosperous and poorer peoples and of other distinct factions; social and economic change, largely involving erosion of self-governing traditions and challenges to the religious establishment; and fear of Indian enemies that created a climate of fear. Today, we as a society need to think about the extent to which people are incarcerated for many of the same reasons: cultural factionalism involving the interplay of white middle-class policymakers and poor minority groups; taking the easy way out in a time of great social and economic change, particularly involving handling of drugs and addiction; erosion of self-governing traditions, where we turn our problems over to the government; a religious establishment that largely looks the other way; and fear of those who are not like us.

Again, not a pretty scene.

THE FAMILIES

Like an iceberg, much of the pain and suffering associated with prison is below the waterline, difficult to see. We often don't see it until it hits us between the eyes. We forget that people who are locked away are missing from other people, who often are hurting almost as much as those behind bars. Inmates are husbands, wives, sons, daughters, brothers, sisters, and parents. Over half of the 1.5 million people held in the nation's prisons at mid-year 2007 were parents of children under age eighteen. They reported an estimated 1.7 million minor children, accounting for 2.3 percent of the U.S. resident population under age eighteen.[22] Ten million young people in the United States have had a mother or father—or both—spend time behind bars at some point in their lives.[23]

These children are a hidden population that pays a stiff penalty for the absence of their parents. If an absentee father is locked up, his incarceration may not make matters much worse. But if he lived at home or provided financial support, his absence will make a difference. The disruption will probably be even worse if the mother, the likely primary caregiver, is taken away. In these cases, children are likely to be moved to another home, separated, or placed in foster care—all situations likely to lead to pervasive anger and misconduct by the child. They frequently have behavioral, emotional, and school-performance problems as a result of their embarrassment, anger, anxiety, depression, sadness, grief, shame, fear, and low self-esteem. Many experience loneliness, sleeplessness, and eating disorders.

Remember Roberta Roberts from earlier in the chapter? Her kids were eighteen and sixteen when she went to prison. Now released, she recalls,

> My youngest son was still living with me at the time of my incarceration and that did pose a problem. I didn't know where he would go or what he would do. His dad was not much help in this area because he is an alcoholic and never really played much of a role in my sons' life. My son went from place to place, mostly living in his car for the first year I was locked up. He found a group of friends that were into methamphetamines and started living that lifestyle. When he would come see me it would break my heart because I felt like I probably started this trend for him. But after awhile I finally convinced him that he needed to get out of it and he moved to New York where he now has a family and two kids of his own. I thank God everyday for taking my son out of that life.

The effect on children of having parents locked away does not end when the parents are released. Both children and parents face a range of problems and challenges when they are reunited. The released parents must find jobs, perhaps find housing, and do a myriad of other new things to reintegrate into the community. Perhaps more important,

22. Bureau of Justice Statistics, "Parents," 2.

23. The Annie E. Casey Foundation, "Partnerships," 8.

they frequently face the formidable task of re-establishing their relationships. New relationships have formed, family dynamics are different, and the released persons are usually facing very different family systems that do not include them. Family members may limit access to children, and spouses who have remained free may have moved to other relationships. The children may have developed close relationships with other adults, perhaps grandparents, uncles, or aunts, and shifting focus back to the long-absent parents may be traumatic and present a stressful transition that exacerbates the children's existing problems. And the struggles are tough to outgrow.

While the reasons for criminality and incarceration are complex and involve a number of factors, it is clear that parental incarceration is an important factor leading to imprisonment of children. Children of prisoners are more likely to go to jail than to graduate high school. They are seven times more likely to go to jail than children whose moms or dads have not served time behind bars. Nationally, 47 percent of inmates in state prisons and 50 percent of all juveniles in custody have a parent or other close relative who has been incarcerated.[24]

Parents of inmates are near the head of the line—perhaps just behind children—of those hurt by prison incarceration. Data on this group is woefully inadequate, seemingly limited to acknowledging that each inmate has two and usually both are severely affected. But anecdotal information paints a picture of fear, concern, and misery.

I visited with Ruth in her small home in southeast Texas. (Her husband Jack chose not to attend our discussion.) She explained, in a subdued, hesitant tone, with occasional tears running down her cheek: "This was his sixteen year old stepdaughter. And it was consensual. It was never—it was more of a touching. And his wife, the mother of the girl, knows it. Steven had talked to Candy and said, 'Now Candy, this has got to stop.' The girl had kept a diary, and mother found the diary. When his wife confronted Steve, he went to the sheriff's office and turned himself in."

24. Califa, "Prisoners as Parents," 3.

Ruth bonded Steve out of jail. He and his wife immediately divorced, and he returned home to live with Ruth and Jack. Steve was fired from his job as a paramedic and then found another one in an auto-parts store, where he worked until he plea bargained a fifteen-year sentence in prison. Steve was in county jail awaiting transfer to state prison at the time of our interview.

Ruth told me she lives in fear that something bad will happen to Steve while he is locked up. She said, "One of the hardest things is seeing him. It's hard on him and it's hard on me too. But I don't let it get to me. I'm going to visit him every time I can. We are able to go twice a week now."

I asked Ruth how this all affected her life. She answered,

> I realize that I am in a depression, and I've got to get out of it. When I come home at night from work, it's all I can do to fix something and then I do not want to do one thing more. There are times now when I don't think all the time about what's he doing, what's happening to him. But I still just can't make myself do what I know needs to be done. When I start to cook things it bothers me, cause I think about what he likes. Brings back the memories. And I don't know about Jack, but I think he is the same way. And we had the financial problems and spent money we didn't have, and the worry. When he gets out, he is gonna have a tremendous child support burden. We will help him when we can.

And then there is the matter of Ruth's friends—or the people she thought were friends and now she is not so sure about. She explained, "I've worked in the same office for twenty-three years. When I came back, my boss knew, they all knew. But nobody in that office said how are you doing or we are here for you if you want to talk or anything. It was just like nothing had happened. I just couldn't believe it. It really hurt. I thought, 'they don't even care what I'm going through.'"

I also visited with Doug and Bonnie Wilson in their beautiful suburban home in a peaceful, forested subdivision just outside Houston. Doug did most of the talking. He told me about their son Michael—how he got involved in drugs in ninth grade, experienced increasing problems in school, participated in various drug programs, seemed to improve and then regressed, and then enrolled in an alternative school. He seemed to be doing well, until he offered to drive some friends in his car to rob a group of kids they had heard had a thousand dollars. The planned robbery went to hell in a handbasket. According to Doug,

> That night two young people lost their lives. And that really changed our life, and obviously theirs, forever. We began to deal with lots of things. The tragedies that happened that night. Two families lost their children and would never see them again. In our own way, we lost our son, or ultimately would lose him. We lost our friends. Those we had know for the fifteen years that we were here—for some reason they really struggled to deal with what we were going through. Either we didn't know how to deal with it or they didn't know how to deal with us. They really kinda walked away from us. Left us kinda hanging, with no one left to hang on to. The defense was unbelievably expensive—insignificant in terms of lives that were lost, but in terms of what it did to change our life, it changed the way we would deal with things forever. And it changed us. A lot of finger pointing. Some of this is this forgiveness thing: dealing with forgiveness of our friends, forgiveness of each other, ultimately forgiveness of the whole system we are involved in. And dealing with forgiveness of our son. He took away from us the hopes and the dreams we had for him. They went up in smoke. And what were these other families going through that lost their children for life. If you look at this as a still body of water, that did not have a ripple one on it, you take a rock, and throw it in there, and you get this ripple effect, and things go out. That's the way all of these families were impacted.

Although Michael was "only" the driver, the judge sentenced him to two life sentences for aggravated robbery. Doug explained, "And a life sentence for aggravated robbery in Texas is thirty years, day-for-day. So Michael is faced with thirty years before he is eligible for parole. We don't claim that, because it will eat us up. It goes back to hope. We have hope that the Lord in some way will deal with this. Or he will deal with it in whatever way he is going to deal with it. We have our hope in him."

Doug told me that the significant thing for him in all this was his anger and bitterness and hatred—of the system and many people involved in it. And also toward their friends, and at times even toward Bonnie. But, he said, "When friends walked away from us, guess what happened? People in our church stepped forward. Some came over and introduced us to a Man who turned our lives around. And that Man was Jesus Christ. The church got more involved and began to help us heal. We got involved in Emmaus, in Kairos, in Bridges To Life. And we began to find that these were some things that we needed, and in fact Christ was significant in our life. He became an integral part of our healing process."

Michael will soon be thirty-three and has been in the system now for a little over fifteen years. Many positive things have happened to him—he has been touched by some men who have a relationship to the Lord, he has shared his story in helpful ways with others, including his victims, and has earned two associate degrees and a welding degree. And Doug and Bonnie have been able to forgive those who hurt them and to hang on to hope. They visit their son every other weekend—have for fifteen years. They have books sent to him, which he reads and shares with others. Bonnie explained, "Another thing that the Lord did—if you look at the whole thing, and how God has done this for us—he knew ahead of time we were not going to desert him. So he had to figure out a way to make us the best we could be. And the most understanding we could be. We know how people desert others, so we know how important it is to visit and not desert our loved one. God added another dimension, and that is unconditional love."

Doug chipped in, "We were in there one day, and I was kinda fussing at him about wanting him to change—want his heart to change—to look for a relationship with the Lord. He turned to me, and said, 'Dad, let me tell you something. For two hours when you visit I'm Michael Wilson. But for that other seven days a week when I have to go back there, I'm 'Little Red.' That's his go-by name. So he lives a different world there than he does for those two hours he is visiting us. And that brought a whole different perspective to me. It is a different world."

Chapter 4 will explore that different world that is home for Little Red and so many others.

4

The Prisons

AMERICA IS HOME TO over 5000 prisons and jails, including 1800 federal and state correctional facilities, with a dog's breakfast of different procedures and practices.[1] Approximately 500 of the 1800 are community-based facilities where a majority of the residents are allowed leaves to work or study in the community. The remaining 1300 or so are confinement facilities such as prisons, prison farms, penitentiaries, correctional centers, work camps, and reformatories. Federal prisons differ from state facilities, every state is different, and even within states there is a wide disparity among facilities, practices, and objectives. Approximately 375 of the 1300 are high-security, tough, and mainly for violent prisoners in the cooler for a very long time with little to lose from behaving like a scoundrel. Roughly 500 are medium security institutions, while the remainder are minimum security lockups, often drug treatment or pre-release facilities. Some are for people with serious mental diseases. Others are like rehab facilities inside a fence. Some are faith-based—others seem not to know God.[2]

Accurately describing the content of this "Pandora's box" in a few pages is impossible. Certain characteristics are so common, however, that one can convey a feel for what life is like inside most prison walls—whether brick, concrete, or barbed wire.

1. Stephan, "Census," appendix table 6.
2. Ibid., 2.

CAULDRONS OF MISERY

I met with Emmit Solomon in his small office on the third floor of the First Baptist Church in Huntsville, Texas, just a stone's throw from the Walls unit, Texas' iconic prison facility. Tall, gangly, slow-talking, wearing blue jeans and cowboy boots, he seems to have changed little since his childhood on a farm near Hereford, in West Texas. But he attended New York Theological Seminary and theological school in Ft. Worth. He then worked in clinical pastoral education, as a prison chaplain for twenty years, and as director of chaplains for the Texas prison system for ten years. Solomon currently is executive director of the Restorative Justice Ministries Network of Texas.

Solomon described prison as "a cauldron of suffering." He explained it this way:

> In a hospital there is suffering, but everybody is aligned against it. In the criminal justice system, you have suffering and it is renewed every day by the system itself. It is not against suffering. It manufactures suffering. And the people who manage it don't want to touch that suffering any more than they have to. They want to keep it at arms length—impersonal—making rules that govern it so they don't have to make the decisions that actually promote suffering. Judges, attorneys, all those associated with courts, police, and the correctional system manage agencies that bring great suffering to society. They do it mechanically. There is a mechanical rule governing everything you want to do. It's designed this way so people who manage it don't have to take responsibility for saying no. They say, "I can't do something because we have a rule against it." There are rules against everything. Problem is, we have never known what to do with our deviants, and since we don't know what to do, we do what we do now. And it's counterproductive.

Just as many different maladies can wrack the body with pain and lead to death, many different conditions combine to create Solomon's cauldron of suffering. But in the end, all boil down to take-aways. Prisons take their residents' freedom, choice, space, privacy, security, and hope.

~

Over five hundred thousand inmates are locked in prisons with a wall or double-fenced perimeter and armed correctional officers stationed in a tower or on patrol. The Department of Justice designates these as high-security facilities.[3] Control-unit prisons, or units within prisons, often called "supermax" units, represent the most secure levels of custody for the highest security risks. The United States federal system has one supermax prison and many states have similar units, either standalone facilities or secure lockups within lower-security facilities. The number of prisoners held in such solitary confinement ranges from a tiny fraction in some states to around 12 percent in others, with a total of approximately eighty thousand human beings locked in these boxes.[4]

The imposition of long-term isolation, which can be for months or years, is ultimately at the discretion of prison administrators. The isolated population typically includes inmates who have assaulted or instigated assaults against staff or other inmates, have violated rules, are associated with gang members, are escape risks, or are isolated for their own protection. Some are highly dangerous and pose a threat to prison discipline, while others are not truly dangerous.

Not surprisingly, the specific conditions of solitary confinement vary from prison to prison. But there is also a numbing sameness in the experience—a sameness that allows Armondo Escatiola to speak for the broader condition. Armondo looks to be about twenty-two, although he is thirty-four years old. He is five feet eight inches tall, slight, bespectacled, articulate, and soft spoken. He seems like a munchkin in the wrong place. He also is a former gang member who has been behind bars eighteen years for the murder of two teenagers in a gang fight when he was sixteen. Armondo was cooped up in administrative segregation—solitary confinement—for almost fourteen of those years. He told me, "I was put in Ad-seg because I was a gang member, was involved in gang activities, which caused administration to seg me and other fellow gang members. Those activities were fighting, carrying out doings for the gang, etc."

Armondo described solitary confinement as follows:

> They are not big cells, depending what unit, and what level, (which is a custody class) determines the size of the cell. But they are small, like 8 x 10 feet. You have a stainless steel sink and toilet, (some have a small table coming out the wall) and bunk, and a mattress, a small window (some have no windows) that is

3. Ibid., appendix table 11.
4. *New York Times*, "Abuse."

> like 2 ½, 3 inches tall by about 3 feet in length, which you mainly look out to another pod/cell block. You have one light, and your door has 2 slot screens—like grill wire, horizontal. The door has a slot where you get your food, and get handcuffed!! Everything is all white besides the screen is black!! You have a locker under your bunk, and a little shelf to put hygien [*sic*] and a few items. Your door slides open and is controlled (also the lights) from a picket in the middle of the Pod. Where I was at they had 2 small rec. yards which each had one basketball basket and ball, one sink and a urinal, and a pull up bar which is connected to the wall, bars and walls and windows close you in. Each section had 14 cells, 7 cells each run, and a shower which is very small, has a door that has a slot and small window. Each section has a day room which is inside recreation for those inmates, which is one inmate at a time, for 1 hour a day, depending on level status.

Armondo explained that his experience involved three levels, or custody classes—and he served time on each. Level 1 assumed acceptable behavior and allowed the most privileges: more personal property, including electrical items such as radio but no television; the privilege of spending more money, if you had it, in commissary; four two-hour visits per month, if you had anyone to visit you, cuffed and behind glass; one hour of recreation each day. Level 3, the other end of the range, was for those with bad behavior, such as fighting. Armondo went to level 3 twice for fighting. Yes, he said, "You can still get into fights in Ad-seg." Level 3 only allowed inmates to have personal pictures, letters, legal work, and basic hygiene items. It allowed no electrical items, and only one-hour recreation three times per week and one visit each month.

Armondo continued, "It was so humiliating. If I went to exercise, I had to strip going out my cell, strip going into the day room, strip coming out the day room, strip going back into my cell, strip going to shower, strip going back out the shower. When my grandmother came to see me before she passed away, I had to go see her in handcuffs. It hurt me just to see her hurt. I couldn't stand for her to see me that way. That's why I changed my life."

I asked Armondo about the worst part of seg. His letter responded,

> All of it. Everything I experienced was and still is a very emotional and traumatizing experience!! Try staying in a closet for 1 day!! Not only are you caged like an animal, but escorted in cuffs, and some officer would put dog leashes on the cuffs. Even though

> I understood the precautions needed of Ad-seg inmates, because your [*sic*] talking about the worse of the worse. But, desensitizing or dehumanizing people does not make them better but worsens the situation and stats show Ad-seg inmates have a high rate of returning if they are released from Ad-seg into the world, and most commit crimes of violence. But losing my grandmother was the hardest part for me. I went into a depression that took me a couple of months to get out of, and only because of my faith and promise to her made me over come it!! Ad-seg can make you or brake you, and for the most, it breaks them.

Armando honed his art and poetry skills during the fourteen years he was locked in solitary confinement. His poem, "Overcoming Darkness" captures the pathos of his life in solitary, and too often in the general population as well.

Overcoming Darkness

Darkness, grows around us all,
Through winter, spring, summer, and fall.
As we seek blissfulness, in life,
we feel much pain.
Cutting our souls, like an acute knife,
driving us insane.
We cry within, as our voices echo inside,
rushing through our bodies
like a horrifying tide!!
Looking around, for a glimpse of light.
Struggling—endlessly!!
Never give up, without a glories fight!!
As we continue forward,
with every felicitous step,
chipping away, at the darkness, we soon, will forget.
Rays of light, reaching through to us.
Feeling the warmth, its caressing touch,
as we build a garden, of internal Bliss.
Filled with glamorous, tenderness.
Be strong, I say,
For you will overcome any darkness!!

Many consider solitary confinement as cruel and unusual punishment, and the practice has been challenged on that basis. Studies at California's Pelican Bay supermax have noted that, similar to what occurred in the Pennsylvania and New York prisons of the early 1800s, after months or years of complete isolation, many prisoners begin to lose the ability to initiate behavior of any kind and often experience chronic apathy, lethargy, depression, and despair. In extreme cases, they may become essentially catatonic. Most develop irrational anger and various fantasies, including illusions of revenge.[5] Advocates of solitary confinement seem to have only one argument for subjecting thousands of people to years of isolation: What else are we supposed to do? How else are we to deal with the violent, the disruptive, the prisoners who are just too dangerous or in too much danger to be housed with others? Not surprisingly, the budget crunches of 2011 have led to reassessments of this question. Use of solitary confinement is declining significantly in many states as prisoners are returned to general population in increasing numbers in efforts to reduce costs.

The majority of people behind bars—everyone not on death row or in solitary confinement—are in the general population, where they are allowed a community with other inmates and more access by people from the outside. People incarcerated for various crimes, such as murder, rape, drug addiction, aggravated burglary, drunk driving, or white collar crime are usually mingled together in a Noah's ark of offenders.

Until the war on crime of the 1970s, a typical general population prisoner in the United States lived in an approximately sixty-square-foot cell—slightly larger than the size of a king-sized bed or a small bathroom. These small cubicles were typically outfitted with a bunk, sink, toilet, perhaps a small shelf or desk, and a locker for storing all the resident's worldly possessions. However, because of the unprecedented imprisonment numbers fostered by the war on crime, federal prisons now house 60 percent more inmates than they were designed for, and state lockups are only slightly less stuffed.[6] Approximately half of state systems are operating at above their design capacities and many are operating at above the maximum number of inmates allocated by rating officials. Some states appear grossly overcrowded, with Alabama at 179 percent of design

5. Weinstein and Cummins, "Crime of Punishment," 2.
6. *The Economist*, "Rough Justice."

capacity and California at 178 percent leading the pack,[7] at least until an uptick in releases due to recent budget problems.

Overcrowding has led prison systems across the country to the practice of "double-celling," or packing two inmates—and sometimes more—into each cell. And when troubled, idle, bored people are arbitrarily stuffed like sardines into a too-small can, arguments inevitably arise—over who gets which bunk, when lights will be on or off, toilet and hygiene habits, property storage, cell cleaning, missing property, snoring, bodily noises, or many other small annoyances that become huge issues.

Overcrowding has also frequently led to housing offenders in large, open-space dorms—sometimes in prison gyms, basements, halls, or dayrooms—where prisoners are assigned crowded bunks with absolutely no privacy. Cal Ray Biggins, introduced earlier, described life in a bunk-room:

> I prefer living in two-man cells rather than a bunk room. Dormitories are too wide open. You never know what's gonna go down, or who gonna hit on you, or when you will get hit by mistake. Even waking up in the morning and yawning too loud is disrespectful, because the bunks are so close together that you may wake up another guy. Everything is based on respect. You never know what's going on. To me, living in dorms was the most uncomfortable time in the penitentiary. Some illegal activity might be going on, and you happen to get out of your bunk at this particular time, and the next thing the law is running in and busting you, and they gonna accuse you even if you really know nothing about it.

David, another person with experience, explained that you learn "the hard way" to deal with it. He wrote, "You refine your manners to coincide with all of the other men you have been crammed into small quarters with; you ask before changing the T.V. channel, say excuse me if you bump into anyone or invade their space or interrupt a conversation. You learn all sorts of games or penitentiary wisdom (shrewdness, knowledge, etc.) and this will include all sorts of cons, lying, tricks, all manner of scams, deceit of all manner. It's very intimidating at first, because all trust is destroyed."

7. Stephan, "Census."

Justin—a large, intimidating Yul Brynner knock-off, sent to the big house after convictions for delivery of methamphetamines, possession of a stolen vehicle, possession of firearm by a felon, and delivery of marijuana—had this to say about life on a general population unit:

> This ain't cool, man. Once you get here, you're a nobody. You're only a number. I didn't know what to expect. I can't really describe the feeling. I'm a big guy, but no matter how big and bad you think you are, once you go through that door, it's a different story. I've never really felt fear like that until I came onto a real unit. Once you come to prison, it's real easy to get caught up. There's lots of things going on. Behind these walls, you see and hear things, and this environment will teach you things you've never learned before. I take a shower every day with at least fifty other guys, buck naked, standing right next to me. I sleep in a dorm with fifty-five other guys. You don't have any privacy. You can't even get up and use the restroom at night without someone yelling at you. You can't go anywhere without a guard giving you permission.

~

Most of the time prison is as boring as a late afternoon math class, and time and again inmates describe the tedious dullness of their lives. Richard Callahan first went to prison, for burglary and criminal mischief, when he was nineteen. This is his third rodeo. He is now thirty-two, surprisingly articulate, and strongly committed to his faith. I asked him about day-to-day life in prison. He wrote, "Every inmate's prison life style can be broken down into categories and sub-categories kinda like; entertainment; development; social interaction, hustling, working; etc. Each of these can be subdivided, for example: Entertainment—watching T.V., playing games such as dominos or chess, gambling, fighting, picking on someone, going to rec., going to church programs, etc. Development—Going to rec. and exercising; going to the library and reading something edifying, going to church programs, pursuing an education, corresponding with loved ones; piddling in the craft shop. Social interaction: going to church programs and participating in programs (also a development), gang affiliation, going to rec. to talk, etc."

David said there is no real way to simply describe life in "a place where calendar years are wadded up like sheets of paper and thrown in the trash can." But he did agree to describe a typical day "of late" for him. In doing so, he confirmed the crushing boredom of most of prison life.

> My alarm clock goes off at 5:00 am. I wake up, brush my teeth, drink three cups of water and a cup of coffee while I wait on work call between 5:20 and 5:50. I go to work in the kitchen which serves the dormitories where I reside. [Ed.: According to the Bureau of Justice, all but 124 of the 1821 correctional facilities have some type of work programs, with approximately 1350 providing work for support services, 560 for prison industries, and one thousand for farming and public works.[8]] After eating a bit of breakfast I go to work cleaning the floor where the grills, pots, etc. are at. I'm usually done by 7:00 a.m. I then go to rec and stretch or play basketball or something until 9 a.m. Then I come back to the dorm and shower and take a nap until 12 or 1 p.m. Brush my teeth and go to dinner at 2:30 or 3 p.m. Write letters or do other writing for a while. They pass out mail between 4:30–6:00 p.m., so that is a highlight of Monday through Friday. I don't watch much television. About 8 or 9 p.m. I'll take another shower to cool off. [Ed.: Think of dormitories on the Texas gulf coast where a heat index of 110 degrees hangs like a curse on crowded, bored human beings.] Then I'll lay down and read a book until 11:00 or midnight, when I'll go to sleep.

David ended his description by noting that this is his base day, but "Never forget that there are all sorts of drama, rumors, fights, stabbings, problems with officers, and on and on that are impossible to predict."

Hustling is as ubiquitous in prison as the stale air the residents breathe. Richard Callahan described it this way: "Hustling involves gambling, trafficking and trading (items, art, tattooing, etc.). Hustling can show positive or negative attributes. Some people manipulate others to score on a hustle, they steal things to sell, or sell tobacco, drugs, all of these are negatives that resemble a criminal mentality. Then you have guys who hustle to make money so they aren't such a burden on their families. These inmates gamble, tattoo, sell art, and piddle in the craft shop. Things repeat themselves in each category because we're limited to what we can do."

David described hustling in much the same way, but with more detail on prisoners who have no support from family or friends on the outside: "A man in prison with no outside help is drifting aimlessly about, totally at the mercy of a corrupt and evil administration. Because

8. Stephan, "Census," 5.

they are indigent or without money on their account to spend at the commissary, they are forced to live on only the necessities we receive, which are five tiny bars of soap, non-anti-bacterial, one cheap razor, and one roll of toilet paper per week. Not to mention you are totally dependent on the state's three meals they provide every day, which is punishment enough, because you cannot buy food—such as soups, refried beans, rice, chips, crackers, snacks—to compensate for the low-grade food and elementary school sized portions."

David digressed and discussed offenders' frustrations in dealing with prison officials. Then he continued,

> But let's return to the commissary thing. How do you get the necessities, like deodorant, real toothpaste, a fan to help with 110 degree Fahrenheit heat indexes? You have to hustle. How do you do that? You learn to tattoo, you wash others' clothes, you steal stuff from work (food from the kitchen, bleach and clothes from the laundry, maybe you are a janitor and can freely move around, so you traffic and trade tobacco, drugs, other contraband) and then people pay you with their commissary. Perhaps you are a gambler or even selling sexual favors for money. But the kick to all these methods? They are all against the rules. So you're always risking disciplinary action which eventually has an impact on your parole decision.

The implications of hustling are much broader than small time games. Take the case of tobacco. Most prisons ban all smoking, which of course immediately creates a supply shortage and a black market for cigarettes and other tobacco products. A correctional officer supplies one cigarette to an inmate, as a favor or for a price. The officer has committed a felony. He is now compromised, and the prisoner can blackmail him into providing hard drugs, weapons, or cell phones. And cell phones, particularly "smart" phones, can have many purposes other than to communicate with loved ones: to plan prison havoc, monitor or supervise outside gang activity, plan a hit, or arrange other unwelcome activity.

Hustling in prison presents an interesting conundrum. The tough on crime crowd—those who see a need for punishment or retribution and believe a tough prison life actually reduces crime—can hardly brook the idea of the state spending money to make an offender's life less arduous, thereby reducing the need for ordinary hustling. But those who see prisons as little more than training grounds for future criminals are offended by a system that provides built-in scarcities and consequent incentives and rewards for learning, or refining, criminal behavior.

Unfortunately, violence and abuse often stir excitement in the otherwise excruciatingly dull prison life. Donald Specter, director of the Prison Law Office in California, noted in his testimony to the Commission on Safety and Abuse in America's Prisons that "If you put poor, underprivileged young men together in a large institution without anything meaningful to do all day, there will be violence. If that institution is over-crowded, there will be more violence. If that institution is badly managed . . . there will be more violence."[9]

Some facility managements maintain a reasonable level of respect for the human dignity of the residents. Corrections officers reduce violence and maintain safety for everyone, in part by engaging with prisoners and bridging race, culture, and class differences. But many prisons host conditions that surface the anger, rage, and passion of their subdued residents. These conditions include overcrowding, insufficient staff training, excessive solitary confinement, insecure facilities, mistreatment of mentally ill inmates, policies that weaken family ties, a culture of disrespect between staff and prisoners, and little accountability of wardens. Corrections officers too often use weapons and force instead of words, and prisoners, acting like the animals they are being taught to be, lash out at each other and at officers.

Johnathan described the situation this way:

> Them dudes are twenty-five, forty, fifty years old. Been locked up twenty, thirty years. These dudes grew up in prison. That's all they know is prison. What they do in prison is take advantage of other people. If a dude wants to get at you, he gonna get at you. If he want to stab you, he gonna stab you. For kicks, just to go back and laugh about it. It's stupid, but that's what happens. That's the life you live in prison. You don't get what you want. You get what they give you. Then you take the rest. You have to be bad to take the rest though, cause somebody else is gonna be bigger and badder than you.
>
> The first night in prison—I was sixteen and I was scared. Anybody gonna be scared. I get put in a cell with two dudes. They gonna try me. I'm outta Houston. They're outta Dallas.

9. Gibbons and Katzenbach, "Confronting Confinement," 12.

> Misfit. They don't like you cause you outta Houston. They lock the doors. Lights go out. They want to take my cigarettes. I later quit smoking, cause I figured out you had to be in shape to fight longer, and I had to fight a long time. You couldn't be fat and sloppy and out of shape, cause they gonna fight you for real. They're gonna try to hurt you. That night, I had to show them that I would fight. If I didn't fight them, I would have to fight every day all day. And that's what happened. We fought. And we fought. The whole night. The only thing that saved me is I got in a corner between two bunks where only one could get at me at a time. And I fought him 'til he got tired and then the other one fought me 'til he got tired. Once they understood I was gonna fight, they backed up. The other people outta Houston heard about it and jumped on them for jumping on me. That's just the way it is. Just a silly game of cat and mouse, who's the baddest and who is not.

Danny, who served fifteen years for burglary, robbery, and possession, says "The level of violence is as high as it gets without being in a war situation." He described his experience this way:

> Even though I wanted to go home and I started out not wanting to get into trouble, or have the snot beat out of me for that matter, prison is not a place where you can easily go unnoticed and then ride off into the sunset. Your heart is going to get checked, meaning that someone (or several someones) is going to come test your heart. If you don't have any heart then you are going to have a hard time and find yourself doing things that you don't want to do. Starting with give your stuff away and it goes downhill from there. If you have a heart, then you are going to have to fight and fight and fight until you convince everyone that you ain't no punk. That might only take one good fight, or you may get "back-doored" (where dudes line up and you fight them one after another) or you might just get "clicked on" (where a few dudes jump on you at one time).

The extent of rape, assault, excessive use of force, and other types of violence in America's prisons and jails is one of the most highly charged and debated aspects of the corrections business. A major reason for the intensity of the debate is that accurate and reliable data on the subject is scarce to nonexistent. Deaths in custody are relatively easy to count, and there is consensus that prisons are less deadly than they were decades ago. But precisely measuring the level of nonlethal violence is virtually impossible for three reasons: a number of facilities do not report assault data; some report numbers of assaults that are improbably low; and the variation between states, and changes within states over time, are inexplicably large. It is clear, however, that prison violence is a major issue. Unofficial studies suggest that levels of victimization in prisons may be ten times greater than official estimates provided by the Bureau of Justice Statistics. If correct, this suggests that in the range of three hundred thousand inmates are victimized each year.[10]

David earlier raised the problem of sexual favors in connection with hustling. He put it in a slightly different context in another letter when he described sex as the foundation, or base energy, of prison:

> Sexual frustration radiates from every single man's core in here, in different wavelengths and frequencies, or on different levels and to varying degrees. This does two things, the first being that what a man gives off is mirrored back to him. The sexual energy, however, is refracted out of a prism and off of a mirror, arriving all ways at you, physical and mental forms of stress, anxieties, worries, fears, insecurities, violence, despair, etc. And second, all those emotional vibrations saturate the environment and become not only tolerable, but often preferred. This greatly fills a man's spirit with a perverted darkness where there was once a light. The implications of being alive in such an environment are astonishing. One's mentality is literally altered, like the unwanted side effect of some psychologically tortuous experimental drug. And this leads to very petty yet incontrollable urges and results (depression, homosexuality, excessive masturbation, confrontational aggression) and has a very raw effect.

Sexual abuse is a much-publicized fact of life. The extent of the problem is difficult to determine with certainty because many reports record inmates' complaints without attempting to verify their validity. However, a Bureau of Justice Statistics survey of inmates in county, state, and federal prisons indicated that 4.5 percent of inmates reported victimization within a prior twelve-month period, with rates as high as 15 to 16 percent in some prisons. An estimated 88,500 inmates nationwide were sexually abused during 2009.[11] Inmates report more abuse

10. Byrne, "Comission,"6.

11. *Houston Chronicle*, "Texas Has Worst Record of Sex Abuse."

at the hands of guards than of inmates. The young, mentally disabled, small in stature, gay, and those with little jail experience are most likely to be abused.

The Prison Rape Elimination Act of 2003 aimed to curb prison rape through research, information gathering, and a "zero-tolerance" policy. A commission was subsequently established and charged with studying sexual assaults in U.S. jails and prisons and presenting a report based on its findings. The report, released in June 2009, stated that approximately sixty thousand U.S. inmates are sexually assaulted each year.[12] However, implementation of its recommendations has been lackadaisical at best. In spring of 2010, the U.S. attorney general issued an Advance Notice of Proposed Rulemaking to solicit public input on the commission's proposed national standards for dealing with the problem—a problem which continues largely unabated.

Prison gangs are criminal organizations that originate and operate within the penal system and often extend into the free world. Typically consisting of a selected group of inmates with an organized hierarchy and an established code of conduct, they are a powerful and destructive force in correctional facilities. It has been estimated that 147,000 documented gang members, of approximately one million total gang members in the United States, are incarcerated in federal, state, and local correctional facilities.[13]

Up to a dozen prison gangs are recognized nationally for their participation in organized crime and violence, including Neta, Aryan Brotherhood, Black Guerilla Family, Mexican Mafia, La Nuestra Familia, and the Texas Syndicate. They vary in both organization and composition. Each group typically is of a single race and has distinctive identifiers in the form of tattoos, specific clothing, signs, or other behavior. Each gang typically has known enemies and rivals as well as acknowledged allies.

Richard Callahan described the rather interesting recruitment practice of gangs in one prison:

> I knew what was coming and what I had to do. When I was assigned to my first Pod I put my stuff in my cell and went to

12. Walton, "National Prison Rape Elimination Commission Report," chapter 1.
13. National Gang Intelligence Center, "National Gang," 6.

> talk to guys who wanted to see where my heart was. A white guy who was AC approached me. First thing anybody wants to know is if you're affiliated with a gang or riding [willing to do favors for some sort of compensation]. He asked me who I was with. Since I wasn't with a gang I told him I was solo. He had to leave for work, but he told me to expect a fight, to handle my business, and the other whites would keep an eye on me. What I learned later was on his way out, he told a guy that I wasn't with a family and that basically he had no interest in me—he thought I would break easily so he really threw me to the dogs. While I was talking to some other men, this guy called me up to 3 row showers, that's where fights take place in those pods. We stood in front of the shower and this guy tried to scare me into riding. I wouldn't budge on the issue, so finally we got in the shower area and fought.

Callahan was badly beaten, but continued to live solo.

Not all prison gangs are an extension of gang activity on the street. Some are self-protective and do not participate in widespread illegal activities. Others, however, are predatory in nature and engage in contract murder, black marketeering, prostitution, extortion, and other such activities within the walls. It is generally conceded that imprisonment does not pose an undue hardship on illegal activity. Members can easily get the goods and services they need and can do anything in prison they could do on the street. Gang members have long been a major source of homicides in prison, and they have a rate of disciplinary violations that is three times higher than non-affiliated inmates. And prison gangs pose a major threat to civil society in the free world through their role in the transportation and distribution of narcotics, as they are an important link between drug-trafficking organizations and street gangs, often brokering the transfer of drugs between the two.

Cal Ray Biggins shared his experience with gangs from his thirty-five years in the Texas prison system:

> Inmates can't teach inmates because you have to congregate—and you can't congregate because they are trying to prevent gang activity. Gangs run the prisons, period. They run the guards. Gangs are so powerful and highly connected on the inside and the outside, which everybody knows. When they tell someone to do something, it's gonna be done. The guards need their jobs, so they do what they are told—also to protect their family on the outside. You also have guards who are in gangs. Everybody

> knows this. You know the guards are bringing drugs in—anything you want. But they blame inmates. You come into prison with a habit, and you never miss a beat. Somebody gonna have it for you and you gonna buy it. It's a world in itself. People support their family from inside prison. Drugs and violence are their livelihood. If you want a cell phone, you go to a gang to get you one. Pay $300 for a $19 cell phone. Everybody got their own territory—the blacks, the whites, the Asians, the Mexicans. Each deals in a different drug, and it's their own territory. And you don't cross the line by selling the wrong thing. If you do, you gonna cause a war. If you respect the territory and follow the rules, you have no problems.

All this combines to form a unique prison culture with its own set of rules or code of conduct for blending in and coping with the consuming fear. The code, amazingly consistent across all facilities, includes the following: "The Man"—anyone in authority in the prison administration—is the enemy and should be treated accordingly. Never snitch. Handle your own business and stay out of others'. Mask your personal feelings and never ask personal questions of another. Don't become indebted to another inmate or to a guard. The debt will always be collected, and in ways you don't like. Don't "diss" or show disrespect for another, even if respect has not been earned. And maintain a low profile, under the radar. The less attention you receive from anyone, the better off you are.

But even cauldrons of misery are not always all bad. Efforts are made in most facilities to rehabilitate inmates to prepare them for release to the free world.

REHABILITATION

We have seen that most prison inmates are young minority men with low incomes and minimal educational attainment. They don't have a capacity for many legal ways of making a living and are highly likely to return to crime after their release. Much of the "training" they get in prison simply teaches them to be more effective and committed criminals. But some things are being done to help prisoners improve their lives.

Rehabilitation theory sees crime as somewhat analogous to medical problems. When you are ill, you see a doctor who diagnoses your problem and prescribes medication to cure your illness. Similarly, the rehabilitation view of criminal justice sees offenders as engaging in crime because of forces largely beyond their control. These forces might be psychological (e.g., mental illness), sociological (e.g., disruptive family environment), economic (e.g., unemployment), or even physiological (e.g., improper diet). Because this line of reasoning places much of the burden for crime causation on society, society is responsible for diagnosing the offender's problems and prescribing a cure. In essence, this model views society as being accountable for changing offenders into law-abiding citizens and successfully returning them to the community—that is, rehabilitating and reintegrating them.

In criminal rehabilitation, prisoners are given opportunities to increase their knowledge, education, and ability to cope in the free world. Programs such as psychological testing, GED education, high school and college education, vocational and skills training, spiritual development, and drug and alcohol counseling aim to help offenders lead law-abiding lives after their incarceration.

Emphasis on rehabilitation has ebbed and flowed over the years, and varies from institution to institution. Rehabilitation was the organizing principle of the American penal system for much of the twentieth century, but encountered great skepticism in the 1970s. However, a report of the Commission on Safety and Abuse in America's Prisons in 2006 concluded that "Increasingly, programs tested through research demonstrate that the old pessimism of the 1970s about rehabilitation was misguided. Targeted interventions work. In particular, highly structured programs that help prisoners understand the motivations underlying their actions and the consequences of their behavior can reduce misconduct in correctional facilities and lower recidivism rates by at least 10 percent."[14] The report also noted that faith and character-based programs that cultivate life skills, anger management, personal growth, faith, family relationships, and victim awareness would reduce the number of people re-incarcerated by tens of thousands if used nationwide.

Approximately 20 percent of adult inmates are illiterate and up to 60 percent are functionally illiterate.[15] There is significant evidence, however, that the recidivism rates for ex-offenders who receive education and training while they are locked up is lower than for those who

14. Gibbons and Katzenbach, "Confronting Confinement," 27.

15. Wagner, "Crime & Punishment."

don't, and that postsecondary education is the most successful and cost-effective means of reducing recidivism. One study of three thousand ex-offenders found that those who participated in prison education programs were 29 percent less likely to return to prison. Misconduct while behind bars is effectively reduced by these programs because of their emphasis on personal responsibility, respect, and tolerance of others.[16]

Not surprisingly, therefore, most prison facilities—more than fifteen hundred—provide some type of educational opportunities for inmates, with basic secondary and GED education and vocational training leading the way. Most also provide some form of special education, study release programs, and basic adult education. Over six hundred facilities provide college courses.[17]

The Windham School District in Texas is among the national leaders in prison education. I visited with Dan Lawrence, a Colorado native with more than thirty years teaching experience in both traditional and prison schools, who is director of operational support for the district. Established in 1969, and the first education system of such scope to be established within a statewide prison system, Windham provides academic and vocational education to eligible offenders in classes conducted in ninety-six prison units across the state. Its aim is to provide confined persons with the academic skills that will allow them to process knowledge and information, the vocational competencies that will enable them to contribute to a productive society, and the social skills that will provide them with self-confidence and the ability to interact successfully with their fellow man. School officials believe such training and education reduces recidivism and the cost of confinement, provides an incentive for positive behavior during confinement, and helps former offenders obtain employment.

Prior to the state's 82d Legislature, the school was funded to the tune of roughly $67 million per year and employed almost thirteen hundred employees.[18] As a result of actions of the 82d Legislature, however, budgets for 2012 were substantially lowered from the level of 2011 expenditures. Paid teachers are required to meet the same standards as those in Texas' traditional schools. A substantial number of volunteers

16. Karpowitz and Kenner, "Education as Crime Prevention," 4.

17. Stephan, "Census," appendix table 6.

18. Windham School District, "2011–2012 Budget," 3.

work as teaching assistants, class facilitators, subject matter experts, and in-class tutors. Classes are conducted 210 days per year.

In 2009, approximately 79,000 offenders received educational services, typically attending classes from fifteen to thirty hours per week. Approximately 40 percent had an educational equivalency of sixth grade. Inmates who are not literate are required to attend literacy classes until they obtain their GED. Those who have no skills are assessed and placed in appropriate vocational training, where the focus is on attaining marketable job skills and even on-the-job training when feasible. Others matriculate in behavioral programs, which they cannot leave after starting.

I asked Dan about the extent to which the Windham school accomplishes its goal of reducing recidivism. He candidly acknowledged the difficulty of obtaining good, defensible data on this subject, but noted that there is a clear, positive correlation between those inmates who complete Windham's programs and those who avoid a return to prison. More importantly, he explained the cumulative effect of various types of prison rehabilitation programs: the more an inmate participates, the less likely he is to return to the big house for a repeat.

Similarly, nearly all prisons provide some type of counseling, particularly drug and alcohol, psychological or psychiatric, life skills, and job seeking. For example, the Windham school district offers its "CHANGES" program—a sixty-day life skills program (Changing Habits and Achieving New Goals to Empower Success) to inmates within two years of projected release. The program includes segments on personal development, healthy relationships, living responsibly, drug education, living well, anger management, and going home.

Most prison populations include significant numbers of inmates with mental health needs. There is a wide diversity as to how they are treated. Some are housed and cared for separately, while others function acceptably in the general population. Generally speaking, those inmates with serious mental illnesses are managed primarily as patients who are incarcerated, eligible for services such as individual therapy, inpatient care, long-term mental health care, and care by a psychiatrist rather than a psychologist. Those with less serious mental health needs are managed as offenders who have additional needs.

Although an overwhelming majority of inmates within the United States have a disorder that involves alcohol or drugs, only 11 percent of those who enter the system with a problem actually receive any counseling or rehabilitation once they are behind bars.[19] While this performance may seem dismal, and perhaps is, before being too critical one should recognize the difficulties of conducting effective counseling programs in prison. Counseling programs usually succeed because people want to participate and change. This is not always the case in prisons, where many do not want to change and have ulterior motives for participating. They are in prison against their will. Their main concern is getting out. If they seek counseling at all, they may look upon it as a hustle—a way of playing the model prisoner role and obtaining an early release, or a way of getting favors from prison officials. Recall the words of Pete, from a previous chapter, "I'm gonna do what I have to do. If it's hard or if its soft, I'm gonna sell it. I loved to sell drugs. I loved the life of selling drugs. I loved the attention I got from the females. The respect from the streets. I loved the clothes I was wearing. I loved the jewelry I was wearing. I loved smoking weed—and getting high. I used to say, 'I can't face the day sober.' I got to blow me a joint. The dope game took me to another level."

Fixing Pete through counseling and therapy is a tough task.

RELIGION

Federal law requires officials to respond to the needs of all faiths claimed by inmates, and a wide variety of religious practices, services, programs, and activities exist in prisons. Nearly every state and federal institution provides support for Catholicism, Protestantism, Islam, and Judaism, and some states do so for as many as 170 faith groups—some with as few as three members—claimed by inmates. While differences in approach exist from state to state, most prisons have chaplains, either paid staff or volunteers, who assist offenders to grow in their chosen faith and provide needed resources. Their goal is moral rehabilitation through religion.

Precise statistics on religious demographics are difficult to obtain because different procedures are followed in each state and many states

19. *Addiction Treatment Magazine*, "Effective."

have not done definitive studies in years. Such anecdotal and statistical information as is available, however, allows for the conclusion that up to 75 percent of inmates declare for some denomination of Christianity, with the remainder claiming other religions, agnosticism, or atheism. An increasing number have converted to Islam or one of its variants in recent years. Anecdotal evidence suggests Islam is the fastest-growing religion in Western jails and prisons.

It is equally difficult to determine why prisoners become involved with religion. Going through the motions can be for many reasons. In some cases inmates are practicing an honest faith that they grew up with or attained later in life, perhaps during incarceration. In addition to their beliefs about the hereafter, they feel that God, or Yahweh, or Allah will provide a direction to their life that is better than their present condition. Belief may give them peace of mind or some level of personal contentment. The acceptance and love from a higher being, or from members of a faith group that are inherent in most religions, helps inmates deal with their guilt about failures in life, their remorse from criminal acts, or the pain of a dysfunctional family background. They feel better about themselves if they practice religion.

Richard Callahan told me how he came to religion and how it has affected him. He related the story of Pops, whom he referred to as an inmate mentor:

> One night Pops brought me a Bible and he asked me to make him a promise. Pops asked me to stop arguing until I read the entire Bible—no more arguments until I read the whole book and then make my decision to worship either God or Satan. I agreed to start reading it and to stop arguing until I finished the book. I remember that conversation 'cause I felt I'd prove Pops wrong, that I wouldn't believe or agree with God. It took me a little over a year to complete the Bible and it still amazes me to this day how the stories in the Bible helped comfort me at different points in prison, it was God comforting me. God was knocking at my heart, but I didn't know it. I read Genesis and Exodus while I was locked in a cell at Diagnostics. The story of Joseph was very inspiring and so were the events of the Hebrew people in the desert. I was trying to work on my attitude, and reading about God's people only having bread and water made me aware that prison food was a blessing no matter how bad it tasted.

Other reasons for inmate religion, often characterized as jailhouse religion, are not so honorable. Inmates may adopt religion to gain protection, perhaps as part of a gang; to meet other inmates for social interaction and satisfaction; to meet volunteers, perhaps of the opposite sex, who may come bearing free goods such as food and coffee, holiday greeting cards and books, musical instruments, or other special favors. And many believe that prison residents often find religion for manipulative purposes, or as a con game, aiming for better living conditions while incarcerated or earlier release on parole. This view is often based on witnessing professed believers who act to the contrary or make repeat visits to the slammer.

David is an inmate with a rather cynical view of prison religion. He considers himself a Christian and for a time participated in prison religious activities. He no longer does. He explained:

> It didn't take long for me to see what was really taking place during the service. I would say that perhaps 10 out of every 100 people that go to church in prison actually attend out of a sincere desire to worship. What are the other ninety in the chapel for, then? Usually the homosexuals occupy the back one-fourth of the pews. It's not uncommon to stumble upon two men making out, hand jobs and other assorted techniques and forms of masturbation, oral sex, etc. The reason for them defiling the chapel with such actions is because if they live on different wings or dorms, the Chapel is a place where they can both be at the same place at the same time and not face disciplinary action for being "out of place." The gang members separate themselves first by race, then by specific gang. They meet up to relay information, record their own members, rival gangs, money, business, drama, etc. It's a twisted thing.

David continued:

> As for the majority of the self-proclaimed "Christians," or those who label themselves as such, they use the term and the Bible to hide behind for various reasons. Perhaps they are scared of a physical confrontation, or they're gay, or they've molested children, or they're snitches, or they're using it as an excuse to get out of a gang. Maybe they like the title and they feel good inside when they claim as much, or maybe they just don't fit in anywhere else. This is the rule for "Christians" in prison. None of them are respected, nor taken seriously in any sense of the word. This would make it impossible for the Christian inmate

> to have any impact on a non-believer's life what-so-ever, and they're the ones that need it the most.

How has this rather cynical view affected David? He explained: "You won't find me in the Chapel. You won't see me on the Rec yard singing hymns with anyone. You won't catch me at a table in the dayroom reading the Bible with anyone. Those are the quickest ways to dissuade a man in prison from the love and mercy of the Lord and Savior."

But the more prevalent view is that religion really does make a positive difference. This view is characterized by the emergence of faith and character-based prisons. Florida governor Jeb Bush announced the creation of an entirely faith and character-based prison at Lawtey Correctional Institution on December 5, 2003. The initiative, according to the Florida Corrections Department website, "is a bold and innovative effort to reduce recidivism and disciplinary infractions in correctional institutions by offering character-based programming in a positive environment to inmates committed to inner transformation. Without regard to religion, this initiative offers inmates a variety of activities and classes (both religious and secular) focused on personal growth and character development."[20]

Florida now has four faith and character-based prisons, housing over four thousand inmates. In addition, the state has instituted faith and character-based dormitories at seven other correctional institutions, with over six hundred inmates. Such initiatives are typically volunteer-staffed, with more than fifty volunteer groups working in each Florida prison. They offer a variety of faith and character-based education programs, varying among facilities. Inmate participation is voluntary and inmates of any faith are eligible. Roughly 68 percent are Christian non-Roman Catholic, 11 percent are Roman Catholic, 4 percent are Muslim, and the remainder are of other, none, or unknown religions.[21]

Richard Lopez, director of chaplaincy support in the Texas prison system, is responsible for implementing faith-based dorms in Texas. He says their basic concept is "accountability, responsibility, presented curriculum, applied to every facet of one's life. Life skills, whether biblical teachings or moral beliefs, are applied to life on a daily basis. In a

20. Florida Department of Corrections, "Faith- and Character-Based Correctional Initiative."

21. Ibid.

faith-based dorm, an individual may have heard about God, but doesn't know God. So they come to know God and as that happens they begin to live God and then they become a testimony to others. Then others want to know God. And they develop a personal relationship with Jesus, and everything changes."

Texas has twenty-nine such dorms housing 2900 inmates and demand for more is high. They are open to people of all faiths or no faith who volunteer and sign a commitment to live by the dorm's principles. The teaching—the majority done by volunteers, including certified volunteer chaplains assistants—is faith-based, but not dogma or traditions specific to a particular religion. Participants get no special privileges and continue their normal life—jobs, school, chow, church, etc. But they do so in a community dedicated full time to the dorm's principles. After they complete the program, ranging from ninety days to two years, they graduate and are sent back into the general population to become "missionaries." This works because other inmates see a "different individual."

The dorms are essentially self-policing as participants informally hold one another accountable for living according to the specified principles. Officers frequently request assignment to faith-based dorms because there is so little conflict, and they too are held accountable. Records to date indicate that disciplinary incidents among participants are 90 percent less than among those same individuals when they were living in the general population.

In 2007, at least ten states had faith-based prison dorms. The Corrections Corporation of America, which operates private prisons, had separate "faith pods" housing about 1,660 inmates at twenty-four prisons in thirteen states.[22] And the numbers continue to grow.

~

Another example that takes the concept further is at Angola, the Louisiana state penitentiary. Angola is located on 18,000 acres—a former plantation—in southern Louisiana, surrounded on three sides by the Mississippi River. For years Angola was considered the bloodiest prison in the country because of the attempted escapes, suicides, attempted suicides, acts of violence between inmates, and assaults upon employees by inmates. It is currently the largest maximum security prison in

22. Crary, "Faith-Based."

the United States, with a large working farm and its share of solitary and segregation units. Five thousand inmates and 1,800 staff members call Angola home. More than 85 percent of the inmates will die there because of the length of their sentences. Many will be buried in the dismal Point Lookout Cemetery on the grounds.

Burl Cain became the prison's warden in 1995 and still presides over the facility. Looking for ways to restore hope for men who had almost none, Cain instituted a number of programs aimed at helping his charges improve their lives. Perhaps the most important involved collaboration with the New Orleans Baptist Theological Seminary. I visited at length with Dr. John Robson, assistant professor of Christian ministry at the seminary and director of its Angola extension. He explained that not long after Cain took over at Angola, he brought in "Experiencing God," a Southern Baptist Convention program that emphasizes obedience based on a relationship with God, in an effort to help Christians cope with difficult situations. This program became the springboard for a collaboration through which the New Orleans Baptist Theological Seminary established an extension center at Angola. This unique "Angola Campus" offers an associate degree and a bachelor of arts degree in Christian ministries that are accredited like those in comparable free-world universities. Students take the same program as other seminarians: 126 hours, with the same requirements for passing. So far about 150 inmates have earned bachelor of arts degrees and another hundred are on track to graduate.

The program was initially established as a way for inmates to educate themselves and grow spiritually. But more emerged. Some inmates who have earned their bachelor's degree now lead services at the prison's eighteen inmate churches and also do one-on-one ministry and grief counseling, while another twenty-three graduates act as missionaries in eight satellite prisons in Louisiana.

Since starting the program at Angola, the New Orleans seminary has begun similar ones in Mississippi and Georgia prisons. And in September 2011 the Texas system launched its first class for a similar program at its Darrington Unit in conjunction with the Southwest Baptist Theological Seminary. The program started with forty inmates. Its purpose is to train offenders to use the Bible to promote moral rehabilitation among their peers. When participants finish the 125-credit-hour program over four years, they will receive bachelor of science degrees in biblical studies and be sent to other Texas prisons to minister to their fellow offenders.

John Robson explained that this all works because men behind bars are ready to be judged. They are accustomed to being judged, by family, friends, acquaintances, society—by people they cannot trust. But all this judging has been to no avail. Prisoners have been shamed and dehumanized rather than made whole. Prison has stripped life from them. But when they meet Christ, he sees them for who they are. They need Christ as a judge and a redeemer. An intimacy develops because the inmates can trust Christ. Atonement is life-changing, because they've never had any before.

~

Faith programs are not without their controversy. Critics argue that the positive reaction to faith-based efforts is fueled by the fervor of devout volunteers, while evidence that such programs reduce recidivism is inconclusive—often based on methodologically flawed research and anecdotal feedback rather than evidence-based practice. Skeptics also maintain there is an evangelical tone in the units that may discriminate against inmates who don't share their conservative Christian outlook.

But Emmit Solomon, and many others, like them. He told me they are for

> people who profess faith and want to use it to hang their new lifestyle on. Housed together, study together, hold one another accountable, talk about their behavior, know and nurture one another. Take a prison with discipline and guidance, add love and nurture, then you have the ingredients for producing a well-rounded human being. For correcting a human being. That's where the prisons should move—where people do not live against each other but live with one another. Where they actually know one another's name—a sign of respect. They usually just know a nickname for others. Prisoners usually don't respect one another enough to learn their names. This approach produces healing and growth—things people in society honor.

Solomon's more comprehensive approach is supported by Byron R. Johnson, Distinguished Professor of the Social Sciences and director of the Institute for Studies of Religion at Baylor University, who has done perhaps the most extensive research to date on the relationship of faith to crime and recidivism. In *More God, Less Crime: Why Faith Matters and How It Could Matter More*, he wrote:

> The reality is that social problems are the product of multiple factors, and such multifaceted problems tend to require multifaceted solutions. Similarly, the challenges facing ex-prisoners, for example, require more than simply introducing prisoners to faith. This is not to suggest that spiritual interventions are not important; they clearly are. However, a conversion experience that happens as an isolated event and is not nurtured or connected to other needed supports is unlikely to transform a life or change a person's long-term behavioral trajectory. Simply put, spiritual interventions must be part of a more comprehensive strategy.[23]

23. Johnson, *More God, Less Crime*, 205.

5

The Aftermath

The aftermath of prison is not pretty. Like a tragic opera, the misery isn't over 'til the fat lady sings, and that rarely happens, or if it does it takes a very long time. The misery certainly isn't over when inmates walk out the prison door. They probably came from the margins of society. Prison afforded them additional training in the criminal lifestyle. And after their release society still has its boot on their necks. Not surprisingly, living successful, law-abiding lives in the free is extraordinarily difficult for them, so there is a high probability they will return through the revolving prison door. This spiral of futility affects both offenders and society at large.

INMATES

A felony conviction usually amounts to a life sentence, regardless of the time an individual is actually behind bars. Escaping the walls is simply a transition from one difficult reality to another. No more controlling guards, but now prying parole officers and the disdain of the community. Forget that bland, monotonous prison food and start worrying about where the next meal will come from. Substitute the hopelessness of incarceration with the despair of being an undereducated felon in a tight job market, relegated to flipping burgers in a fast-food joint or actually selling a few joints. Face the reality that longed-for loved ones and friends have moved on, and can still only be longed for.

The continuing misery comes in various forms. The most basic is that released felons have to live with continuing guilt and shame for what they have done in the past as they try to build new lives. Danny, recently released after a long sentence, described it this way, "For any individual coming out of prison, returning to the family unit is hard. Shame, guilt, and remorse are the clothes you walk out with. You can never measure the pain, hurt and resentment you have caused your family. Seeing my family magnifies the hurt, the pain. I became the victim of my own actions."

Emmit Solomon, who you met earlier, believes that once people become felons, they are never not felons. He described the problem this way: "The system is designed to continually punish people. Forgiveness in not in its purview at all. Never was really, but in the past it would let up on a guy. Now, once labeled, there are consequences the rest of your life. Employment, housing, interaction with government. One of the most difficult issues is finding a way into the working world. Couple of hundred professions a felon cannot hold—largely to do with jobs requiring licenses."

In her book *The New Jim Crow: Mass Incarceration in the Age of Colorblindness*, Michelle Alexander refers to the time after release as "the period of invisible punishment." This term describes "the unique set of criminal sanctions that are imposed on individuals after they step outside the prison gates, a form of punishment that operates largely outside of public view and takes effect outside the traditional sentencing framework."[1]

I observed the daunting reality of being released from prison one hot spring day in Huntsville, Texas. In recent years roughly 90 percent of inmates in the Texas prison system have been shipped to Huntsville's Walls Unit as their last stop before injection back into society. Opened in 1849, its thirty-foot-high, red brick walls topped with razor wire and box-like guard towers manned by rifle-wielding uniformed guards create a fortress with the intimidating feel of a movie prison—straight out of *The Shawshank Redemption*, *The Green Mile*, or *Alcatraz*. The people

1. Alexander, *The New Jim Crow*, 186.

who exit through its front door are not all that different from the estimated 700,000 others released each year nationwide.[2]

The inmates who have served their flat time—their entire sentence, with no parole required—are discharged at 9:00 a.m. each day. Flat-timers often arrive at the exit door in handcuffs, having come directly from "ad-seg." Parolees are released shortly thereafter. Each person is given a transparent, ten-gallon sized "onion sack" to carry all his earthly possessions. Flat-timers are given one hundred dollars and released with no strings attached. Parolees receive fifty dollars and are promised another fifty when they meet with their parole officer. The second fifty often barely covers the parole fees.

Roughly 15 percent of released inmates are met by family or friends at the small, austere "Offender Release Family Waiting Area" just across the street. This former craft shop with concrete floor and benches is surrounded by magnificent oak trees and parking lots filled with pickups, well-used cars, and more than a few motorcycles that will haul fearful passengers into a free world that has moved on without them. The remaining 85 percent are directed to the bus station a couple of blocks down the street, where the state provides a ticket to Dallas or Houston, and thence to whatever Texas town is to be their new home. Some estimate that as many as 30 percent of those who board the buses have no idea where they will spend their first night of freedom. They can only hope that friends or relatives will come through, or that a church shelter will offer a meal and a cot.

Johnny described what it feels like:

> You know, after thirty-one years they put me out on the street. Have you been to France? I haven't been there either, but getting outta prison after thirty-one years and going to the streets is like dropping me off in France or dropping me off in Afghanistan. I don't know the language. I don't know the people. I didn't have nobody. They sent me to Houston. I didn't know nobody in Houston. I didn't have no job, no money. You know what they gave me? What they gave me was a used shirt, some baggy pants, and some old raggedy shoes I couldn't wear and fifty dollars. What's fifty dollars, man? After working and slaving hard labor for thirty-one years they gave me fifty dollars. They opened the door and said "get out—go—and don't do nothing wrong cause you will come back. We'll be watching you every

2. *The Released*, directed by Karen O'Connor and Miri Navasky.

> moment, every day." Then Johnny showed me his ankle monitor as further evidence that his current situation was only one small step beyond prison.

Bill Kleiber runs a Welcome Back Ministry in Huntsville. Bill is a wiry, balding, fast talking, middle-aged man who personally experienced the release and transition process about ten years ago. He concedes he looks "like a little old grandpa," but in the next breath explains, "See all these scars on my knuckles. That's why they called me the dentist." Kleiber's ministry takes teams of volunteers into prison to meet with inmates just prior to their release. They provide information about the release process along with local phone numbers for help with food, clothes, shelter, and other challenges the released offenders will be facing. Offenders can fill out forms asking for special assistance, which are forwarded to volunteers in the local communities the offenders will call home. All are provided with a toll-free number for requesting additional assistance. Bill summarizes his ministry quite simply, "Many of these men don't even have money for a phone call. We are their family."

Bill and a couple of volunteers go each morning to visit with families, friends, and brand new ex-cons sampling their taste of freedom. More than two hundred inmates were released on the day I visited. Bill repeated his prescribed speech to several small groups of ex-inmates along with the teary-eyed parents, children, wives, or significant others who had not forgotten them: "Hello. My name is Bill. I'm from the church. I was in your place a few years ago, and I'm here to help. Welcome home, brother." He then answered questions and invited those being released and their families to participate in a prayer circle. About half joined in.

One individual in the waiting room seemed to characterize the complexity and paradox of the moment. She sat alone on one of the concrete benches—a strikingly beautiful, stylishly dressed blond, probably in her late thirties. She was the woman every man notices and many women pretend they don't see. The young lady must have been there to greet a loved one—a husband, lover, or perhaps a brother. It would seem to be a happy, exciting time. But her face radiated sadness rather than happiness. Her melancholy eyes communicated gloom rather than excitement. I wondered. Was she just worn out by the miseries of having a loved one locked up? Was she more fearful than happy about meeting this man she might no longer know? Did her concern for the realities of the future overcome her excitement about the present? What are the realities of her future with a felon who has served time? And what about all the others who were not so attractive?

We walked two blocks to the bus station, a worn-out looking storefront with a large veranda for busses on one side and a grimy secondhand shop on the other. The only sign on the shop front read "We Cash Release Checks Free." The station was dimly lit and cool, with a small ticketing area, four iron mesh benches in front, a pool table in the rear, and drink, candy, and video machines around the edges. The five pay phones on one wall—those vestiges of a bygone time, except for prisons—were in continual use. Nothing suggested the station is used by anyone other than released inmates with no one to take them home. The lobby opened directly to the secondhand shop, with its racks of used clothes, cheap gimme hats, knock-off athletic shoes, and incredibly expensive cigarettes.

The population at the station grew over a couple of hours as more and more newly free men arrived in their "clown suits"—the state provided, used clothes that were grungy without intending to be. Many were old industrial uniforms with insignia removed. The frumpy, ill-fitting clothes and the onion sacks with all their worldly possessions conveyed the unmistakable message—ex-con. This seemed to be the state's parting shot at the inmates' humanity.

Cam approached me—said he was hungry but was afraid to walk down the street to buy something to eat. Doing so would be too much too soon. "I'm not used to having so much open space, to making so many decisions." I informed him that Bill had ordered some cheeseburgers and they were available out front. Cam had just completed twenty years flat and was returning to Ft. Worth. He was slight, small boned, and slightly emaciated, with the translucent skin of someone who had spent his entire adult life on a dimly-lit cell block. He spoke softly, almost timidly. Made me wonder how he had fared in prison. The man appeared to be in shock, said the feeling of freedom "was really surreal. After twenty years of doing the same things, seeing the same walls, being with the same people every day, now all of a sudden it's like I was sitting dead still and they kicked me out the door. Told me to go wherever I want, do whatever I want to do. I am afraid of not making it, but that's not an option." Cam was unusual, in that "My family is behind me, has been waiting for me to come home. My mom has a place for me to live and transportation. My father has said he will make sure I have work at a local body shop." He admitted that adjusting to his new life will be a problem: "I can already tell, just from being here, that the pace of life on the outside is much faster, with no set regimen every day. All the years, I knew exactly what to expect every day, the few decisions I would have to make. Now there is a whole lot more options and decisions to be made." Cam told me that the biggest problem of his incarceration had been the set-offs, the hopelessness of going time and again for parole and always being turned down. He said, "I had the misfortune of being locked up just after they slammed the revolving door. That pretty much nailed it shut for me." Cam went outside and paid Bill $5.95, 6 percent of his net worth, for a cheeseburger and fries.

Brian was so different from Cam, yet the two were so much alike. They had a different life, but were equally fearful, anxious, uncertain. Brian had a lumpish body, a ruddy complexion, a slightly puffy face, and a loquacious nature. He volunteered that he was a former corrections officer and city policeman who lost his job when he got involved with marijuana: "This all started my downward cycle. Then I started doing cocaine. Decided I didn't like that, and moved on to meth. It all caught up with me. In the end, I turned myself in, cause I knew it was coming." Brian served seven months in county jail and was now completing two years in state prison. "Last time I saw my mom and dad was the day I left for prison. Both of 'em are in a nursing home now, but I'm not sure where. My first thing is to find out where they are and go see them." Brian is afraid he will be sent back to prison because he doesn't have the money to pay some traffic tickets from before he was sent away. He is estranged from his sister and other relatives because of what he did to the family reputation, has no money, and doesn't know where he will stay. An older cousin told him to go to the Motel 8 and call her. She promised to put him up for a day or two.

And the stories go on and on. Eighteen-year-old Jose is returning to Austin, but he's not sure where in Austin. He never had a visit during the year he was locked up. The old man, limping aimlessly around on his walking cane, is reluctant to reveal anything about himself. The young, burly Hispanic with tattoos—literally—from the top of his head to his feet, spent his last six months in solitary for fighting. The young man with his arm in a fresh sling—he claimed a guard intentionally slammed a cell door on it the night before. The tall, lanky, freckled-faced farm boy whose onion sack revealed a four-inch stack of letters, no doubt his main sustenance for several years. The Scottish citizen on his way to Beaumont, although he doesn't know a soul there. All are facing an uncertain future and a mountain of challenges in making a new life that's any better than their old one.

Three buses—decrepit retreads with pealing paint and more than their share of road grunge—finally arrived. The anxious passengers loaded as quickly as possible, as though this were all a dream and if they missed the bus the dream would end. Bill visited each bus and led a short prayer for safe travel and a better life. And then they drove away into scores of uncertain futures.

Jack has seen that future. Now in his mid-fifties, he was a guest of the Texas Department of Criminal Justice for eighteen years and was released on parole approximately a year ago. While incarcerated, he supported himself as a "writ-writer," doing legal work for other inmates for pay. Like Bill, his knuckles are crushed and scarred. He now assists Bill with the welcome home ministry. Jack was not reticent when I asked about the problems ex-cons face.

Jack mentioned first things first—those immediate needs for survival. "The biggest problem is their medical needs. Seventy to 75 percent of the inmates are on some kind of medication. And when you get out and want a copy of your medical file, they say it will cost you a dollar a page. I had eighteen years worth of medical files. Fifty dollars doesn't go far. And they have ten days of medication, and no money to buy more when that runs out. What are they gonna do?"

Jack says the second problem is identification, typically access to a social security card and driver license. Inmate's birth certificates and social security cards are often lost during their travels through the criminal justice system, leaving them with no form of identification upon release. According to Jack, the state claims identification documents are available, but often they never show up. A nationwide survey indicated that in most states individuals who are released from prison do not receive the appropriate identification documents. If they are given any at all, the documents usually are not adequate for obtaining proper state identification. Without proper identification, people with criminal records are at an even greater disadvantage in finding employment, securing housing, or applying for public benefits that may be necessary to obtain medication or other life support. If they are fortunate enough to find work, the lack of an acceptable ID can make cashing paychecks or opening a bank account extremely difficult.

Jack continued: "Transportation is also critically important. I am on parole, and they told me I have to go to AA. How? I picked up aluminum cans and bought a bicycle so I could go to meetings. They don't care how you do it, just do it. Here I am, a grey-haired old man, driving down the middle of the neighborhood on a bicycle. It's very humbling, but I did it. If you are on parole, you gotta have a way to get around. And people need a place to live. Only about 15 percent of people have families waiting when they are released. Most of the others don't have a place to stay."

He continued, shifting back and forth from first person, to second person, to third person,

> Learning how to communicate and relate to others is really hard. On the other side of that wall, you cannot let down your demeanor, you can't show a weakness, you can't show that you're afraid of anything. Because you have predators in there, and they are gonna take advantage of you. You have to carve out your own niche in that society. When you walk down those steps and leave prison, you have to be honest with yourself. This is new. I've got to learn how to live all over again. I have to admit this is scary business. But if you open up, shed a few tears, and admit you need some help, you can win the battle. You can't be ashamed of who you are. He needs help in regaining some ego, some self-respect, some admiration, learn how to communicate—particularly how to communicate with a female. When you get out you have to re-establish your whole life energy. The longer you're in, the longer it takes to re-establish your life. They need opportunities to earn their way back into society.

Jack summed it all up, "When you get out you are like a fledgling bird in a nest. If you flex your wings too soon and fall outta the nest, something's going to eat you. And you're going back to prison."

Felon exclusion laws, a mishmash of legislation with little consistency from one jurisdiction to another, generally prohibit released felons from exercising a host of rights that most of us take for granted. The most notable aspect of such laws is probably their restriction on the right to vote. Although a number of states implemented reforms in the late 1990s and early 2000s, in 2004 over five million Americans were disenfranchised due to felony convictions. Seventy-four percent of those were no longer in prison and were living in the community. One in twelve African Americans was disenfranchised because of a felony conviction, a rate nearly five times that of non-African Americans.

A felony conviction can also be used to deny other rights or to terminate existing relationships. Depending upon the jurisdiction, a convicted felon can be prohibited from serving on a jury, obtaining public employment, holding public office, or owning a firearm. Moreover, a felony conviction can be cited in some jurisdictions as a reason to terminate a marriage or parental rights, or to require an individual to register with local law enforcement officials. Some felon exclusion laws, especially for particular drug felonies, deny people public housing, federal educational assistance, and even food stamps—for life.

These laws make attaining employment extraordinarily difficult. A 2010 study found that incarceration reduces former inmates' earnings by 40 percent and limits their future economic mobility.[3] Employers may ask job applicants whether they have been convicted of a crime, and may bar felons from consideration if they show that a conviction-based disqualification is justified by "business necessity." More importantly, a number of statutes authorize agencies to suspend or revoke a dizzying array of licenses or permits based on conviction of a felony. The following examples are listed to illustrate the breadth of the exclusions:

> A felony conviction generally leads to suspension or revocation of licenses for architects; private detectives, watchmen, guards, and patrol services; professions under the jurisdiction of departments of health, specifically including healing arts, medicine and surgery, osteopathy, chiropractic, natureopathy, podiatry, physical therapists, nursing, nurse's aides, dentistry, optometry, opticians, psychologists, marital and family therapists, clinical social workers, professional counselors, veterinary medicine, massage therapists, dietician-nutritionists, acupuncturists, paramedics, embalmers and funeral directors; barbers, hairdressers and cosmeticians; and hypertrichologists; attorneys, judges, family support magistrates, and workers' compensation commissioners; radiographers and radiologic technologists;

3. Pew Charitable Trusts, "Collateral Costs," 1.

> midwives; electricians; plumbers; heating, piping, and cooling contractors; elevator contractors and craftsmen; solar contractors and journeymen; fire protection sprinkler contractors and journeymen; irrigation contractors and journeymen; sheet metal contractors and journeymen; automotive and flat glass contractors and journeymen; lead abatement consultants, contractors, and workers; public service gas technicians; certified public accountants; psychologists; individuals and businesses selling insurance; licensed social workers; athlete agents; pawnbroker; professional bondsman or a bail enforcement agent; guard, watchman, or patrolman.
>
> Other licensing and permit statutes include provisions on suspension or revocation on conviction of certain crimes (such as those related to the profession, fraud, or extortion) or lack of good moral character. These statutes include consumer collection agencies; real estate appraisers; occupational therapists; real estate brokers and salespersons; television and radio service dealers, electronics technicians, apprentice electronics technicians, and antenna technicians, radio electronics technicians; sanitarians; landscape architects; interior designers; hearing aid dealers; community association managers; pharmacy licensees; practitioners distributing, administering, or dispensing controlled substances; new home construction contractors; physical therapists and physical therapy assistants.[4]

Sometimes it never ends. The May 17, 2010 edition of the *Houston Chronicle* contained an editorial by Texas state representative Harold V. Dutton Jr. Dutton wrote, "In Texas, we give every felon a life sentence. Oh, I don't mean 'we the jury.' It's more like 'we the public.'" He then recounted the story of a man who wanted to move his family into another apartment complex. His truck was loaded for the move, he had notified his previous landlord, the utilities were turned on at his new place, and he was there, ready to move in. He was then denied his new home because a background check showed he had a felony conviction on his record, and the complex "had a policy of absolutely never, ever renting to an ex-felon." The fact that the conviction was in 1960, more than fifty years ago, the man was eighty years old, and his wife, a recent

4. Coppolo et al. "Consequences of a Felony Conviction Regarding Employment," para 7.

cancer patient, was sixty-five years old, did not dissuade the apartment manager from the position that "a rule is a rule, and there are no exceptions." To his credit, Dutton condemned the decision and argued, "A life sentence should come from the court jury, not from the public jury."[5] But things seem not to change, and felons rarely get to the point where they are no longer punished.

SOCIETY

Let's take stock of where we are. In this and earlier chapters we have seen that prisons are largely punitive cauldrons of suffering, with some attempts to rehabilitate offenders. And punishment of felons never really ends, even after release from prison. We noted the explosive growth in the number of people, largely poor and nonwhite, locked away in prisons and the general decline in crime rates for the last couple of decades. One might conclude that the system is working: That the recent decline in crime is the result of the increase in incarceration throughout the 1980s and 1990s. That somehow the cost of the corrections system is worth it, because prisons reduce crime. But the truth is much more complex.

Researchers have credited the decline in crime to many and varied causes. Some have cited the waning of the crack cocaine epidemic and its associated violence, the movement toward community policing in some cities, and behavioral changes among young people.[6] One study estimated that the growing economy was responsible for 30 percent of the decline in crime during the 1990s. Others credit the change in the age structure of the population—fewer men in the high crime age group of fifteen to twenty-four.[7] One controversial study concluded that the U.S. Supreme Court's 1973 *Roe V. Wade* decision was a major crime deterrent because a subsequent increase in abortions prevented the birth of a large number of children who, had they been born, would have been in the high-crime group.[8] All agree that prisons had some effect on crime rates. Few agree on the extent of that effect.

5. Dutton, "Every Felon."
6. The Sentencing Project, "Incarceration," 5.
7. Conklin, *Why Crime Rates Fell*, 145.
8. Levitt and Dubner, *Freakonomics*, 139.

Determining whether incarceration really reduces crime is a complex and difficult problem. Three theories—incapacitation, deterrence, and rehabilitation—are often discussed. Incapacitation is a philosophy that argues that more arrests and incarcerations take more offenders off the street and thereby reduces crime. As one journalist somewhat indelicately put it, "A thug in prison can't shoot your sister." Deterrence suggests that offenders are rational, thoughtful individuals, and an increased risk of arrest and punishment increases the likelihood that they will refrain from crime. Rehabilitation sees offenders as engaging in crime because of psychological, sociological, or economic forces largely beyond their control. Thus, crime is reduced if prisons "diagnose" the offenders' problems and prescribe a "cure." (These are covered in more detail in the following chapter.)

But the extent to which the factors are effective is not clear. While it may seem obvious that locking up more people would lower the crime rate, the reality is much more complicated. Incarceration and crime do not comprise a simple cause-effect relationship, but instead are parts of a Rube Goldberg-type system of interacting, interrelated parts that form a complex whole. The extent to which each of the philosophies of incarceration contributes to a decline in crime is intertwined with the effect of the others, and is almost impossible to determine. And going beyond the specific philosophies, the more general question of whether incarceration, regardless of the underlying philosophy, reduces crime is equally troubling. Many factors affect both incarceration levels and crime in very nuanced ways. Sending more people to prison might reduce crime. But less crime, resulting from a growing economy or changing age demographics, might mean fewer people are sent to prison because there are fewer offenders or less public demand that offenders be sent to prison. And one should not assume that one event causes another just because the events occur together or in a particular sequence. For example, we saw in an earlier chapter that crime rates rose dramatically from the 1960s to the 1980s, incarceration rates escalated by 700 percent in the four decades following the mid-1970s, and crime rates began to decline in the 1990s. But it is a mistake to make a causal conclusion because of the sequence. As discussed earlier, factors such as the war on drugs and changes in sentencing and release policies, not criminal behavior, were the main reasons incarceration rates escalated. And various external environmental factors, not the number of people incarcerated, most likely drove the crime rates down. When looking at the data, one hardly knows whether he is coming or going.

Another problem is that many who look at data see what they believe rather than believe what they see. A February 22, 2010 *Time* magazine article entitled "What's Behind America's Falling Crime Rate" is a good example. The writer, David Von Drehle, in an otherwise generally balanced article, wrote that "In his book *Why Crime Rates Fell*, Tufts University sociologist John Conklin concluded that up to half of the improvement [in crime rates] was due to a single factor: more people in prison."[9] Von Drehle also, with equal accuracy, could have written, "as little as an estimated 15 percent" of the crime reduction resulted from incarceration. In fact, Conklin's book states, "Elasticities indicate that 13 to 54 percent of the decline in crime rates in the 1990s was due to growth of the prison population."[10] The book also noted that calculation of elasticities is a controversial issue where criminologists reach different conclusions, and "It is possible to support practically any conclusion by selecting a time frame consistent with one's arguments. Sometimes rates of incarceration and crime move in the same direction, sometimes they move in opposite directions, and other times they appear unrelated to one another."[11]

Considering the effect of incarceration on crime makes the Mad Hatter's Tea Party seem like a paradigm of order. The three largest states offer a useful example. During the period 1991 to 1998, the state with the smallest increase in incarceration rate had the largest decrease in crime rate. Texas experienced a 144 percent increase in incarceration with a 35 percent drop in crime rates, California had a 44 percent rise in its incarceration rate with a 36 percent drop in crime rates, and New York saw its incarceration rate increase by 24 percent and its crime rate drop by 43 percent.[12] Go figure.

One study concluded that only 10 percent of the crime decline in the 1990s was due to increased use of incarceration. Further, between 1998 and 2007, states that had the greatest increases in incarceration rates did not necessarily see a corresponding drop in crime rates. Some

9. Von Drehle, "What's Behind."

10. Conklin, *Why Crime Rates Fell*, 95.

11. Ibid., 83.

12. Alexander, "Michigan," 4.

states (Maryland, Massachusetts, Nevada, New Jersey, New York, North Carolina, South Carolina, and Texas) lowered their incarceration rates and still experienced a drop in crime rates.[13] In fact, during the last ten years, all nineteen states that cut their imprisonment rates also experienced a decline in their crime rate.[14]

On the other hand, many criminologists believe that incarceration is in fact a significant factor in reducing crime. A recent report by The Sentencing Project notes that incarceration rates have risen by 24 percent and violent crime has declined by 33 percent since 1994, with about 25 of the decline attributable to the increased incarceration and the other three-quarters to other factors.[15] Other studies reach similar conclusions.

In summary, prisons probably help suppress crime and make our lives safer. While prisons as such do not seem to deter future crime, they do keep some habitual criminals off the street and help to rehabilitate others. One cannot seriously question the need to incarcerate some offenders. Society has to protect itself from Capone, Dillinger, Bonnie and Clyde, Manson, and many other less notorious but equally bad actors who commit violence against others and wreak havoc wherever they go. But, what does society get for the more than seventy billion dollars it spends each year? For all the money it spends locking away every Tom, Dick, and Harry who is convicted of committing a crime, regardless of the consequence of that crime? A look at three issues suggests the get tough on crime movement has been suckered into a deal that satisfies its proponents at the time, but which sadly offers no basis for satisfaction in the longer term.

The first issue is the high rate of recidivism among released inmates, many of whom are in a revolving door relationship with the law. They do time, are released, commit another crime or violate the terms of their parole, and are returned to prison for more of the same. Richard Callahan, who has been sent away three times, is a good example. He wrote,

13. Justice Policy Institute, "Pruning Prisons," 5.

14. Pew Center on the States, "State of Recidivism," 12.

15. The Sentencing Project, "Incarceration," 4.

> I've been to prison 3 times beginning when I was 19. I turned 20 right after I hit the system in 1998. I had a 5 year sentence, I pulled 2 ½ and made parole. I messed up twice on parole, but eventually I completed my parole term. Five months after being off paper I caught two new felonies in regards to dating a woman who was split up with her husband. I didn't physically hurt anyone, but I scared them. I received two, two-year sentences. I knew I had to serve the whole two years because one felony was a state jail sentence. Because of my victimized mentality I took the whole thing hard. I never thought I'd go back to prison after I got out my first time. I was so blind I never saw a need to change anything about myself during those two years. When I left prison in 2005 I planned to do the same things I did which was basically smoking weed, working, looking for sex. Within 4 months of my release I was headed back to prison. I was charged with two felonies, but one was dropped to a misdemeanor. The other felony was a second degree burglary of a habitation. In light of my past, and my resistance to cooperate with the investigation I was sentenced to 25 years and that is what I'm serving now.

Someone has said, "There are lies, damned lies, and recidivism statistics." A kinder—and perhaps less accurate—statement is that recidivism statistics are like a fruit salad because they have so many different components. While the word is usually defined as the number of releases from a particular program who are returned to prison because of a new violation, jurisdictions use different definitions and methodologies to compile their data. Some states have several different, simultaneous procedures for data collection, which allows interested parties to use whichever best responds to their self-interest. Some define a person as released when he leaves prison, others when the offender graduates a post-release program, still others after the individual has a job. One state defines recidivism as recommitment to a correctional institution within five years after release, another as recommitment within three years, and still another as re-arrest within five years. Sometimes offenders are released in one state and get incarcerated again in another state—so they don't count as recidivists. An inmate released on state probation or parole is seldom counted as a recidivist if later jailed for a federal crime. There are just too many variables and diverse influences to draw precise conclusions.

Notwithstanding all this, it can be said that recidivism rates give little hope that prisons are preventing crime or rehabilitating a significant number of inmates. At least 95 percent of all state prisoners will be released from prison at some point—and roughly half will return to prison within three years.[16] A major study concluded that 67 percent of prisoners released in 1994 were rearrested within three years and 52 percent of prisoners released during the year were back in prison either because of a new crime or because of a technical violation of their parole.[17] A subsequent study concluded that 45 percent of people released from prison in 1999 and 43 percent of those sent home in 2004 were re-incarcerated within three years, for a new crime or for violating provisions of their release.[18]

Recidivism varies somewhat by the type of crime for which a prisoner served time. The 1994 study cited above indicated that although rates are high across all criminal categories, they are marginally lower for those serving time for the most violent crimes. Forty-one percent of murderers released were rearrested. Robbery and assault had re-arrest rates of 70 percent and 65 percent respectively. The property crime category saw a re-arrest rate of 74 percent. The offense category with the highest re-arrest rate was motor vehicle theft (78.8 percent) and the offense category with the highest rate of return to prison was drug offenses other than possession or trafficking (71.8 percent).[19] The numbers clearly show that those offenders who commit crimes that arguably should be dealt with in ways other than prison—the nonviolent ones—seem to be more likely to reoffend and return to prison.

The second issue, the war on drugs, is even more discouraging. By most accounts, this continuing struggle has been the mother of all failures. President Obama's drug czar, Gil Kerikowske, noted in early 2010 that "In the grand scheme, it has not been successful. Forty years later, the concern about drugs and drug problems is, if anything, magnified, intensified."[20] In a detailed and sophisticated 2005 report, the RAND

16. Lanagan and Levin, "Recidivism of Prisoners," 1.

17. Ibid.

18. Pew Center on the States, "State of Recidivism," 2.

19. Lanagan and Levin, "Recidivism of Prisoners," table 9.

20. Associated Press, "After 40 Years."

Drug Policy Research Center, while acknowledging the complexity of assessing a generations long program with unclear and changing objectives, concluded that "some simple measures show the war on drugs might be considered successful; others show it generally as a failure." Also, "There appears to be a sense that the United States has spent too many billions of dollars over too many years to have just gone through a decade in which youth drug initiation actually increased and heroin and cocaine dependence declined only modestly."[21] And in a similarly sophisticated report in June, 2011, the Global Commission on Drug Policy issued a report stating that, "The global war on drugs has failed, with devastating consequences for individuals and societies around the world."[22]

The facts supporting an "F" are compelling. In the last forty years, taxpayers have spent thirty-three billion dollars marketing "Just Say No" style messages, $49 billion for border law enforcement, 121 billion arresting 37 million nonviolent drug offenders, and 450 billion dollars to lock these people up in federal prisons alone. None of this has stopped the carnage. According to the Office of National Drug Control Policy, about 330 tons of cocaine, twenty tons of heroin, and 110 tons of methamphetamines are sold in the United States every year, plus vast amounts of marijuana.[23] And a 2008 study showed that of those aged twelve and over in the U.S., 41 percent had tried marijuana in their lifetimes, 15 percent had tried cocaine, 5 percent had tried methamphetamine, over 1 percent had tried heroin, and more than 5 percent had used Ecstasy.[24]

The large numbers of drug offenders have overwhelmed justice systems. Many simply are not prosecuted, while others are stuck in prison for very long terms. There has been some decline in cocaine use, drug abuse among American youth has been on the decline for the past decade, and counter-drug efforts in recent years have resulted in record seizures of drugs. But, we in the United States, comprising 5 percent of the world's population, consume 66 percent of the world's illegal drugs.[25] It is estimated that the U.S. consumes more than 70 percent of

21. Caulkins et al., "How Goes the 'War on Drugs?'," 5.

22. Global Commission on Drug Policy, "Report of the Global Commission," 2.

23. Smith, "Prohibition: Drug War is a Failure," 1.

24. Substance Abuse and Mental Health Services Administration, "Results from the 2008 National Survey," section 2.

25. Califano, "Criminally Unjust."

the world's supply of legal medicinal opiates—poppy-based pain drugs related to heroin.[26] In 2004, the last year for which the Centers for Disease Control has numbers, nearly 31,000 people died from drug abuse and related illnesses.[27] And America's streets are swimming in cheap, powerful narcotics. Hundreds of thousands of people are now pouring out of prisons, many having served fifteen to twenty-year sentences for drug offenses. For the most part, they are returning to the neighborhoods they came from, and usually they lack access to rehabilitative programs, drug counseling, and job training. Traffickers continue to operate in the free world and in prisons. Circumstances approaching anarchy in Mexico seem to be on an inexorable northern march, threatening a massive invasion of our country.

Clearly, the war on drugs has not led to substantial decreases in the severity of America's drug problem, and many critics argue that the increasingly tough policy has done more harm than good. It seems simply to have provided the calories that led to the obesity of our prison system.

The third consideration in assessing the get tough on crime policy is the extent to which high rates of incarceration have broad collateral effects that actually lead to more crime. Under this view, the system will eventually reach a "tipping point," where so many people in a given neighborhood are in prison that the community is destabilized and crime increases.

Families of prisoners are affected most. For example, when a low-level drug offender is sent to prison, that person's crime potential is removed from the community for a period of time. But so also are whatever positive contributions the person was making, whether as a parent, worker, consumer, or neighbor. This effect is exacerbated when the people involved are concentrated in relatively compact communities, as is so often the case.

More than 2.7 million, or about one in every twenty-eight, children in the U.S. have a parent in prison. One of every fourteen African American children has a parent behind bars on any given day.[28] A study

26. Olsen, "Feds Are Slow."

27. Barba, "America's."

28. Pew Charitable Trusts, "Collateral Costs," 4.

in Hudson County, N.J., found that one in fifteen children experienced the trauma of having a parent go to jail for at least six months. In sections of South Central Los Angeles, an estimated 70 percent of the young men are in the clutches of the criminal justice system.[29] Prior to prison, two-thirds of male inmates had been employed and more than half had been the primary source of financial support for their children. In such communities, shame, stigma, and loss of financial and psychological support become a profound aspect of the population's life experience. So many young men are missing that the formation and stability of families are affected. Families are disrupted due to the loss of economic support, the burdens brought on by visiting and supporting loved ones in prison, and the social stigma of having an incarcerated family member. As a result, there is a fraying of social bonds between families and neighbors, and the loss of informal controls that normally contribute to public safety. There is strong anecdotal evidence that children of people who are imprisoned are more likely to be imprisoned themselves, although there is no reliable research information to confirm this idea.

Andrew Romano, writing in the April 28, 2012 edition of *Newsweek*, eloquently summarized the situation:

> Of all the problems in America today, none is both as obvious and as overlooked as the colossal human catastrophe that is our criminal-justice system. Prisons are overflowing. The government is broke. Communities are being destroyed. And yet the country's cowed, uncreative politicians are still stuck in lock-'em up mode: a stale ideology that demands stricter drug laws, tougher policing, and more incarceration, then tars every dissenter as "soft on crime." As a result, the U.S. is now paying $200 billion a year, according to the late Harvard criminal-justice scholar William Stuntz, to arrest, try, and incarcerate nearly 25 percent of the world's prisoners, even though it's home to only 5 percent of the world's inhabitants. Crack use may have subsided, violent crime may have plummeted, and so-called superpredators may have gone the way of Bigfoot. But that hasn't stopped us from separating millions of disproportionately poor, disproportionately black men from their families and communities

29. Fletcher, "High Incarceration," para. 21.

> and consigning them to a vicious cycle of stigmatization and recidivism instead.[30]

We need to acknowledge that imprisonment has some effect on reducing crime. But this effect comes at a high cost, and other options such as drug treatment, school completion programs, and interventions with families at risk often do more to reduce crime than prison. The fact remains, however, that as a society we are where we are. Over thirteen million of our fellow human beings will be locked behind bars within the next year. Christians need to visit them.

30. Romano, "Jailbreak!", 22.

PART 2

Prison Ministry

6

System Building Blocks

PART 1 DISCUSSED THE U.S. prison system, warts and all. Prisons came into popular usage largely as a Christian movement devised to encourage penance by offenders and move beyond harsh corporal or capital punishment, banishment, and public humiliation. Some level of imprisonment, at least for incapacitating and controlling socially destructive persons, continues to be necessary today and the best idea going for protecting the safety and security of the country's population. But prisons generally have become overused cauldrons of misery, holding hoards of suffering people.

Part 2 explores the biblical charge for Christians to help these people. Our current system of corrections is comprised of three important building blocks: the contemporary criminal justice system, a restorative justice movement that is transforming the margins of that system, and a network of prison ministry programs that, more often than not, are faith-based. This chapter explores these building blocks as a context for later, more in-depth discussion of the role of Christian prison ministries and prison volunteers in helping people who are incarcerated.

CONTEMPORARY CRIMINAL JUSTICE

The criminal justice system in the United States, often called our "contemporary criminal justice system," covers a range of actions, from offenders' first encounters with law enforcement through their incarceration or other penalties, to their return to society. Its basic concepts came into being in Western civilization during the eleventh century. After invading England, William the Conqueror expanded the state's role in criminal law in order to strengthen his fragile reign over his people. He made most actions committed against persons or property offenses against the "king's peace," or the crown, rather than private matters among the parties. Fines paid to the crown, as well as capital, corporal, and other types of punishment came to be used increasingly as supplements to or replacements for offender restitution to victims.

This focus on the state rather than the victim continues in our contemporary criminal justice system. A crime is defined as a violation of criminal law, typically state or federal, rather than as harm to another person. When someone is alleged to have committed a crime, the matter is resolved in an adversarial judicial proceeding between the state and the accused offender, or the offender's lawyer. The lawyer often negotiates a plea bargain with the state in which the offender is convicted of a less egregious crime than he actually committed. Crime victims—the persons who were actually hurt by crime—often have little or no role or say in the matter, and their needs are given little weight.

Ron Carlson, introduced more fully in chapter 8, lost his sister in a particularly brutal murder. He was his sister's closest family member. This is the way he described the system that prosecuted her killers: "I respect victims, because I remember what I went through. They [the system] focus on the crime, they show the scenes, the bodies being wheeled out and loaded on the van. They always focus on the criminal. They don't do anything for the victims. The only time I was ever contacted by the system was through a subpoena on the day they sentenced Daniel Ryan Garrett to death. I was advised by a man that 'We got the death penalty for the guy that murdered your sister.' Then he asked me, 'Is this what you want?' My reaction was that I guessed they got what they deserved. I had no choice in the matter either way."

Similarly, an offender is often little more than a silent pawn in a courtroom drama that will so affect his or her life. He has scant understanding of what is taking place as the state focuses on proving his guilt and imposing a punishment he deserves. The punishment, which often includes probation (along with a threat of incarceration if he doesn't comply with stated terms) or actual time in jail or prison, may be based on either of four theories.

The retributive theory focuses on giving offenders their just desserts. With roots deeply set in religious and theological ideas, this theory largely equates crime with a moral wrong, or sin, and holds that it should be atoned through the suffering of the offender. The infliction of harm on an offender—an eye for an eye and a tooth for a tooth—is the only way justice can be restored, as the punishment rights the wrong done by the criminal act. It gives the offender his due, and through this he pays back his debt to society. The problem, of course, is that the suffering of the offender does nothing to address the loss and harm suffered by the victims, to mend the broken relationships with victims and society, or to address the cause(s) of the crime. In practice the punishment often greatly exceeds the hurt the crime caused, demoralizes and dehumanizes the offender, and increases the likelihood of future crime.

The other three theories, introduced in chapter 5, focus less on the morality or sinfulness of crime and more on pragmatic efforts to reduce crime and protect society. Incapacitation locks offenders away, not for what they have done, but to prevent them from doing future harm to the community. This philosophy holds that more arrests and incarcerations take more offenders off the street and thereby reduce crime. Scholars have disagreed as to the crime suppression effects of incapacitation, and estimates vary greatly. One study concluded that the crimes prevented by incapacitation amounted to as few as 1.2 percent, and no more than 8 percent, of the total crimes actually committed. A second study concluded that crimes prevented amounted to 25 percent of crimes committed.[1] A third indicated that incapacitation strategies prevent an estimated 10 to 30 percent of potential crimes.[2]

The deterrence philosophy holds that imposing pain and suffering, including prison time, on offenders is the most effective way of deterring potential offenders and protecting society from crime. Under this view, the primary function of criminal punishment is to enforce legal and social order and protect the welfare of citizens by preventing future crime. The problem is that the emphasis on protecting citizens from future victimization essentially ignores the harm done to existing victims. Further, there is substantial evidence calling into question whether prisons actually deter potential offenders. A 1999 study of the effect of California's "Three Strikes" law, one of the most punitive

1. Law Library—American Law and Legal Information, "Incapacitation," para. 3.
2. Visher, "Incapacitation and Crime Control," 1.

sentencing statutes in recent history, noted that "Virtually no evidence could be found supporting the law's deterrent or selective incapacitation effect on targeted populations . . ."[3] Another study looked at teenagers in Florida around their eighteenth birthday, when their probability of being sentenced to prison for an offense jumped from 3 percent to 17 percent after they were considered adults. The study concluded that there was no sizeable decrease in the arrest rate corresponding to the bump up to an adult penalty in the weeks after people turned eighteen.[4]

The rehabilitation approach aims to fix offenders. This approach, which in theory rejects the punishment aspects of the deterrence philosophy, is rooted in the social and behavioral sciences. Offenders tend to be viewed either as patients or victims, which sometimes allows them to believe they have been absolved of moral responsibility for their actions or of any obligation to take control of their situation. Some argue that conditions in the average prison, which often encourage criminal behavior just to survive, are far more detrimental to inmates than any good served by rehabilitative programs. However, as noted in chapter 4, studies indicate that many of these programs have met some level of success.

In summary, corrections imposed by the contemporary justice system often bear little relationship to the harm offenders have done and generally impose no obligations on offenders other than to rot behind bars for their allotted time. Almost nothing in the system aims to put right offenders' wrongs, address the needs of victims, or attack the root causes of criminal activity. Instead, prisons often are so rife with violence and degradation that they by and large impede the transformation of offenders and even turn nonviolent people into violent criminals. Excessive prison sentences alienate offenders from their families and communities, and perpetuate the poverty that in many cases contributed to the incarceration in the first place.

But a movement, with roots in the 1950s, aims to improve many aspects of this system. The movement is called "restorative justice."

3. Males et al. "Striking Out," 10.

4. Lee and McCrary, "Crime, Punishment and Myopia," 16–17.

RESTORATIVE JUSTICE

Restorative justice seems to have originated with a series of articles by Albert Eglash in 1958, and to have gained steam with the publication of the highly influential book, *Changing Lenses*, by Howard Zehr (often called the grandfather of restorative justice) in 1990. Over the years the field has developed in piecemeal fashion in different parts of the world. Even today the concept is often badly misunderstood. Some people give it a bum rap, while others pigeonhole programs or interventions as part of restorative justice that are not truly restorative or that are in stark contrast to its principles.

For example, one major news personality gave the concept a bum rap by describing restorative justice as an affront to justice and common sense which advocates that all punishment is bad and society should literally hold hands with criminals. On the other hand, another personality defended restorative justice programs that keep nonviolent offenders out of the court system and force them to make amends for their misdeeds, thereby saving society money and valuable court resources.

I asked chaplain Jerry Bryan about his take on restorative justice. He put it in an entirely different perspective with a story from his experience.

> I grew up in a Christian home in Abilene, Texas. My dad was a Gideon—a member of the Christian organization dedicated to distributing Bibles in schools, prisons, and elsewhere. He and a couple of his Gideon friends started going out every Sunday afternoon to the city jail. Now it was basically just a drunk tank. I was growing up in this home, and when I was twelve I asked Dad, "Do you think I could go into the jail with you?" It was pure curiosity, that's all it was. "Sure," he responded. So I went, and his Gideon friends made a big deal of it—a young man with no skeletons in his closet talking to a room full of drunks. And those drunks would stumble forward to receive the Lord, and I thought, "Man, move over Billy Graham." But I went back next week, and these same drunks had gotten out and gotten drunk and gotten back in. My disillusionment grew by leaps and bounds. Mainly, I had smelled all the urine I wanted to smell and had looked at all the smoky walls I wanted to look at. One day I told my dad, "I don't think I want to go back in there with you." He said, "Why not?" "Well Dad, we are not doing any good. These are just a bunch of drunks and they keep getting

> drunk and we are not accomplishing anything." At that point, I got the greatest talking-to I've ever had in my life. Lovingly given, but he got down to eye level, put his hand on my shoulder, and he said, "Jerry, boy, let me tell you something. Jesus Christ came from heaven about 2000 years ago as a baby in Bethlehem's manger, just so he could die on the cross for the sinners of the world, including every one of those drunks in that tank. Don't you think that we can go spend an hour on Sunday afternoon to talk with them?" I was soundly rebuked. So I repented and went back in. I haven't been out of jail or prison ministry since then.

These three examples, ranging from cynical condemnation to what is better defined as a Christian ministry, demonstrate the range of views on this broadly misunderstood and sometimes controversial topic. They set the stage for our discussion of what restorative justice is and is not.

~

Restorative justice principles are deeply rooted in history and in all of the world's major religions. In ancient times, harms done to a person or property were generally handled as private matters between offenders and victims, and perhaps their families, according to existing community norms. Indigenous justice systems, including American Indian, Australian Aboriginal, and Eskimo traditions contained elements, such as sentencing circles, seen in modern restorative practices. And major religions such as Islam, Hinduism, and Buddhism contain many similar elements. While Christianity's restorative justice principles have roots in the Bible, they became institutionalized in the late sixth century when Celtic monks developed a new approach of reconciliation with God that involved personal penance and confession.

With its worldwide use and piecemeal development over several decades, no single source articulates a set of universally accepted restorative justice principles. Instead, various academics, practitioners, and agencies have described restorative justice in their own words—words that may vary somewhat in their detail but that are amazingly consistent in their fundamental essence. The following, based on *Changing Lenses: A New Focus for Crime and Justice* and *The Little Book of Restorative Justice* by Howard Zehr, and *Restoring Justice: An Introduction to Restorative Justice* by Daniel Van Ness and Karen Heetderks Strong, reflects that essence.

At its core, restorative justice recognizes that all people are connected to one another and to the larger world through a web of relationships. These relationships create a system in which each part affects and is affected by other parts, and no person or action stands alone. However, restorative justice also respects the individuality and worth of each person—even those who are different from us, seem to be our enemies, or who have violated society's rules and caused harm to others. Howard Zehr has defined the concept this way: "Restorative justice is a process to involve, to the extent possible, those who have a stake in a specific offense and to collectively identify and address harms, needs, and obligations, in order to heal and put things as right as possible."[5] Similarly, Van Ness and Heetderks Strong say, "Restorative justice is a theory of justice that emphasizes repairing the harm caused or revealed by criminal behavior. It is best accomplished through cooperative processes that include all stakeholders."[6] This foundation supports three key elements.

First, restorative justice focuses on the harm crime does to people and communities, rather than on violation of laws creating crimes against the state. This implies an inherent concern for victims, their injuries, and their need to regain control over their lives and have their rights vindicated. Although its first concern is the victims, restorative justice is also concerned about injuries offenders may have suffered that contributed to their crime or resulted from it. Restorative justice does not excuse individuals' criminal choices. It is concerned about threats to the sense of safety, order, and common values in the communities where crime occurs.

Second, restorative justice requires offenders to be accountable for the consequences of their actions and responsible for repairing the harm they have done, whether concretely or symbolically. Unlike the legal system that is largely limited to making sure the offender is punished, restorative justice seeks to put right the wrongs. It expects that those responsible for harm take responsibility for repairing the damage and addressing the underlying cause to the extent possible.

Third, restorative justice empowers the affected parties—victims, offenders, and the state—to find solutions through mutual, consensual decision making after the offense has occurred. In the contemporary

5. Zehr, *The Little Book of Restorative Justice*, 37.

6. Van Ness and Heetderks Strong, *Restoring Justice*, 43.

legal system the government is considered to be the primary victim, and consequently it has a virtual monopoly over the apprehension, prosecution, and punishment of offenders. Restorative justice, on the other hand, involves practices such as victim-offender mediation programs in which victims and offenders meet with the assistance of a trained mediator to discuss the offense and agree on steps toward justice; conferencing, where groups of affected people meet with a facilitator to agree on a plan of action; circles, where community members express their perspectives and feelings, and propose and commit to solutions; and victim-offender panels that provide willing parties who are linked by a common type of crime an opportunity for a kind of surrogate encounter with like-minded people.

The idea of restorative justice has deep roots in biblical concepts of justice. Christian faith communities, particularly Mennonites, along with Christian prison ministry programs, are a major force behind the contemporary movement. While today one cannot speak of a single "Christian" view, statements or policies of various Christian churches reflect an amazing consistency with the principles discussed above. For example, a resolution of the American Baptist Churches USA states:

> "Restorative justice" offers a framework with which to bring a reparative and holistic focus to the center of the criminal justice system. At its core, restorative justice views crime as a violation of people and relationships and justice as a process that actively works to repair those harmed by crime. Central to the justice process are victims, the harms that they experienced as a result of the crime and the resulting needs for reparation. The offender is held accountable to these harms and needs and encouraged to take responsibility for them, making things as right as possible with the victim and others affected by the crime. This process of repairing the harm to the victim has as an equal and parallel goal the restoration of the offender to the community. Restorative justice also provides an active role for the community as a facilitator of this justice which has a vested interest in the well-being and integration of victims and offenders within the community. This relational approach to justice invites victims, offenders and communities to be actively involved in the justice process.[7]

7. American Baptist Churches USA, "American Baptist Resolution," section 8212.

Father Michael Bryant, PhD provided a Catholic perspective on these issues. Father Bryant served for thirty years as the staff chaplain at the Washington, D.C. jail and continues, after retirement from that position, to volunteer at the facility. He is past chair of the National Convocation of Jail and Prison Ministry, co-editor of the book *Criminal Justice: Retribution Vs. Restoration*, and founder and president of Welcome Home, a faith-based prisoner reentry program in the Washington, D.C. area. We met on a beautiful April day on the patio of San Antonio's, a surprisingly good Mexican restaurant in the shadow of our nation's capital. His balding head, piercing eyes, comfortable smile, and depth of experience reminded me of the best of my college professors.

Father Bryant was among those who researched and drafted *Responsibility, Rehabilitation, and Restoration: A Catholic Perspective on Crime and Criminal Justice*, published in 2000 and currently the stated view of the Catholic bishops of the U.S. on matters of criminal justice. This document recognizes the paradoxical nature of restorative justice. On one hand, it does not tolerate behavior that threatens lives and violates the rights of others. It maintains that the community has a right to establish and enforce laws to protect people and property, and to hold people who violate those laws accountable for their actions and for the harm they cause. On the other hand, restorative justice holds that both victims and offenders are important human beings, and their lives and dignity should be protected and respected. Society should seek justice, not vengeance. Punishment must have a clear purpose: protecting society and rehabilitating those who violate the law.

The teachings and process of the sacrament of reconciliation (also called the sacrament of penance) are, in Bryant's view, at the heart of restorative justice. The traditional elements of this sacrament call for those who have done wrong to be genuinely sorrow for their wrong and commit not to repeat it, to acknowledge and take responsibility for their hurtful behavior, and to exhibit their desire to amend their life by a form of restitution for their wrongs and the harms they have caused. When these changes have been made, the offender's wrongs are forgiven and the person is welcomed back into the community.

The Global Ministries of the United Methodist Church describes restorative justice as follows: "Restorative justice advocates restitution rather than retribution; it is concerned neither with blame and punishment nor with forgiving and forgetting but with remembering, truth telling, repenting, forgiving, and healing. The goal of restorative justice is to change wrongdoers and, insofar as possible, to make wrongs right."[8]

Restorative justice can address the same issues as the contemporary criminal justice system, and many proponents dream of the day when the entire range of system activities is based on a restorative foundation. At the present time, however, restorative justice practices serve mainly to augment contemporary processes in those situations where the parties choose to use them rather than or in addition to the normal process. Use of restorative practices varies greatly from country to country, jurisdiction to jurisdiction, and among varying parties. Goals vary, from providing alternates to the judicial system, to healing or therapeutic programs, to assisting offenders in their transition from prison back into society. And they may be used at any step of the process. Police may use processes such as conferences among victims, offenders, and others in deciding what to do with offenders who come to their attention, or offenders may be referred to community peace committees rather than the normal judicial process. Prosecutors may divert cases to mediation or dismiss cases entirely if the parties have reached a settlement. Judges may substitute mediation for trial or allow the parties to pursue agreement on the appropriate sentence after conviction or a guilty plea. Probation officers may arrange encounters between offenders and victims or others. Inside prisons and jails, restorative processes may be used to help inmates develop empathy for victims, participate in programs of symbolic restitution, meet with their victims or estranged family members, or move toward a culture of peace within the institution. And reintegration programs may be available upon release.

Although restorative justice has deep roots in the world's religions, much of today's practice in the U.S. involves secular attempts to augment the contemporary criminal justice system. But for Christians, this is not enough. Christian prison ministries focus on part of the broader system—prisoners, prisons, and their aftermath—and aim largely to improve the material and spiritual well-being of those people in the system.

8. General Board of Global Ministry of the United Methodist Church, "Restorative Justice," para. 3.

CHRISTIAN PRISON MINISTRY

Opportunities abound for restorative justice proponents and Christians to improve the contemporary criminal justice system: to work for inclusion of restorative principles throughout the system, to lobby for reforms in sentencing procedures, to promote a sane drug policy, to pursue programs that foster victim's rights, to attempt to limit the lifetime punishment of ex-felons in society, and on and on. Like this book, however, the purpose of Christian prison ministries is more limited. Prison ministry is a subset of restorative justice that focuses on opportunities for people of faith to work within the system to improve the material and spiritual lives of individuals who are incarcerated or otherwise affected by it.

Several biblical teachings combine to call Christians to prison ministry. One is the Great Commission, contained in several biblical passages, including Matthew 28:16–20: "Then the eleven disciples went to Galilee, to the mountain where Jesus had told them to go. When they saw him, they worshiped him; but some doubted. Then Jesus came to them and said, 'All authority in heaven and on earth has been given to me. Therefore go and make disciples of all nations, baptizing them in the name of the Father and of the Son and of the Holy Spirit, and teaching them to obey everything I have commanded you. And surely I am with you always, to the very end of the age.'"

The Great Commission is one of the most significant passages in the Bible. After Jesus' death on the cross, he was buried and resurrected on the third day. Before he ascended into heaven, he appeared to his disciples in Galilee and gave them these last recorded personal instructions. Although Jesus gave the command directly to his apostles, it has been broadly interpreted as a directive to all Christians of every time and place. Christians are instructed to step out in faith and take specific action: "to go and make disciples of all nations, baptizing them in the name of the Father and of the Son and of the Holy Spirit, and teaching them to obey everything I have commanded." This requirement is Christian theology's foundation for evangelism and missions work, and Christians of all generations have embraced it. People who hear this calling cover the globe spreading the word of Jesus Christ. While many work in remote regions, uncivilized jungles and deserts, or war-torn countries, mission fields can also be close to home. They can include a neighbor who has not heard the good news, or a poverty-stricken area just across town, or a prison, which may be as dark, as forbidding, as dangerous, as hopeless, as lost, as any place on earth.

Matthew 28 contains three charges that relate to prison ministry. The first is to "go." Jesus told the apostles to go and make disciples of all nations. While some believe the Great Commission only applies to the apostles and ordained preachers and teachers, it is usually interpreted as a command for all believers to go witness to their neighbors, including those behind bars, and make disciples of them.

The second charge is to baptize them. Many questions, conflicting ideas, and differing doctrines and practices regarding baptism have developed over the centuries. My purpose here is not to try to resolve them. It is fair to say, however, that Christian traditions generally hold that baptism shows one's commitment to the Lord and to his call. This suggests that a role of Christian prison ministry, at a minimum, is to foster that commitment from those who are incarcerated.

The third charge is to teach them to obey Jesus' commands—"everything I have commanded you." This, then, includes not only teaching to bring them to Christ, but also teaching them to let him be Lord of their everyday lives.

~

The second biblical call to prison ministry is the admonition that "whatever you did for one of the least of these brothers of mine, you did for me" and the statement that "I was in prison and you came to visit me" from the story of the sheep and the goats in Matthew 25:31–45:

> When the Son of Man comes in his glory, and all the angels with him, he will sit on his throne in heavenly glory. All the nations will be gathered before him, and he will separate the people one from another as a shepherd separates the sheep from the goats. He will put the sheep on his right and the goats on his left. Then the King will say to those on his right, "Come, you who are blessed by my Father; take your inheritance, the kingdom prepared for you since the creation of the world. For I was hungry and you gave me something to eat, I was thirsty and you gave me something to drink, I was a stranger and you invited me in, I needed clothes and you clothed me, I was sick and you looked after me, I was in prison and you came to visit me."

> Then the righteous will answer him, "Lord, when did we see you hungry and feed you, or thirsty and give you something to drink? When did we see you a stranger and invite you in, or needing clothes and clothe you? When did we see you sick or in prison and go to visit you?"
>
> The King will reply, "I tell you the truth, whatever you did for one of the least of these brothers of mine, you did for me." Then he will say to those on his left, "Depart from me, you who are cursed, into the eternal fire prepared for the devil and his angels. For I was hungry and you gave me nothing to eat, I was thirsty and you gave me nothing to drink, I was a stranger and you did not invite me in, I needed clothes and you did not clothe me, I was sick and in prison and you did not look after me."
>
> They also will answer, "Lord, when did we see you hungry or thirsty or a stranger or needing clothes or sick or in prison, and did not help you?"
>
> He will reply, "I tell you the truth, whatever you did not do for one of the least of these, you did not do for me."

This passage, like so many others, has been interpreted in various ways, particularly concerning to whom the reference to "all nations" and "these least brothers of mine" applies. The preponderant view, however, is that Jesus is speaking to all people, and that "These least brothers of mine" must be understood to include all those in need. Thus, we cannot be a follower of Jesus without having compassion for those in need, including those in prison. Our relation with people in need is a metaphor for our relation with God. Followers of Christ will produce good works, will treat others with kindness, will deal with others as if they were Christ—to honor and worship God.

And finally, James 2:14–18 explains what Christians with a true faith will do: "What good is it, my brothers and sisters, if someone claims to have faith but has no deeds? Can such faith save them? Suppose a brother or a sister is without clothes and daily food. If one of you says to them, 'Go in peace; keep warm and well fed,' but does nothing about their physical needs, what good is it? In the same way, faith by itself, if it is not accompanied by action, is dead. But someone will say, 'You have faith; I have deeds.' Show me your faith without deeds, and I will show you my faith by my deeds."

The social implications of these scriptures were summarized and endorsed by the Lausanne Covenant, a 1974 Christian religious manifesto that is one of the most influential documents in modern evangelical Christianity. The Lausanne conference, called by a committee headed by Billy Graham, brought together Christian religious leaders from over 150 countries at the International Congress on World Evangelization in Lausanne, Switzerland. The covenant, written and adopted by 2,300 Christian leaders, contains a section on "Christian Social Responsibility" which reads as follows:

> We affirm that God is both the Creator and the Judge of all people. We therefore should share his concern for justice and reconciliation throughout human society and for the liberation of men and women from every kind of oppression. Because men and women are made in the image of God, every person, regardless of race, religion, color, culture, class, sex or age, has an intrinsic dignity because of which he or she should be respected and served, not exploited. Here too we express penitence both for our neglect and for having sometimes regarded evangelism and social concern as mutually exclusive. Although reconciliation with other people is not reconciliation with God, nor is social action evangelism, nor is political liberation salvation, nevertheless we affirm that evangelism and socio-political involvement are both part of our Christian duty. For both are necessary expressions of our doctrines of God and man, our love for our neighbor and our obedience to Jesus Christ. The message of salvation implies also a message of judgment upon every form of alienation, oppression and discrimination, and we should not be afraid to denounce evil and injustice wherever they exist. When people receive Christ they are born again into his kingdom and must seek not only to exhibit but also to spread its righteousness in the midst of an unrighteous world. The salvation we claim should be transforming us in the totality of our personal and social responsibilities. Faith without works is dead.[9]

Thus, Christians are called to help meet the needs of people who are locked in cages. And they have many needs. Most prison inmates need to have their rationalizations about their criminal acts challenged. They need to learn to be more responsible and accountable. They need to develop employment, interpersonal, and other life skills. They need emotional support, help in dealing with guilt, and help developing a healthy self-image. They need to learn to channel anger and frustration in more appropriate ways. They need spiritual guidance. And on and

9. Lausanne Congress on World Evangelization, "The Lausanne Covenant," 760.

on. Prison ministries can meet prisoner needs such as these. Not all of them, all the time. But some of them, as time and talent permit.

Many people do many things every day to minister to prison inmates. Debbie Van Dyke, director of volunteer services for the Texas Department of Criminal Justice, responsible for coordinating more than 19,000 volunteers working in a wide range of programs across Texas, emphasized the extent of the possibilities. She said that programs range from mentoring, to teaching job skills and GED classes, to preaching and teaching the gospel, to quilting classes, to Girl Scout troops for mothers and their daughters, to "Patriot Paws" that trains dogs that are given to disabled veterans, to programs that help veterans with their own peculiar issues. Some programs aim to help inmates be accountable for what they have done. Others help them be more aware of the hurt they have caused and develop empathy with their victims. Some help inmates grow in their faith, while others teach job skills that can be used after release. Some minister to the needs of inmates' families. The opportunities are unlimited.

How does one think about a Christian prison ministry in the face of so many, disparate needs and so many possible responses? How does one integrate biblical teachings with inmate needs? I suggest a model comprised of the following elements, each of which represents both a biblical teaching and a generalized inmate need: spreading the gospel, fostering forgiveness, building shalom, and encouraging restoration.

These four elements make up a system of interrelated parts. They overlap, and each element affects and is affected by the others. They are circular, and there is no start or finish point. What applies to one element may also apply to several or all. Therefore, discussing them is a messy proposition, but I will try in the following chapters. My aim is to help Christians think about their obligation and role in Christian prison ministry and consider what Jesus may have intended for today's world when he said, "I was in prison and you came to visit me." One thing He must have meant is that Christians need to spread the gospel.

7

The Gospel

CONCERN FOR SPREADING THE gospel and, presumably, for the spiritual welfare of prisoners has a long and sometimes sordid history. For example, during the Middle Ages, when confinement on charges of heresy was common, clergy were responsible not only for convincing the imprisoned of the seriousness of their errors and offering communion to those who renounced their heresy, but also for helping elicit confessions from those who were slow to come around. Church rules provided that a prisoner could not be considered to have been tortured properly unless a cleric had been present. And from the middle of the seventeenth century to the early eighteenth, a number of Huguenots were imprisoned on French ships, where priests where charged to provoke conversions, often using brutality rather than logic. Prisoners who failed to doff their caps in the presence of the communion bread and cup received one hundred lashes.

During the 1700s, John Howard, John and Charles Wesley, Sarah Peters, and others involved in the eighteenth-century English reform movement believed that faith could help rehabilitate prisoners, and that religion held the best, perhaps the only, hope for their transformation. They believed that criminality (and poverty as well) indicated a defect in character, and religious conversion offered the only hope for rising above the defect. "In one model, the profligate might be won to conversion by hearing of the horrible wrath of God; if nothing else, fear might motivate them to regain governance of their passions. In a different model, the poor and the criminals were encouraged to give over control of their passions to a loving God who would bring order into lives that had been allowed to slip into disorder."[1] This view led some reformers to adopt a style of prison visitation that comprised sitting with inmates and reading the Bible. Some prison chaplains required memorization of lengthy biblical texts and compulsory attendance at chapel services. In the United States, the move to the penitentiary system, intended to avoid the brutality of earlier approaches, emphasized the reformation of prisoners by nurturing penitence through solitude and liberal use of clerics and the Bible. As noted in chapter 4, religion of various types and degrees is present in most prisons today, often the work of outside volunteers and prison ministries.

There is still much work to do. Prisoners by and large continue to be isolated in a godless environment of hopelessness and despair. In such an environment, how does one deliver the good news that God has not abandoned them, that Christ died for their sins, that there is hope? How does one teach love to the unloved? Some prefer to emphasize explicit evangelizing in an effort to convert inmates to a particular religious belief. Others suggest teaching biblical principles through the example of Christian living. This chapter explores the two approaches and suggests that on balance the latter is more likely to transform the lives of inmates.

PROSELYTIZING

One approach to prison ministry involves evangelism through explicit preaching, teaching, and persuasion. This type of ministry aims to spread the gospel of Jesus Christ, save inmates' souls, and—quite often—convert inmates from their sinful lives to the particular Christian tradition of which the minister is a member. As a volunteer from a midwestern state explained, "I see my role as an Evangelist in every aspect of my sphere of influence and this includes openly speaking the truths of scripture that Christ mandated and instructed his disciples to do. What can be more important? I believe that overt evangelism in or out of prisons supersedes all other approaches. The world is full of humanitarian organizations with good works which we know is not

1. Griffith, *Fall of the Prison*, 166.

adequate to change lives or lead to sanctification. All our good works are constrained by the love God has for us and should thus lead to a forthright approach to the very simple question, 'Would you like to accept Christ as your personal savior?'"

Overt evangelizing is a legitimate way to spread the gospel, but within prisons it is fraught with dangers and concerns. As a practical matter, under certain circumstances proselytizing may raise separation of church and state issues, and many prison administrations are reluctant to allow it. The U.S. Supreme Court has held that a state may not directly fund programs that involve "explicitly religious content" or that are "designed to inculcate the views of a particular religious faith."[2] One circuit court of appeals has ruled that a prison crossed the line when it promoted religious indoctrination by supporting an evangelical Christian program. And prison systems often limit or prohibit it. According to Debbie Van Dyke, director of volunteer services for the Texas Department of Criminal Justice, Texas prison policy provides that a volunteer may not proselytize inmates, teach the unique practices, beliefs, or traditions of a particular denomination, or press the unique beliefs of one faith against another. In fact, Texas' online training program for volunteers provides, "Volunteers shall not proselytize or induce someone to convert to one's faith or recruit someone to join one institution, or cause while serving as a volunteer."[3]

Perhaps more importantly, one can question whether proselytizing is really effective. Does an inmate who responds to an impassioned plea "convert" temporarily until the passion cools and become a religious criminal rather than a changed person? Is a claimed conversion part of the hustling game? Does it involve honest repentance or a grab at cheap grace? Does the minister cut a notch on his belt each time an inmate comes forward? Are we talking about faithfulness or religion?

Lee Griffith, author of *The Fall of the Prison: Biblical Perspectives on Prison Abolition*, characterized such concerns as follows:

> It must be noted that the biblical call to visit prisoners is a call to faithfulness, but it is emphatically not a call to religion. Faith has to do with God coming down to us—with God redeeming and reconciling us. Faith is a gift. Religion is the exact opposite. Religion has to do with our efforts to climb up to God . . . And above

2. *Bowen v. Kendrick*, 621.
3. Texas Department of Criminal Justice, Volunteer Services, "Handbook."

> all, religion has to do with the conviction that we are the ones who reconcile people to God. Religion is that which inspires us to be hucksters in approaching both prisoners and victims of crime. When people are vulnerable, they are far more likely to listen to hucksters and peddlers, and people are certainly vulnerable when they are homeless, hungry, victimized by crime, or sitting in a cage. It is an opportune time for conversion. But conversion to what?[4]

Proselytizing runs the risk that ministers' efforts will not lead to restoration and a Christian life, but instead to jailhouse religion. Those who accept jailhouse religion are in fact religious criminals—people who wear a claim of religion like a coat when it seems needed but take it off when things heat up just a little. Or, as my friend who is a criminal court judge says, "They get on the 'Jesus Train,' but they get off at 'Parole Station.'" They want to get out of prison more than they want to get prison out of them.

Proselytizing often leads to a one-dimensional approach to a multifaceted problem. Byron R. Johnson, introduced earlier as author of *More God Less Crime*, has written: "Simply put, spiritual interventions must be part of a more comprehensive strategy. Though this observation should be obvious, for many religious volunteers and workers it is not. The reason is that most volunteers tend to be evangelical Christians, and churches these volunteers come from tend to take a very simplistic, shortsighted view of the problem. In other words, most people are taught in churches that prisoners need Jesus, but are not told they need housing, transportation, counseling, life skills, and ongoing mentoring, or that the church should be willing to enthusiastically embrace and support this population."[5]

In *Generous Justice: How God's Grace Makes Us Just*, Timothy Keller asks the question, "What is the relationship between the call to help the needy [ed.: including, in my opinion, essentially all of those locked behind bars] and the Biblical command to evangelize?" His answer is "that they should exist in an asymmetrical, inseparable relationship." Keller argues that "Evangelism is the most basic and radical ministry possible to a human being," but that it is a grave error to "see the work of doing justice as a distraction for Christians that detracts from the

4. Griffith, *The Fall of the Prison*, 226.

5. Johnson, *More God, Less Crime*, 205.

mission of evangelism." Further, "Deeds of mercy and justice should be done out of love, not simply as a means to the end of evangelism. And yet there is no better way for Christians to lay a foundation for evangelism than by doing justice."[6]

Keller concludes a discussion on this subject with the following helpful perspective: "Christians who live or work in needy communities in order to do evangelism must inevitably become involved in helping their friends and neighbors with their pressing economic and social needs. To fail to do so is simply a lack of love. It is also impractical. If you wish to share your faith with needy people, and you do nothing about the painful conditions in which they live, you will fail to show them Christ's beauty. We must neither confuse evangelism with doing justice, nor separate them from one another."[7]

Richard Lopez, director of chaplaincy support in the Texas prison system captured this idea when he explained that "Proselytizing would be forcing somebody to do something, whereas living it [your faith] would be much more powerful, more inclusive for everybody, no matter what faith they are. We should be there, teaching, talking, giving examples of living it. Give them a choice to live the faith, as long as the message is biblical. You are talking fundamentals, you are talking the truth that would fit everybody. I believe the scriptures were made to be lived, not to be argued."

And finally, an old Presbyterian minister once said, "Some people are so heavenly minded that they do no earthly good." Let's turn to the earthly good.

MINISTRY OF PRESENCE

St. Francis of Assisi suggested a different approach: "Preach the Gospel at all times and when necessary use words." This suggests that Christians are called to a ministry of presence, where they teach the love of Christ by doing things to help the lives of those who are incarcerated. The story of the Good Samaritan from Luke 10 is a great model for this approach to prison ministry:

6. Keller, *Generous Justice*, 138.

7. Ibid., 143.

> On one occasion an expert in the law stood up to test Jesus. "Teacher," he asked, "what must I do to inherit eternal life?"
>
> "What is written in the Law?" he replied. "How do you read it?"
>
> He answered: "'Love the Lord your God with all your heart and with all your soul and with all your strength and with all your mind'; and, 'Love your neighbor as yourself.'"
>
> "You have answered correctly," Jesus replied. "Do this and you will live."
>
> But he wanted to justify himself, so he asked Jesus, "And who is my neighbor?"
>
> In reply Jesus said: "A man was going down from Jerusalem to Jericho, when he fell into the hands of robbers. They stripped him of his clothes, beat him and went away, leaving him half dead. A priest happened to be going down the same road, and when he saw the man, he passed by on the other side. So too, a Levite, when he came to the place and saw him, passed by on the other side. But a Samaritan, as he traveled, came where the man was; and when he saw him, he took pity on him. He went to him and bandaged his wounds, pouring on oil and wine. Then he put the man on his own donkey, took him to an inn and took care of him. The next day he took out two silver coins and gave them to the innkeeper. 'Look after him,' he said, 'and when I return, I will reimburse you for any extra expense you may have.' Which of these three do you think was a neighbor to the man who fell into the hands of robbers?"
>
> The expert in the law replied, "The one who had mercy on him."
>
> Jesus told him, "Go and do likewise."

The parallels to prison ministry are striking. The man was "half dead" and needed help, like so many inmates. The Samaritan took care of the man, which is what so many inmates need. Jews and Samaritans hated each other for religious and political reasons, just as many people today feel fear or animosity toward inmates. The fact that it was a Samaritan who helped the Jewish man shows that love does not allow limits on the definition of neighbor, and that all people are our neighbors, including those in prison. A human being cannot be a non-neighbor. Humanness defines "neighbor," and we cannot limit the definition to our own group or to those with whom we are comfortable.

The parable "exposes any religion with a mania for creeds and an anemia for deeds."[8] It also shows that compassion, mercy, and love are

8. Jones, *Studying the Parables*, 314.

key factors in living for God and demonstrating the teachings of Jesus. Our first priority should be to ensure that justice is carried out around us, that we show mercy to our neighbors, and that we practice our faith rather than just talk about it, while letting go of all stereotypes, discrimination, and hatred. The Samaritan was truly present, spoke through his actions, and actually interacted with the man who was hurting.

The parable of the Good Samaritan, along with the story of the sheep and the goats discussed in chapter 6, raises for many the theological question of whether salvation is a matter of faith or something that can be earned through good deeds. Some scholars and preachers fear that such a concern for moral action can lead to hypocrisy and an attempt to earn salvation through works. Klyne Snodgrass, theologian, author and professor of New Testament studies at the North Park Theological Seminary in Chicago, discussing the parable of the sheep and the goats in language that applies to both parables, has responded to this concern as follows: "The judgment evidenced in this narrative does not ask if a person has accumulated *x* number of merciful acts but asks 'What kind of person are you?' Identity is always the issue. Are you a person characterized by the love and mercy evidenced in Jesus's kingdom—which is what faith is all about, or are you one characterized by no concern for those in need? Salvation requires such acts. The point is that a person cannot claim the identity without evidencing it in acts of mercy. Sins of omission are judged as harshly as overt sinful acts."[9]

The New Testament tells us who we need to be rather than specifically what we should do. And we need to be people who, like the Good Samaritan, love the least of our brothers and carry out the Great Commission while helping offenders get their lives together. Christians can be witnesses of Jesus Christ through the natural outcome of living for him. We don't always have to preach, lecture, or proselytize to teach the saving grace of Jesus. Inmates aren't as interested in what we say as they are in seeing how it's working in our life. I once heard one say, "I would rather see a sermon than hear a sermon."

One can view a ministry of presence—teaching through actions—in several ways. One is reflected in the idea of a "secular parable." This term, proposed by famed Swiss theologian Karl Barth, contemplates

9. Snodgrass, *Stories With Intent*, 559.

the presence of authentic Christian actions outside explicitly Christian contexts. Briefly stated, Barth holds that Jesus Christ is the one Word of God, true, complete, and sovereign; all other words are derived from Jesus' words and cannot compete with them; Jesus' words speak for themselves; but "Jesus Christ as the One word of God is the truth which miraculously calls forth parables of itself, not only in the inner sphere of the Bible and Church, but also in the outer sphere of the world."[10]

Thus, Barth concludes that human words that say materially the same thing as Scripture are also true when used in the same context. They stand along side and support the Scripture, and reflect the Word of God. Just as the everyday happenings of a biblical parable are transformed into real testimonies to the real God, human words are transformed and elevated to serve and enjoy the power and authority of the Word of God. Thus, Barth suggests, we should celebrate authentic Christian actions wherever they are found, whether in the context of other of the world's religions or of no religion at all. Such actions and words, he believes, can illuminate Scripture and the teachings of the church and move us more deeply into them.

George Hunsinger, professor at Princeton Theological Seminary, has noted: "They [secular parables] will always encourage the community in the execution of its sometimes dispiriting task. For they will indicate that, despite appearances, the Word itself is at work in the world incognito, not leaving it destitute but raising up 'witnesses to the truth from the darkness of the nations' outside the community's own sphere, as the Bible itself well knows. These secular parables will therefore demand a real hearing from the community, not deflecting it from 'its own mission to preach the one Word of God,' but assisting, comforting, and strengthening it on the way."[11]

Another way of viewing a ministry of action is from Crosswalk Ministries USA, a ministry for incarcerated youth headquartered near Atlanta, Georgia. Board member Bill Ward sent me the following:

> Under the Influence . . . typically evokes a negative connotation that might cause us to wonder who has been inebriated while behind the wheel. But in its broader sense the term applies to everyone. The truth is we are all under the influence of someone or something every day. Conversely people around us are also

10. Hunsinger, *How to Read*, 250.
11. Ibid., 255.

> under our influence every day. So the real question is not if we're making a difference in our world; the question is what kind of difference are we making.
>
> This influence thing is really a pretty simple concept. It was God's, you know. His idea. Community. Doing life together. Each person a combination of every other person whose path he has crossed, for good or for bad. Jesus said we are the light of the world and the salt of the earth. Think about that. Light and salt have a great deal of influence on whatever or whoever is in their paths, but they don't really have to try. Light and salt only have to be what they are—light and salt.
>
> By that same logic, we don't have to try either. We have only to be what we are—flawed but forgiven human beings filled to overflowing with God's Spirit who lives in us. Then and only then will we have the kind of influence that God created us to have.[12]

And finally, I rob another explanation from friend, author, and blogger Edward Fudge who notes that like news correspondents who are "embedded" with the troops in a war zone, "We believers are God's embedded agents, scattered throughout the general population with the unique assignment of being 'salt' and 'light' in our designated place."[13]

~

We can exercise our influence and teach the lessons of Jesus through many kinds of actions when we are in contact with prison inmates. The first is how we handle the matter of judging, or not judging, the offenders we contact. The people we meet behind bars are no angels. They have done bad things. They have violated the laws of man and God—usually often and sometimes egregiously. They have been judged by governmental authorities and often by a jury of peers and found guilty. They are locked up because civil society says they deserve it and should not be allowed to live in the free world.

What attitude toward these individuals is appropriate? How can we avoid making judgments about them? And should we? What is the meaning of Matthew 7:1–2, "Do not judge, or you too will be judged. For in the same way you judge others, you will be judged, and with the measure you use, it will be measured to you?" And Luke 6:37, "Do not judge, and you will not be judged. Do not condemn, and you will

12. Crosswalk Ministries USA, "Under the Influence."

13. Fudge, "God's Embedded Agents."

not be condemned?" And Romans 14:13, "Therefore let us stop passing judgment on one another. Instead, make up your mind not to put any stumbling block or obstacle in your brother's way?"

Not judging in the face of obviously unacceptable, sometimes truly evil, behavior can be a difficult and confusing task. On one hand, we are commanded to not judge or we too will be judged. On the other hand, the Bible and civil society have established standards we all are to live by, and most inmates have failed miserably and obviously in doing so. How can one avoid judging? And how does one help an inmate wrestle with his responsibility for his bad actions and be accountable for what he has done without judging those actions?

Some form of judging is necessary to truly serve an inmate. Failure of parents, family, and friends to make good judgments and take action on them is one reason many are incarcerated. We need to judge, because we need to help inmates understand that making choices and acting upon them requires judgments about right and wrong, good and bad. And biblical teaching supports appropriate judging. Skye Jethani, senior editor of *Leadership Journal* and author of *The Divine Commodity: Discovering a Faith Beyond Consumer Christianity* has a take on judging that fits the prison context perfectly. The following draws extensively from his ideas.

The word "judge" is ambiguous and is used in two different ways in the New Testament. Sometimes it means to judge between things, to differentiate, or discern—to discern between right and wrong, good and evil, righteous and unrighteous. "Judge" may also mean sitting in judgment, or even condemning, people.

Christianity does not forbid judgment as an act of discernment. In fact, the Bible commands us to discern. When the whole sentence in Luke 6:37 is read, "Judge not, and you will not be judged; condemn not, and you will not be condemned" it is clear that Jesus forbids the second definition, to condemn. Jesus is saying the same thing in two ways, a common linguistic device at the time. He is calling us to not condemn people, or pass final judgment, or declare them guilty beyond restoration. And later in Luke 6:43–45, Jesus talks about having the discernment to see the difference between good people and evil people when he compares them to good trees that produce good fruit and bad trees that produce bad fruit.

Much Christian teaching suggests that we are supposed to exercise a righteous kind of judgment, with careful discernment, while we are not to judge hypocritically or condemn another. Matthew 7:2–5 declares, "For in the same way you judge others, you will be judged, and with the measure you use, it will be measured to you. Why do you look at the speck of sawdust in your brother's eye and pay no attention to the plank in your own eye? How can you say to your brother, 'Let me take the speck out of your eye when all the time there is a plank in your own eye?' You hypocrite, first take the plank out of your own eye, and then you will see clearly to remove the speck from your brother's eye."

What Jesus was condemning here was hypocritical, self-righteous judgments of others. If a believer sees another believer sinning, it is his Christian duty to lovingly and respectfully confront the person with his sin (Matt 18:15–17). This is not judging, but rather pointing out the truth in hope, and with the goal, of bringing repentance in the other person (Jas 5:20). We are to speak the truth in love (Eph 4:15). We are to proclaim what God's word says about sin. Second Timothy 4:2 instructs us, "Preach the Word; be prepared in season and out of season; correct, rebuke and encourage—with great patience and careful instruction." We are to "judge" sin but always with the goal of presenting the solution to sin and its consequences (John 14:6). In the words of Bonhoeffer, "The old man and his sin are judged and condemned, but out of this judgment a new man arises, who has died to the world and to sin."[14] It is a judgment that serves mercy, reconciliation, and a new life.

Today's prisons are similar in many ways to the biblical context. In the culture of Jesus' day, some people were acceptable and others were not, and people defined themselves, their identity, and place in the world by comparing and contrasting themselves with others. For example, Jews saw themselves as better or more acceptable to God than non-Jews. Many Romans were dismissive of the Jews. Rich people were seen as more blessed and acceptable to God than poor people. The healthy were seen as righteous, and those with diseases or disabilities were judged to be sinners receiving their due.

Similarly, inmates today often are seen as unacceptable human beings, defined by the bad things they have done and by their incarceration, dismissed as simply sinners receiving their due. So how does one judge them without condemning them? The conventional wisdom

14. Quoted in Jones, *Embodying Forgiveness*, 14.

is that we must remember that we really know very little about their situations. We must judge them from the inside and accept that there are reasons why they act as they do. And if we really look inside them deeply and clearly enough, we even begin to see a reflection of ourselves. Thus, when we know their reason(s), and perhaps can see ourselves, we can much more easily understand, sympathize, forgive, and be patient and tolerant toward them.

But no circumstance or reason can justify a brutal murder, child rape, or other such heinous act. Most of us cannot honestly see ourselves doing such acts. Therefore, looking inside for the reason for inmates' behavior seems to suggest that if we can't find the reason, or can't see ourselves in the action, it's okay to condemn them. This, however, is the judgment that Jesus forbade.

It's okay, even advisable or necessary, to conclude that inmates have acted badly. We need to call a spade a spade, and refuse to justify their inappropriate actions. That is the essence of discernment. But when discernment causes us to value them less, then we've crossed the line into condemnation. When we condemn someone, we declare that they have no value and do not matter to us or God. We exclude them from the status that we feel privileged alone to occupy. This causes us to see the other not as a person, but as a thing—less human and therefore less valuable. And once we see an inmate or a group of inmates this way, the next step is to condone injustice and abuse. When we see inmates as wrong, not just in what they have done, but in their core identity as people, then it's easy to convince ourselves that we don't have to love them; we don't have to serve them; we don't have to respect them. But Jesus says the Christian is never to judge, never condemn, never exclude, never to see anyone as without value or dignity, even the person who has done the most heinous things. We are to see every inmate as worth Jesus dying for.

~

A second way of teaching the gospel through our actions is to listen. Paradoxically, effective listening is an important way of both receiving and sending information, and each is a critical element of spreading the gospel. Effective listening allows you to receive information from incarcerated people: you perceive what they want or need, how they feel, all the things to which you need to respond. If you don't receive information properly, you will not respond appropriately or helpfully. Receiving information and learning from it is the most commonly understood meaning of listening and is most often seen in biblical teaching.

The Bible teaches people to listen to one another. Proverbs 12:15 teaches that "The way of a fool seems right to him, but a wise man listens to advice," and Proverbs 18:13 notes that "He who answers before listening—that is his folly and his shame." Matthew 11:15 says, "He who has ears, let him hear." And James 1:19 underscores the importance of listening, "My dear brothers, take note of this: Everyone should be quick to listen, slow to speak and slow to become angry, for man's anger does not bring about the righteous life that God desires." Thus, listening is our way of learning about other persons and how we can help them. People's words carry their soul's longings, beliefs, purposes, and feelings. Through careful, caring listening, we can see into the depth of the soul and begin to understand the hidden desires, convictions, goals, and emotions, for "Out of the overflow of the heart, the mouth speaks" (Matt 12:34).

One may ask whether he can depend on what an offender, probably incarcerated for dishonest acts, tells him. Perhaps, perhaps not, similar to most other populations. Problems of memory, bias, and sometimes outright fabrication may skew any communication. Certainly this happens sometimes with people who are locked in cages and have bones to pick with many people. When this happens, with close observation and discernment, we can usually fill in the gaps and deal with the interpretations and biases to form a workable view of the truth. We can discern if a person's communication reveals suffering—physical, emotional, spiritual—or hopelessness, or lostness, or other of prison life's unhappy situations. The details don't matter if we connect the dots to understand the needs of another human being, and how we can help him or her.

We can also try to understand the filters through which we listen and make adjustments if they are leading us astray. Remember that our worldview and personal attitude often color what we hear. They may lead to habits of negative responses, generalized assumptions, labeling, or other ingrained acts that cause us to hear what we want to hear and suit reality to our own needs and wants. For example, if we fundamentally believe all inmates are inherently liars, we are not likely to hear what is being said or will hear selectively, if at all, and dismiss the real message. Critically examine and understand yourself and separate what the inmate is communicating from your feelings, personal agendas, biases, and beliefs. Acknowledge your differences, control your own biases, put yourself in the inmate's shoes, and listen with empathy.

Empathy is probably the most fundamental characteristic for effectively helping people who are behind bars. You have empathy when you experience as your own the feelings of another, when you move into their life with understanding and feeling. Empathy requires you to acknowledge your differences, control your emotions, and put yourself in the other person's shoes. It goes beyond an intellectual understanding of their circumstances, and involves an understanding in your heart and soul. When you are empathetic, you do not try to change the other person's feelings or necessarily understand why he has them. Instead, you try to feel as he feels, see what he sees, and appreciate the emotions that are present within him. Listen, observe, and feel in order to identify and appreciate his feelings. With empathy you are able to see an inmate's behavior from her point of view, react to bad behavior with love and understanding, and make judgments about her behavior while avoiding them about her motives.

To develop empathy with another person, acknowledge that each of you has different beliefs, biases, and experiences. The other person's are his, they may be wrong or inappropriate, but they are his. To understand his, you have to deal with yours. You cannot understand that another person is different from you, with different feelings, beliefs, and needs, unless you acknowledge your own feelings, beliefs, and needs.

Sending information by listening effectively may be even more important than receiving information. At some level of abstraction, when a person speaks to us he expects us to show that we value him and his ideas. We respond to this expectation just by the act of listening. We cannot not respond. Even if we remain silent and show no reaction, we are still sending a message. Failure to listen effectively tells the other person something about himself and is likely to contribute to low self-worth. When we don't listen we are telling him that he isn't worth listening to. On the other hand, listening carefully conveys the idea that he is valuable and worth listening to.

Rachel Naomi Remen, in her book *Kitchen Table Wisdom*, says it better than I can: "Listening is the oldest and perhaps the most powerful tool of healing. It is often through the quality of our listening and not the wisdom of our words that we are able to effect the most profound changes in the people around us. When we listen, we offer with our attention an opportunity for wholeness. Our listening creates sanctuary for the homeless parts within the other person. That which has been denied, unloved, devalued by themselves and by others. That which is hidden."[15]

Like a tree that crashes in a forest makes no sound unless someone is there to hear, a speaker is diminished if someone doesn't really listen. On the other hand, one moment of being listened to in an accepting, nonjudgmental, loving way can call into question a lifetime of feeling unworthy, lonely, or unloved. Real listening—active, empathetic rather than just being quiet while another is talking—is perhaps the most powerful tool for showing respect and love for another. Listening is a gift of our time and attention to the speaker. This gift validates her importance and helps the speaker realize she is not alone in her life. And our listening helps the speaker listen to herself and make her own judgments about who she is.

The words of three inmates explain why it is so important for ministry volunteers to listen. One explained, "My family never came forward to hear me out, and it's a lot of offenders within prison who have a lot within themselves that family and loved ones has denied them to say." A second noted that some inmates get regular visits from family or friends, but "people like me, once a year if lucky, but I haven't had one in years." And the third explained, "Inmates can be open and honest with volunteers, while they can't with their peers because of fear of ridicule or of being seen as weak." Thus, many—probably most—inmates yearn for someone just to listen to them.

To demonstrate through your love, patience, and attention that you care about an inmate, pay close attention to your listening habits. Concentrate completely on what he is saying as though he were the only person in the world and you have nothing else to do or think about. Assume that whatever is being said is in good faith and try to understand the essential theme being expressed. Avoid thinking about how you will respond rather than really listening, and instead paraphrase in your mind what the offender is saying. Show by your verbal response and body language that you really care. Make an effort to erase any thoughts of yourself and give the other person 100 percent of your attention.

15. Remen, *Kitchen Table Wisdom*, 219.

Commit to ensuring that he is able to get his point across, and don't worry about yours. And, as discussed above, don't judge or try to advise an inmate too quickly, but do offer feedback. Providing feedback, often in the form of asking questions, keeps you actively involved in the conversation and lets the other person know her message is being received. It keeps both of you engaged, facilitates a better exchange of ideas, communicates that you care, and confirms that the speaker has value.

A third way of teaching the gospel is by demonstrating Jesus' charge in Matthew 22:34–40 to love our neighbors as ourselves: "Hearing that Jesus had silenced the Sadducees, the Pharisees got together. One of them, an expert in the law, tested him with this question: 'Teacher, which is the greatest commandment in the Law?' Jesus replied: 'Love the Lord your God with all your heart and with all your soul and with all your mind.' This is the first and greatest commandment. And the second is like it: 'Love your neighbor as yourself.' All the Law and the Prophets hang on these two commandments."

Christians are charged to teach a message of love—love that is unconditional, foundational, and unshakeable—given completely and without reservation to God and to one's neighbor. Every other commandment flows from this, and every effort to transform the lives of people behind bars also flows from this charge. Most inmates, however, don't know what this kind of love means or looks like. Most have no models for loving others, no experience in loving others, and no motivation to love others. Prison volunteers need to lead by example and provide the models, experience, and motivation.

Volunteers can be an example of love in many ways. One way is by just showing up and treating inmates with respect and dignity, no matter what they did that sent them to the slammer. Just visiting, playing cards, or engaging in other social interaction makes the point. Jesus treated people right, even when they mistreated him or were condemned by society. Volunteers can do the same. If you do this, inmates will wonder how you are able to show this kind of respect for them, and begin to see a small ray of goodness that typically has been missing in their lives. Your presence alone demonstrates the love and forgiveness that shows how Christianity should really work.

And you can tell them you love them. Beverly worked with four kids in a twelve week program in a juvenile facility. Each day she told every kid, "I love you." At the last session, one of them reported, "Every day Miss Beverly told me she loved me. I couldn't understand it, because she didn't even know me. But after a while, when she kept on saying it, I finally decided she really did love me."

Love can also be demonstrated in more organized ways to show those behind bars that volunteers are not phony, that they live what they believe. Two prison ministries demonstrate different, but equally appropriate, ways of demonstrating love. Let's start with Kairos Prison Ministry International, Inc. Kairos is a body of ministries addressing the spiritual needs of incarcerated men, women and children, their families and those who work in the prison environment. It aims to "offer to prison residents, their families, and those who work with them, the opportunity to receive God's forgiveness through faith in Jesus Christ, and to grow in their faith and servant hood in Christian community."[16]

Kairos volunteers, 20,000 strong worldwide, come from many Christian denominations, but the program presents only those basic principles that all share in common. Its most notable effort is a four-day, in-prison weekend involving coordinated talks, discussions, chapel meditations and music, described as a short course in Christianity. This weekend is followed by small, three to six person prayer and share groups within the institution that meet monthly to share their lives on a deep spiritual level and pray with and for one another. Each program, typically for forty-two inmates, may create in participants a desire to become a Christian or to continue his/her personal Christian growth.

I attended the closing session of a four-day Kairos weekend on a hot June day at the Carol Vance unit just outside Houston, Texas. Approximately fifty visitors—Kairos volunteers and hangers-on like me—stood for thirty minutes in a broiling Texas sun amidst prison corn fields before being allowed to enter the chapel. We entered silently, as the inmate participants were in a nearby room and the large visitor attendance was to be a surprise. We were joined by an almost equal number of inmates who were former Kairos participants, returning to encourage the new participants.

The session was, mainly, an opportunity for the forty-two inmate participants to go to a microphone and share with the assembled group

16. Kairos Prison Ministry International, "Kairos."

their answers to three questions: What was your spiritual condition when you came to Kairos? What did you find here? What are you taking with you? Most of them said they came as broken, weak in their faith. The overwhelming majority stated that what they found was love. One middle-aged, balding inmate with a bulging midsection said "These folks didn't know me, or who I am, or what I did to get me locked up. But they came anyway, as friends. They didn't even ask me what I did, cause they didn't care. I was forgiven and loved. And that's what counted." And he spoke for the group when he said, "I'm taking God's love, and when I give it away I will still have it."

Kairos' basic theme is "listen, listen, love, love" or, slightly different, "love, listen, and laugh." Love is exhibited in many ways. Just showing up is a starter. But they did more. The Kairos weekend at the Vance prison was supported by forty-one volunteers working on the outside in support roles and another forty-six on the inside, working directly with the offenders. Each of the eighty-seven volunteers wrote an individual, personal "agape letter" of encouragement, based on scriptural belief, to each of the forty-two participants. Nancy Darley, a longtime Kairos volunteer who was leader of the outside team (women are not allowed to work the program inside a men's prison), explained,

> When I write my letters, I pray about them, open my Bible and point to a verse, and then share my thoughts as to how the verse applies to me and might apply to the participant. God always leads me. It's an incredible experience for these guys to get eighty plus personal letters from someone who loves them. Many of them rarely get a letter. They can't believe a stranger has the love to write them when their family and former friends don't. And the celebration cakes. On Sunday, each inmate receives his own personal cake, like a birthday cake, with a candle and his name written on it. It's overwhelming for someone who has never celebrated a birthday or other special occasion. Oh—and just the food. Not the bland prison chow, but real, quality food. And all they can eat. We usually have a person, or several, who gets sick from overeating. And the letters and pictures and posters from churches and others on the outside. For so many, it is the first time in their life that they have been loved unconditionally, and once a person feels that in their lives, they learn to love others.

The closing ended with everyone—participants, former inmate participants, volunteers and guests—forming a mammoth circle, almost too big for the large room, holding hands and singing "Surely the Presence of the Lord" by Lanny Wolf:

> Surely the presence of the Lord is in this place.
> I can feel His mighty power and His grace.
> I can hear the brush of angels wings.
> I see glory on each face.
> Surely the presence of the Lord is in this place.

If Kairos is a soft approach to demonstrating love, the Bridges To Life prison ministry often shows a tougher side. Bridges To Life, mentioned in the introduction, is a faith-based organization founded by John Sage in 1998, following the brutal murder of his sister. Its mission is to connect communities to prisons in an effort to bring peace into offenders' lives while they are incarcerated and reduce the recidivism rate when they are released. The program's spiritual mission is to minister to offenders and victims of crime in an effort to show them the transforming power of God's love and forgiveness. Victims of crime and offenders participate in a restorative justice process involving face-to-face discussion sessions inside prisons. I observed the tougher side of love in a small group discussion exchange between Jan and Lawrence.

Lawrence grew up in a middle-class community. He had a better-than-okay childhood: loving parents, Boy Scouts, football, prom, graduation, trade school. He married at age twenty-two and supported his young family by working in a series of auto repair shops. At age thirty-one, Lawrence and his best high-school friend pooled their savings, borrowed heavily, and purchased a used car dealership. The business was a struggle but eventually began to do well.

Over a period of time Lawrence came to the conclusion that his partner was taking money from the till and decided to confront him. They agreed to go to a local park to talk in private. Heated words were exchanged, emotions escalated. Lawrence went to his truck, got his .22 caliber pistol, and killed his friend. Lawrence is now serving twenty-five years. The Bridges To Life program requires inmates to discuss the offense for which they are incarcerated. Lawrence did initially, but on most occasions in small group meetings he avoided discussing the murder by noting he was in prison because he "caught me a case."

Jan had enough. When Lawrence one more time talked only about "catching a case," Jan responded with just the right combination of love, concern, and frustration. She told him, "Lawrence, don't try to feed me that BS. You didn't catch a case. You got mad, went to your truck, got a gun, and murdered your best friend. You need to go to that man's mother and beg for forgiveness."

Lawrence's startled reaction showed that Jan had gotten his attention. But Lawrence knew she had acted out of love for him and a desire to help him get his life together. Jan saw the truth when Lawrence would not, forced Lawrence to see the truth as well and acknowledge responsibility for his actions, and did so with love and concern. Jan had demonstrated her love, and Lawrence knew it.

~

In this chapter we have explored how prison ministry volunteers can teach the gospel by overtly evangelizing, and through their lives and behavior by not condemning those behind bars, by listening to them, and by demonstrating love through all their actions. The next three chapters will focus on some substantive ideas and principles the Bible calls volunteers to teach that inmates need to hear. We will start with the threshold concept of forgiveness.

8

Forgiveness

Ron Carlson first met Karla Faye Tucker in the Harris County jail where she was being held for an evidentiary hearing relating to her capital murder conviction. They talked briefly, and Ron told her, "Karla, whatever comes out of this, I just want you to know that I forgive you and that I don't hold anything against you."

Ron's life had never been the same since his father called, "You need to come over to the shop right away. We have reason to believe your sister has been murdered." The police arrived soon after Ron. They showed his father a picture, and he confirmed it was Debbie, Ron's sister. Ron asked to look at the picture, but his father told him, "You don't want to see it." That's how he learned about his sister's death.

After a weekend of drugging and partying, Karla Faye Tucker and Danny Garrett had entered Jerry Dean's home intending to steal his motorcycle and do a little intimidating. In the process they impaled Dean twenty-eight times with a pickax. When they discovered that Debbie Thornton, Ron's thirty-two year old sister, was there and had seen them, they decided to silence her as well. Tucker wielded the pickax. The bodies were discovered by a coworker who came looking for Dean when he didn't show up for work. The pickax was lodged in Debbie's chest.

Unbelievably, Ron's father was murdered about a year later by a shotgun charge to the head.

Ron still seemed shaken when I interviewed him several years later. He told me his mother had passed away when he was five and his sister was ten. His adopted father worked two or three jobs to take care of the children, so Debbie became his mother figure. They were close, and grew closer after they were grown. After a number of years, he established a relationship with his biological father. And then the murders. Ron recalled, "I was shocked, stunned. I was angered, horrified. I utterly hated those people that destroyed my family, and I hated them with such a passion that I wanted to resort to the same things they had done. I wanted to take that same pick-ax and leave it in the heart of Daniel Ryan Garrett and Karla Faye Tucker, just as it was left in my sister's chest. And I wanted to take that same shotgun that Elbert Homing used on my father the following year and blow his head off, just like he killed my father. Some people call it revenge. Some people call it vengeance."

Ron Carlson had been into alcohol and drugs before the carnage, and for roughly seven years thereafter he abused them even more in an attempt to assuage his hatred, pain, and grief. Then he forgave the killers.

~

Forgiveness is typically defined as granting pardon or giving up resentment for a harm or debt. It involves looking back at what happened but not for the purpose of analyzing, blaming, or condemning. Forgiveness looks back for the purpose of leaving the offense behind and moving on to a better future. It does not change the past or the bad things that have happened, but it does change the present and can change the future.

L. Gregory Jones, formerly dean of the Duke Divinity School, is the author of *Embodying Forgiveness: A Theological Analysis*. His views are a major influence on this chapter and will be cited frequently, starting with his definition of forgiveness that is especially pertinent for people who are locked in prison, often after a lifetime of crime:

> This suggests that people are mistaken if they think of Christian forgiveness primarily as absolution from guilt; the purpose of forgiveness is the restoration of communion, the reconciliation of brokenness. Neither should forgiveness be confined to a word to be spoken, a feeling to be felt, or an isolated action to be done; rather, it involves a way of life to be lived in fidelity to God's Kingdom . . . .
>
> That is, forgiveness is at once an expression of a commitment to a way of life, the cruciform life of holiness in which people cast off their "old" selves and learn to live in communion with God and with one another, and a means of seeking reconciliation in the midst of particular sins, specific instances of brokenness.[1]

1. Jones, *Embodying Forgiveness*, 5.

Jones believes that such forgiveness requires confession, repentance, and love of enemies, to be practiced in specific and concrete ways. Therefore, forgiveness is risky, because sometimes it leads to disappointment and further hurt. This risk, the vulnerability of forgiveness, imposes a high cost. There are no shortcuts or easy techniques to replace it. That is the cost of true forgiveness.

Jones distinguishes true forgiveness from "therapeutic forgiveness," or what Dietrich Bonhoeffer called "cheap grace." The cheap approach expects forgiveness without confession or repentance, or it offers forgiveness without love. It aims to make people feel better and get beyond hate rather than to restore communion with God and one another. Cheap grace, or therapeutic forgiveness, sees forgiveness as self-help rather than pursuit of holiness and community.

Cal Higgins, introduced in chapter 4, was offered cheap grace. He was locked up at age seventeen for murdering two people in a drug deal gone bad and had a history of bad behavior while in prison. He told me,

> One day I was in my cell and they called me to the Administration. Two women I had never seen before were waiting on me—said they represented Joe. Until they explained, I couldn't figure out who Joe was. They explained that he was the grandson I locked in the closet when I murdered his grandparents, and he wanted to meet with me. First thing that came to mind was this cat's up to something. But after thinking about it for several days, I agreed to talk to him. It was a very emotional meeting. He wasn't the person I was expecting. He was a spiritual guy, with a good attitude and he had a good heart. Most important thing was that he forgave me for the crime I committed against his family. That was one of the hardest times I ever had, to face someone like that. This was a new challenge. I exchanged letters with the granddaughter who was born on the day of the murder, but I refused to talk to her. Just didn't want to talk to her. I wrote her and sent a tape recording. She wrote saying she forgave me.

Cal said it was one of the hardest times he ever had. But it was free, cheap. He did nothing, took no risks. He didn't even have to look into the eyes of the granddaughter of the people he murdered.

Contrast Cal with Ernst Werner Techow and Mathilde Rathenau. In 1922, Techow and two others, motivated by political ideology and anti-Semitism, murdered Walter Rathenau, Germany's Jewish foreign minister. When the police captured the assassins, the other two killed themselves, and only Techow faced trial. Three days after the assassination, the victim's mother, Mathilde Rathenau wrote the surviving assassin's mother as follows: "In grief unspeakable, I give you my hand . . . say to your son that, in the name and spirit of him he has murdered, I forgive, even as God may forgive, if before an earthly judge your son makes a full and frank confession of his guilt . . . and before a heavenly judge repents. Had he known my son, the noblest man earth bore, he would have rather turned the weapon on himself. May these words give peace to your soul."[2]

Mathilde demanded confession and repentance as the cost of forgiveness, and Techow paid the price. He was sentenced to fifteen years and released after serving five. He joined the French Foreign Legion. After France surrendered to Nazi Germany in 1940, he left the Legion, smuggled himself into Marseille disguised as a dock worker, and began helping Jews escape Nazi-dominated France. He enabled over seven hundred Jews, many penniless, to escape to Spain, and Jews came to regard his as a "one man relief committee." Mathilde Rathenau reached out in compassion and forgiveness, but she didn't offer cheap grace. The life of a murderous assassin was redeemed, and hundreds of innocent Jews were saved.

True forgiveness, the restoration of communion and the reconciliation of brokenness, requires mending and sustaining relationships. Later chapters of Ron Carlson's story present an incredible example. He explained that after he told Karla Faye Tucker he had forgiven her, "I felt a great weight had been lifted off of my shoulders and some of that anger went away." But importantly, they began a friendship. They exchanged letters frequently, and Ron drove hundreds of miles to visit her on many occasions over the years. They always opened and closed each visit with prayer. Karla Faye invited Ron to join her family on the day she was executed after fifteen years on death row. He was there for her.

I asked Ron if he thinks it is possible to separate forgiveness and reconciliation. His response was interesting: "Karla answered the question this way: 'To forgive was one thing. But to actively come up and to love me . . .' Jesus said we are supposed to hate the sin but love the sinner. Forgiveness is just the tip of the iceberg. Just the beginning. Everything I've done was steps in faith. I didn't know where this would lead the day I went and said 'I forgive you.' All I know is I stepped out in faith like God commanded me to do."

2. Gershon, "Life Is Too Short," 1.

There can be no better place for the practice of forgiveness than prisons. When ministry volunteers go into prison, they need to consider forgiveness from two perspectives: whether they can or should forgive inmates, and how they can help inmates learn and apply the craft of forgiveness. These issues will be examined in the remainder of this chapter.

VOLUNTEERS FORGIVING

Should volunteers forgive inmates to whom they are ministering? Can volunteers forgive people behind bars if they haven't been hurt by them or significantly affected by crime? Does it matter?

Volunteers typically want to forgive inmates to whom they are ministering. Like those locked behind bars, prison ministry volunteers are themselves sinners in need of forgiveness. We may not be murderers or burglars or drug dealers, but the common refrain, "There but for the grace of God go I," often is more than a little true. We all have done things that place us in the "sinner" category along with those to whom we are ministering, and we can only guess what our behavior would have been had we experienced the same influences as they have. We all, inmates and volunteers alike, are in need of forgiveness. And we are commanded to forgive if we want to be forgiven. According to Mark 11:25, "And when you stand praying, if you hold anything against anyone, forgive him, so that your Father in heaven may forgive you your sins."

Forgiving inmates makes it easier for them to remember the bad things they have done. If offenders believe God and others are out to get them and will not forgive, their only recourse is to deny or forget their offenses. Doing otherwise exposes them to psychological and perhaps even physical danger. On the other hand, if offenders understand that they can be forgiven by God and others for their offense, no matter how egregious, it is more feasible for them to truly remember what they have done, acknowledge it, and do something about it. Knowing that forgiveness, even cheap grace, is possible reduces the fear and makes the risk worth taking. It allows recollections of the threats, destructiveness, and despair of the past to become a basis of hope for the future. Think about Cal. It must have been much easier for him to remember and accept what he had done after he knew the grandchildren had forgiven him.

So forgiveness seems helpful and perhaps necessary. It may be easy, particularly if crime hasn't really hurt us. It shows love and compassion, while avoiding the appearance of a chip on one's shoulder and a condescending, holier than thou attitude. Forgiveness may lubricate the tension of communication with offenders. And importantly, forgiving makes volunteers feel better. But the idea of corporate forgiveness by non-victims raises serious questions.

~

Corporate forgiveness means forgiving a group for non-specific offenses. While biblical references generally involve forgiving individuals for specific personal hurts and grievances, they seem to suggest that a comprehensive, all-powerful forgiveness is also appropriate. But different traditions have interpreted the Scripture differently. The Christian tradition emphasizes the all-powerful forgiveness embodied in the life, death, and resurrection of Jesus. While we should not aim to play God, we are called to act as he does: to love as he loves, to be holy as he is holy, and, it would seem, to forgive as God forgives. God's forgiveness provides a model for how we are to forgive others. And both the Old and New Testaments tell of a God of judgment, grace, and merciful forgiveness. If God forgives a group of inmates, shouldn't we as well?

The Jewish tradition, on the other hand, holds that only one who has been wronged can offer forgiveness. French philosopher and Talmudic commentator Emmanuel Levinas explains: "Jewish wisdom teaches that He Who has created and Who supports the whole universe cannot support or pardon the crime that man commits against man . . . No one, not even God, can substitute himself for the victim. The world in which pardon is all-powerful becomes inhuman."[3]

Thus, Levinas posits that corporate forgiveness becomes inhuman because too little attention is paid to the victim. But an even more powerful objection may exist in the prison setting. Cheap grace, forgiveness offered too easily by people who haven't been hurt to people who didn't hurt them, seems to encourage an abdication of responsibility and create a culture in which inmates can wallow in the notion that they are the true victims. This victim's culture allows them to pretend what they did was not very hurtful, and believe that they, like everyone else, are simply fallible people, and all they need is God's forgiveness. In this

3. Levinas, *Difficult Freedom*, 104.

situation, offenders may begin to trade on their victim status, certainly to get off the hook for what they have done, and sometimes to enhance their power with volunteers or elicit inappropriate favors.

Jones maintains that seemingly all-powerful corporate forgiveness is not inhuman as suggested by Levinas, but at the same time does little or nothing to transform lives. He notes, "On the cross, God enfleshed in Jesus Christ is the substitute for all of the world's victims, bearing the judgment of the world's brokenness—its universal situation of disaster—so as to bear it away. But God does so in a way that does not ignore, but actually *requires*, the conversion of victimizers through a turning to their particular victims to seek forgiveness and reconciliation."[4] Forgiveness in general and abstract terms has destructive consequences and, in particular, "Forgiveness without repentance invites the perpetuation of sin and the condoning of wrongdoing"[5] and "makes no transformative difference in people's lives, because there is no means to actualize that forgiveness in the dynamics of human relationships. Consequently, the difference that it makes is often a destructive one, as the illusions of either a cheap grace or an ineffective redemption wreak havoc and even death on particular people's lives and relationships."[6]

Thus, volunteers need to carefully avoid the slippery slope that begins with our essential likeness as human beings and goes on to equate lives of crime with lives lived generally in accord with society's, and hopefully God's, standards. We should acknowledge the downside of forgiving a group of inmates without any knowledge of whether they want forgiveness, have repented for their action, or are willing to do so. We need to confront the truth, acknowledge criminal activity for what it is, and refuse to offer cheap grace to those who have been involved in pervasive and persistent crime without any accountability or repentance.

~

We need instead to love them. In Matthew 5:43–45, Jesus taught his disciples: "You have heard that it was said, 'Love your neighbor and hate your enemy.' But I tell you: Love your enemies and pray for those who persecute you, that you may be sons of your Father in heaven."

4. Jones, *Embodying Forgiveness*, 126.

5. Ibid., 136.

6. Ibid., 143.

This candid acknowledgment that Christians will have enemies sets the stage for dealing with offenders who have been enemies of society. We are charged to love them, pray for them, and help them.

The parable of the Pharisee and the tax collector from Luke 18:9–14 shows us what this love looks like:

> To some who were confident of their own righteousness and looked down on everyone else, Jesus told this parable: "Two men went up to the temple to pray, one a Pharisee and the other a tax collector. The Pharisee stood by himself and prayed: 'God, I thank you that I am not like other people—robbers, evildoers, adulterers—or even like this tax collector. I fast twice a week and give a tenth of all I get.' But the tax collector stood at a distance. He would not even look up to heaven, but beat his breast and said, 'God, have mercy on me, a sinner.' I tell you that this man, rather than the other, went home justified before God. For all those who exalt themselves will be humbled, and those who humble themselves will be exalted."

Like most prison volunteers, Pharisees were highly respected individuals, considered righteous and scrupulous in their efforts to obey God. Attitudes against tax collectors, as with most inmates, were quite negative. They were considered dishonest, along with murderers and robbers. The parable shows the contrast between self-righteousness and humility, and condemns those who show disdain for others, even the worst of the worse. It shows that apparently righteous acts—by Pharisees or prison volunteers—that are without compassion and love are not really righteous. God is not impressed by pious acts and feelings of superiority. God is a God of mercy who responds to the honest prayers of people in need.

~

Prison ministry volunteers sometimes have to walk a fine line between love and compassion on one hand, and thoughtful detachment with reasonable expectations on the other. We shouldn't pretend offenders have done nothing wrong, nor should we condemn or demonize them or turn them into scapegoats for society's ills. We shouldn't give them a free pass for what they have done or let them off the hook through cheap grace, but we should hold them accountable for their actions. We shouldn't view all inmates as an abstraction, each just like all others. Instead, we should acknowledge that each individual has a personal history, with mother, father, family, likes and dislikes. We should see each of them as a unique human being, made in God's image and called to be like him. We need to love each of them and behave so they know it. But we should leave considerations of forgiveness to God and their victims, and move on to help inmates with their own forgiveness issues.

INMATES AND FORGIVENESS

In prisons we often think of forgiveness in terms of the desire, perhaps need, of inmates to be forgiven for their crimes and the beneficence of crime victims who forgive those who have done them harm. Inmates did the wrong. If there is forgiveness, it is in the hands of others—an easy, one-dimensional view of the world. But forgiveness is more complex, with various elements, pushes and pulls in different directions, and tough questions calling for difficult answers. Importantly, most inmates need to wrestle with forgiving as well as being forgiven.

Thinking of forgiveness as a craft helps one sort through the complexity. Like carpentry or quilting, forgiveness is a process in which people learn through experience and move from apprentice to excellence. For inmates, the process includes unlearning habits and patterns of abuse, crime, hate, or vengeance and learning habits of peace and reconciliation. They need to build skills for discerning what to do and how to do it; develop a deeper, wider range of appropriate responses to particular situations; and continue to practice and grow such skills.

Volunteers can help inmates develop the craft of forgiveness by helping them learn in six principle areas: getting the truth out, forgiving others, being accountable for their actions, accepting God's forgiveness i.e., forgiving themselves, repenting, and maintaining hope. Each of these will be discussed below.

~

Inmates are not notoriously great truth tellers. They live in a society that punishes the truth, and it's nearly always easier to shade the facts to their advantage or blame someone else. It's easier to think like criminals—to pretend to be victims, continually minimize what they have done, blame others for their own situations, and claim they are the ones who were really wronged. For example, when asked about the crime for which he is serving time, Jose predictably replies, "VOP"—violation of parole. It takes some pressing to get to the truth. He was on parole after serving time for aggravated burglary, and he violated it with a dirty urine test. Or Sally, a woman inmate, sees herself only as a victim of her live-in boyfriend's abuse and cannot bring herself to say that she was a drug dealer and prostitute who grossly neglected her children.

Inmates often allow such self-deception and self-indulgence to trivialize their crimes. They abdicate responsibility for their actions and pass the buck to others: parents, schools, police, drug dealers, society at large. Or they define themselves as victims and see their victimhood to the exclusion of their criminality. This identity allows them to project an image of innocence, even in the face of clear lawlessness, and provides currency for their purchase of compassion and cheap grace from volunteers and others. Their intellectual dishonesty becomes a major roadblock to forgiving and being forgiven.

Telling their life stories works like a truth serum for most inmates and provides an excellent form of confession, an integral part of forgiveness. Telling their personal narratives requires offenders to open up and let it all hang out, like they are writing a play or a song or doing a rap, with themselves as the main character. Stories cover factual information, such as where they were born and lived, a little about their parents, the names and ages of their siblings, and so on. But they go far beyond the bare facts and cover why things happened as they did, how they have been hurt and how they have hurt others, their beliefs and feelings, their vulnerabilities, their loneliness and isolation, their relationships, their dreams and hopes. Their stories reveal who they are as well as what they have done, and begin to generate the honesty that makes forgiveness more costly yet more worthwhile.

Inmates need a critical listener to help them tell the truth and avoid "autobiographical exhibitionism," as few have the best or most truthful perspective on their lives. Having someone listen helps an offender listen to herself and focus on the important things in her life. A good listener who is willing to ask questions helps her fill in the gaps between the events, feelings, and circumstances that she can remember and form a more complete picture of her life. This picture typically reveals both the possibility of goodness and the capacity for great destructiveness, as well as what she has done to others and what has been done to her.

Carrie, an inmate at the Henley facility for women in southeast Texas, tells of her drug-addicted mother who loved and favored her brothers but hated her, and of her feelings of fear, loneliness, and isolation when she was locked up in a juvenile facility as a teenager. Carrie describes her feeling of loss and betrayal when her father got himself killed in a bar fight, her fear of her abusive husband, her belief that no one loved her because she was not lovable, her suicide attempts, her attempts to change, and her dream of becoming a better mother than hers had been. But her whole story also requires her to talk about, and confront, her drug use, forgery, and shoplifting, and acknowledge the fact that she is also a victimizer and a criminal. This gives her a more complete picture of herself that she can examine, criticize, think about, and reconcile through both forgiveness and forgiven-ness.

Stories are the foundation for empathy. Telling them helps inmates develop insights into other people without needing to change them, walk a mile in their sandals, and see things from their points of view. When offenders put themselves in the place of those who have hurt them or whom they have hurt, forgiveness is more likely. And this forgiveness, based on an honest assessment of all the circumstances, can be authentic.

Jones describes the power of stories as follows: "As we learn so to renarrate our lives and to listen so that we can help others narrate theirs, we are unlearning the destructiveness, violence, and depression—indeed, any and all ways in which we diminish and destroy one another and ourselves—so that we can learn the forgiving and reconciling love characteristic of mutual edification. But we cannot do so unless we take the time to hear each other's stories, to know the particular pasts of people's joys and griefs, hopes and fears, sin for which they need to repent and grace that they need to claim and celebrate."[7]

In summary, when offenders tell their stories it's often like removing the lid and smelling the sewer of their broken and hurting life. The first thing they smell is the need for forgiveness, as they see more clearly how they've hurt others and been hurt.

Forgiving others raises very significant and highly personal issues for most inmates. Like Carrie, most are themselves victims, who have been

7. Ibid., 168.

seriously abused, neglected, or trained in their criminal ways by family members or supposed friends who should have loved them. Many, perhaps most, are angry, resentful, or bitter about what has been done to them. Carl is five feet ten, slightly built, with red hair cut very short and an abundance of freckles. He seethes with anger but holds it just below the surface until the conversation shifts to his father. Then he explodes. His father made a decent income and spent much of it on booze. He seemed to relish abusing Carl's mother and whipping Carl. Carl's main memories are of the big black belt, of dreading returning from school to face the whipping, of the many nights his bleeding buttocks stuck to the sheets. He finally escaped, hit the streets, got into trouble, and ended up in prison. He is angry with the world but particularly resents his father, who he blames for his broken life. He wears his bitterness on his sleeve, like a badge of honor. Forgiving his father seems unthinkable. His life of anger and resentment is easier and more comfortable. Some would argue that holding on to his anger is okay, that it simply reflects the moral significance of what has happened to him and motivates him to make changes that will improve his life.

As with Carl, patterns of destruction and violence sometimes have been so egregious, long lived, and deeply embedded that forgiveness seems either impossible or morally unjustified. This is particularly true when those who have done the hurting are more powerful and will use forgiveness as a weapon to justify continuing their exploitation of the weak, or when the lack of repentance suggests that the offense will persist or get worse. How does a woman inmate, incarcerated for drug abuse and prostitution, forgive others when she has been betrayed by a world in which men rape women and by her grandfather who raped her from childhood and is probably still raping her niece? Or think of the wife who forgives her abusive husband. He abuses her again and again, presuming that she will offer unconditional forgiveness each time. Only sincere accountability and repentance can cause the husband to take his actions seriously and remember the hurt he has caused.

However, a strong thread of Christian belief holds that even in the most egregious cases people must forgive those who have sinned against them in order to be forgiven. Ron Carlson, introduced at the beginning of this chapter, reflected this view when he explained how he managed to get beyond his hatred and forgive the three people who had murdered his family before they had shown any remorse or repentance:

"It comes back to the scriptures. My Bible still says the same thing. What really matters in the long run is what I, Ron Carlson, do with my life. Each one of us is accountable for our own actions. Each one of is accountable for our life. It doesn't really matter whether or not they accepted my forgiveness. What matters is that I, Ron Carlson, took the time to say 'I forgive you.' When push comes to shove, the only thing I have to answer for is what I have done in my life. The Bible plainly says, 'We will be forgiven as we forgave.'"

How do volunteers help inmates deal with their anger and forgive those who have hurt them? Not with a simple "I understand," because we really don't understand unless we have been there. And not by trying to pressure a person to forgive someone who has victimized her or him. A hollow forgiveness in the face of real anger and bitterness leads, not to reconciliation and a new life, but to repressed bitterness and exacerbated hatred. Even suggesting forgiveness may tend to trivialize the victim's valid feeling of anger, hatred, and desire for revenge. Encouraging inmates, or others, who have been hurt by family, friends, or others to forgive too cheaply seems to blame the sufferers for suffering. It can add insult to injury by making them feel guilty or ashamed over a reaction that under the circumstances is natural, fitting, and proper.

Forgiveness of any significance is not a one-time event that happens overnight. How long it takes will depend on the relationship of the parties, whether the hurt was deliberate or accidental, the magnitude of the damage, whether it was a one-time event or a continuing problem, and other such factors. Sometimes people have to hurt enough to want to forgive. They have to go through an "acceptance time" during which the mind and heart learn to live with what has happened and the hatred and resentment gradually subside. Therefore, volunteers can encourage inmates to commit to work toward forgiveness, and then accompany them on their journey.

This journey can start by helping them think about their anger. Ephesians 4:26–27 acknowledges that people will be angry and perhaps even suggests that there are things about which one should be angry: "In your anger do not sin: Do not let the sun go down while you are still angry, and do not give the devil a foothold." But uncontrolled anger, resentment and bitterness make forgiveness almost impossible. One cannot blame and hate others and change one's self. One cannot square bitterness with love, resentment with moving on. The last verses of the chapter, Ephesians 4:31–32, tell us to get rid of it: "Get rid of all bitterness, rage and anger, brawling and slander, along with every form of malice. Be kind and compassionate to one another, forgiving each other, just as in Christ God forgave you." Thus, anger and resentment seem inevitable, even okay in some situations. But we are to get rid of it, to forgive. At the end of the day, Jones has concluded, "We are not allowed to endorse hatred, moral or otherwise, as a normatively good response to sin or wrongdoing. This is even true if the sinner or wrongdoer remains persistently impenitent. We are called to 'love our enemies.' Still, we ought to recognize that even this call, part of the way of life of forgiveness, may involve a phenomenally difficult struggle. We should not trivialize it as easily accomplished or suggest that it is always clear what such love entails, particularly in relation to the importance of accountability and punishment."[8]

During the forgiveness journey, volunteers need to help inmates deal with their victim mentality and put their hatred into context: to be truthful about what happened, to see that it has also happened to others, to recognize that they have themselves voluntarily made the choices that put them where they are, and that they are subject to God's forgiving and reconciling love. As prison ministers, our focus should be on inmates and their needs, not on our own need to preach a particular view of forgiveness. Inmates may be counseled to forgive those who hurt them where the other person sincerely confesses and repents of his guilt. But sometimes the victimizer refuses to acknowledge culpability or commit to change, or makes an insincere, cynical claim of penance. In these cases, inmates can be helped to disown the hurtful action and engage in communal practices of forgiveness that "situate forgiveness and repentance as an embodied way of life that enables us to become holy people."[9] This includes the indispensible feature of forgiveness, loving one's enemies, and living a life that embodies both love and forgiveness. Hopefully such love will lead to repentance by the victimizer and eventual reconciliation. This focus leaves the specific question of forgiveness to God, who is better able to handle it. And the prison minister will have accomplished her role of serving the hurting with loving care without imposing her own beliefs that she thinks will be quick solutions to very difficult problems.

8. Ibid., 261.

9. Ibid., 154.

In addition to forgiving, inmates need and want to be forgiven. But they should not be let off the hook too easily. They should be accountable for what they have done. And volunteers should hold them accountable—not just to themselves, but to others—for the crimes they have committed. "Christians ought to insist more than anyone else on the importance of accountability and culpability—but they should do so within a context in which the judgment of *grace* is the determinatively prior aim and where eschatological holiness is the ultimate goal."[10] Thus, volunteers should hold inmates accountable without condemning them, for the purpose of helping them change to a better life.

Accountability means being answerable and implies a legal, moral, or other obligation to someone as though she is sitting in judgment and can in some way call you to account. A person is accountable when he has a duty to another and accepts that duty to meet or respect the other's valid need, expectation, or right. An accountable person acknowledges his culpability, accepts responsibility for his actions, takes the consequences, and makes things right with those who have a legitimate expectation.

Accountability is usually informal, based on relationships and unstated expectations of those who care about or love one another. Offenders typically should be accountable to many people and groups, including their victims, families, friends, the judicial system, and society at large. Inmates are accountable to prison ministry volunteers for their behavior while together and for responding honestly to volunteers' attempts to help. And volunteers need to help inmates be accountable to those to whom they have a broader, more fundamental obligation.

Accountability and forgiveness are not the same, but they work hand in glove, as suggested in Luke 17:3: "If your brother sins, rebuke him, and if he repents, forgive him." Forgiveness does not require those to whom an inmate is accountable to look the other way, act as if no wrong has been committed, excuse the inexcusable, tolerate the intolerable, or sweep things under the rug. Instead, they are charged to rebuke their brother for his crime. Failing to do so, and forgiving without accountability, can cause an inmate to infer that his life has been okay and work to prevent him from confronting his past and making needed

10. Ibid., 156.

changes in his life. Forgiveness with accountability, on the other hand, encourages the individual to make much needed changes in his life, as accountability is a necessary component of repentance. Jones has noted that "The path of forgiveness, which aims at reconciliation, nonetheless requires a call that enemies become accountable, repent of their evil, and take responsibility for their actions (even if, or perhaps as, they begin the process of learning to accept forgiveness for those actions)."[11]

Inmates often rebel against being accountable, as answering for wrongs flies in the face of their criminal thinking. It's easier to deny, rationalize, blame, or forget than to answer. Therefore, volunteers need to help inmates understand why accountability is important and to whom they should be accountable. Sometimes this isn't easy. It may involve their answering to victims who offenders believe felt no hurt, to the police whom they believe have shafted them, to family members who have abused them. And sometimes people who are normally entitled to an answer just don't seem to deserve one.

Demarcus is a twenty-two-year-old inmate, serving a five year sentence in the Kyle unit for an aggravated assault that occurred when he was high on cocaine. He is six feet four inches tall, good looking, and has the muscular build of a person who has more than a passing acquaintance with the prison's barbells. Tears rolled down his face in a group discussion on accountability as he talked of his mother:

> I didn't have a real mother. Sure, she gave birth to me. But she was never there for me when I was a kid. She was more interested in alcohol and drugs with her boyfriends. Then she was sent to prison, although things weren't all that much different with her locked away. I was moved from my auntie to my grandmother to a foster home. I'll never forget the time my grandfather gave me some new shoes for school, and my mother stole them and sold them for drug money. My mother caused me a lot of pain, and she didn't have to. I tried to keep the pain inside and just put her out of my mind. I was mad—but mostly sad. I didn't think about accountability when I was a kid, but no way did I owe her an answer for anything. She did wrong by me.

Demarcus was quiet for several long seconds as he wiped tears from his face. Then he continued, "One day, probably when I was about seventeen, I said some really mean things to her. I'll never forget the

11. Ibid., 269.

look on her face. I knew then that she really loved me. As I have thought about her over the last few years, I've realized that although she did me wrong, she tried to look out for me. She had her own problems. And she was my mother, who still loves me. And I now feel accountable to her. I have to answer to her as to why I'm locked up."

Demarcus had it right. Being accountable often is not easy. Volunteers may need to help offenders deal with their accountability to others in tough, unclear situations. Volunteers can also refuse to condone criminal thinking or let offenders off the hook, while also showing empathy and love. Inmates may need to be prodded, sometimes repeatedly, to get beyond their denial, rationalization, and blaming. And, at the end of the day, inmates need to be accountable to themselves, which leads us to the question of whether, and if so how, they can forgive themselves.

~

The greatest wish of many inmates is to be able to "forgive myself." Many, perhaps most, are filled with guilt, shame, and self-loathing at the lives they've lived and the crimes they've committed. They have lost a sense of self, live with hopelessness, and see their behavior as so unacceptable that it leads to some level of self-hatred. Their negative feelings may not arise from some abstract notion of having defied a legal or moral law, as many offenders are not deeply pained by such facts. Instead, they feel so bad because they have failed to meet their own expectations of themselves or live up to their own standards. They have done a string of things, criminal or not, that they regard as wrong and shameful. Failing themselves nearly always leads to the realization that they have badly hurt others, and in particular, people they love. They say they just cannot forgive themselves.

Richard Callahan is on his third rodeo for drug offenses and assorted other crimes. I asked him about the worst part of being in prison. He answered, "The separation, then personally living with the shame and guilt every day. When I look around at my environment, I'm constantly reminded of my mistakes. And every night my mistakes throughout life are a barrage assaulting any sense of peace I might have felt over the course of the day."

Ronnie, with a somewhat similar criminal history, grew up in a stable, God-fearing, middle-class family. He had all the advantages but saw them go up in the smoke of a methamphetamine lab. After being arrested several times, he plea-bargained a twenty-year sentence in the Texas Prison System. He knows his family has forgiven him, but he continues to condemn himself. The following portion of a letter he wrote to his family speaks to his struggles:

> My throat is sore from the lump in it. Knowing every time I dream of either you or Aunt Pat, my very being breaks down. Aunt Pat, every time I think of the last time I saw you I weep out of remorse and still at times shame. I am so sorry. As I look back at the last time I saw you I can now see you knew what I was doing. The last words I can remember hearing you tell me as your feet dangled on the edge of the ground from you sitting on your bed with the tubes that brought oxygen to your lungs was "Ronnie, you know I love you." It breaks my heart knowing the reason I went to your house was to get some new syringes so I could shoot more dope. You knew it and you told me you loved me. I wish I could make it up to you but I can't. From what I've been told I was the last person to see you alive. Monica found you two days later on the couch dead. I don't think I can ever forgive myself. The closest I can come to making this up to you is a living amends. I have finally sobered up that's a start.

Can Richard, Ronnie, and others like them really forgive themselves? Does anyone have the right or authority to forgive himself for hurting others? Reasonable people might disagree, suggest that self-forgiveness is not biblical, and equate it with an inappropriate self-love. But inmates generally are not that nuanced. They often say they understand their victims and God have forgiven them, but they just cannot forgive themselves. And volunteers need to help them deal with their dilemma.

Self-forgiving in this context is not a religious or spiritual act, nor does it involve a relationship with another. It has to do with self-worth and dignity as a human being. Laura Hillenbrand, wrote in *Unbroken*, a compelling story of one person's journey through numerous Japanese POW camps, that one's self-respect and sense of self-worth, "the innermost armament of the soul, lies at the heart of humanness; to be deprived of it is to be dehumanized, to be cleaved from, and cast below, mankind. Men subjected to dehumanizing treatment experience profound wretchedness and loneliness and find that hope is almost impossible to retain. Without dignity, identity is erased. In its absence, men are defined not by themselves, but by their captors and the circumstances in which they are forced to live."[12]

Without in any way equating modern prisons with Japanese POW camps, a sense of self-worth is equally important for today's inmates. They need to accept themselves as humans and let go of self-anger and the feeling of shame over grievous offenses of the past. They need to calm their self-rejection, quiet their sense of failure, and lighten their burden of guilt. And forgiving themselves, regardless of the theological implications, helps them do these things, restore their self-worth, find their own identity as valued human beings, and maintain hope.

The starting point on a journey of dealing with self is for inmates to remember that, regardless of how they feel about themselves, God loves them and will forgive them. Both the Old and New Testaments describe a God of judgment, grace, divine justice, and merciful forgiveness. God invites inmates, and all of us, to friendship with him and others. It is not a casual friendship, but is a friendship that requires us to see the world and ourselves truthfully and engage in a substantive and enduring relationship with him. Confessing our sin to God and then receiving his grace and forgiveness should result in humility and gratitude. On the other hand, saying, "I can't forgive myself," is prideful and ungrateful. It places one's own evaluation over God's, and says his forgiveness is not adequate. Thus, offenders need to get beyond their pride and accept God's forgiveness as evidence that they are valuable human beings.

One reason forgiveness of self seems so difficult for inmates is that the cost is higher than they think it is. They typically think in terms of cheap grace, a one-time experience that says even in the face of all the bad they've done, suddenly everything is okay and they can think better about themselves, feel good, or simply cope with their situation. This seems too easy, so they find forgiving themselves very difficult. It's a different matter if they view self-forgiveness as more costly, involving accountability, confession, repentance, and love. If they pay a price—even if Christ has already paid the price—they can more readily accept God's forgiveness. They can forgive themselves, not in the sense of a free pass, but in the sense of a changed life. "Those who are forgiven by Jesus are called to embody that forgiven-ness in the new life signified by communion with Jesus and with other disciples. Indeed, that forgiven-ness

12. Hillenbrand, *Unbroken*, 182.

calls believers to live *penitent* lives that seek to reconstruct human relationships in the service of holiness of heart and life. For Jesus, forgiveness cannot be earned, whether through repentance or by forgiveness. This shifts the emphasis from Judaism's assumption that repentance precedes human forgiveness to an assumption that repentance will become an indispensable component of the habit of forgiveness."[13]

Within the prison setting, discussing whether repentance precedes forgiveness or is an indispensable component of God's forgiveness seems like arguing over how many angels can dance on the point of a needle: all clearly need to be penitent and dramatically change their lives, as soon as possible. Accepting God's forgiveness can confer a new identity on an inmate where the prior identity was mainly a dehumanized or dehumanizing burden, precipitated by having been abused for a lifetime or by having preyed on others for many years. Whether this new identity is one of judgment, worry, conflict, chaos and confusion, or of trust, peace of mind, love and joy is up to the inmate. God's forgiveness has provided him the power to react to any circumstance, any time, and in any way he desires. God's forgiveness opens the door to a changed life that gets beyond the self-rejection, sense of failure, and shame that characterized his need for self-forgiveness. Thus, whether an offender calls it forgiving himself, or God forgiving him, or both, this forgiveness will help give him the self-esteem and personal peace he so desires.

~

The call to live a penitent life in peace and communion with God and others is a key component of forgiveness. To do more than accept cheap grace, to live a forgiving and forgiven life, inmates have to behave differently in the future. But simply changing their behavior is not enough. They need to repent. Dietrich Bonhoeffer has observed that "the preaching of forgiveness without requiring repentance. . ." is one element of cheap grace.[14] Forgiveness and repentance are inexorably linked, and both are necessary for a holy life.

Repentance requires remorse or sorrow for what one has done. A sincerely repentant person hates that aspect of himself that engaged in the hurtful behavior he now regrets. He is remorseful, sorry for what

13. Jones, *Embodying Forgiveness*, 121.

14. Quoted in Jones, *Embodying Forgiveness*, 13.

he did—not just sorry that he got caught. Each time he thinks of his wrongful act, he wishes he had made a better choice. Paul described the sorrow of true repentance in 2 Corinthians 7:10: "For God sometimes uses sorrow in our lives to help us turn away from sin and seek eternal life. We should never regret his sending it. But the sorrow of the man who is not a Christian is not the sorrow of true repentance and does not prevent eternal death."

Richard Owen Roberts has described this sorrow, the sorrow inmates need to feel, as follows: "Godly sorrow is concerned with the heart and soul rather than merely the body. Its quality of shame, pain, and agony of conscience may vary from season to season, but it will never totally disappear. It plumbs the depths of sin rather than merely scratching its surface. Because it goes deep, it may be less showy than the sorrow of the world, but once visible, it remains where all who care to see it can."[15]

But repentance is more than sorrow or remorse. It also involves drastic change—a transformation that is more than a temporary change of mind or behavior, or a jailhouse conversion until the problems die down. True repentance is a transformation in which a person's fundamental character and being, not just his surface behavior, become permanently different. Repentant people leave their sins and bad behavior behind and radically and deliberately change their hearts and attitudes as well as their actions. They change not just what they do, but who they are.

When a person repents, deep remorse leads to a firm resolve to do better in the future, and she becomes a new person. Paul wrote in Ephesians 4:20–24: "That, however, is not the way of life you learned when you heard about Christ and were taught in him in accordance with the truth that is in Jesus. You were taught, with regard to your former way of life, to put off your old self, which is being corrupted by its deceitful desires; to be made new in the attitude of your minds; and to put on the new self, created to be like God in true righteousness and holiness."

Repenting admits one to the imperfect, fallible human race. It frees one from guilt and shame, enlarges one's capacity to love, provides a special understanding that works closely with forgiveness and reconciliation, and propels one forward on the journey toward becoming more Christlike. Honest, sincere repentance also enables other people

15. Roberts, *Repentance*, 178.

to have confidence that one is a different person who will behave differently in the future, and who deserves forgiveness.

Like forgiveness, repentance is not a one-time event, but is an ongoing, daily, hourly attitude and change of life. Quoting Richard Owen Roberts again: "If someone comes to me with a report about repentance sometime in their past, I want to cry out, 'So what? Who cares what happened years ago?' It is never enough to say, 'I repented.' You must be able to say, 'I am repentant. Day in and day out, month after month, year after year, unceasingly, I live as a repentant person. I live in the spirit and attitude of repentance.'"[16]

And quoting Jones: "Neither should forgiveness be confined to a word to be spoken, a feeling to be felt, or an isolated action to be done; rather, it involves a way of life to be lived in fidelity to God's Kingdom."[17]

So what should inmates be advised to do about repentance? While they are locked in prison their options may seem limited. But remember, repentance is a change of who they are, not where they are. And they can do many things to change who they are. They should give serious thought to the harm they have done to other people and to their offenses against God, particularly by reflecting on their stories: the good, the bad, and the ugly. They should not view repentance as a general repentance, but instead should endeavor to remember and discuss, to the extent possible, each individual crime—what they did, who their victims were, and who they are accountable to. They can write letters to family members, and under some circumstances to other victims, asking forgiveness for the hurt they have caused. They can read the Bible, pray for help, and reflect on the goodness of God. They can take advantage of programs available in many prisons to improve their lives and demonstrate changed attitudes. They can withdraw from gangs or change their prison friendships. They can obtain help with their substance abuse and begin refusing drugs while incarcerated. And they can identify a role model—perhaps you—to emulate as they try to live a genuinely repentant life.

Hope is our quiet, never ending faith regarding the future. When our present situation doesn't satisfy us, we hunger for more. And sometimes

16. Ibid., 108.

17. Jones, *Embodying Forgiveness*, 5.

that's where inmates are with forgiveness. Forgiveness is a two-way street, and one individual is not in position to control all aspects of it. A person may want an enemy or someone who has harmed him to repent, accept forgiveness, and reconcile, but the person is hardened and refuses even to acknowledge the hurt they have caused. Sometimes an inmate wants forgiveness from a victim, but the crime was so egregious that forgiveness seems unreasonable.

Attempts to pursue forgiveness can easily backfire. Offering words of forgiveness to an unrepentant victimizer may be inferred as an accusation that will make reconciliation more difficult or encourage similar victimization of others. And asking for forgiveness from a crime victim may, at a minimum, be logistically impossible. In many cases asking for forgiveness may be seen by the victim as an attempt to trivialize an egregious crime. Thus, sometimes the most inmates can do is to live forgiving and forgiven lives that will buttress their hope for forgiveness and reconciliation in specific situations as time passes. The importance of hope will be discussed in a broader context, and in more detail, in chapter 10.

In summary, forgiveness is a complex craft, particularly in a prison setting. But volunteers can help inmates deal with the complexities by helping them be honest with themselves and others, by encouraging them to love those who have hurt them, by holding them accountable for their actions, by helping them understand that God will forgive them so they should not continue to condemn themselves, by encouraging them to repent and transform their lives, and by fostering hope for forgiveness in the future.

Importantly, forgiveness is an important ingredient of peace, the topic of the following chapter.

9

Shalom

PRISONS ARE NOT PEACEFUL places. Richard Callahan, a longtime prison inmate introduced earlier, told me, "While I lived in cells on Connally I was what they call a 'cell dweller,' meaning I stayed in my cell as much as possible. I saw a guy get jumped by five inmates at rec. I saw a guy fighting off another inmate with a trash can. What I didn't realize is that the inmate was getting shanked [stabbed with a homemade dagger]. It was not surprising to get locked down out of the blue for a murder. The worst murder was when an inmate was killed on Christmas day." Stopping such violence would be a good idea, but it would not bring peace. It would not address the alienation, the worry, the fear, the wants and needs, the fundamental immorality that are so prevalent in prisons. This broader struggle of prison life can only be addressed through building shalom.

Shalom is generally understood to mean peace. While it is the Old Testament word for peace, it means much more. Shalom comes from the root verb *shalom*, meaning to be complete, perfect, and full. Other words that have been used as synonyms are wholeness, completeness, health, peace, welfare, safety, tranquility, contentment, soundness, prosperity, rest, harmony, the absence of agitation or discord. *Eirene* is the New Testament Greek word for harmony or peace. In Greek culture, the idea of peace was not passive or an absence of conflict. Rather, peace was active, with parties working to find common ground and maintain relationships.

Old Testament scholar Perry Yoder, whose writing in *Shalom: The Bible's Word for Salvation, Justice, and Peace* heavily influenced this chapter, believes that shalom, or *eirene* in the New Testament, reflects the essential theme of the biblical message—the core belief around which many other important beliefs are organized. The biblical basis of shalom is God's act of salvation and liberation, an act that involves mutual understanding between God and people and among people. Shalom is not a tit-for-tat justice based on reciprocity, merit, or just desserts. Instead, it is a response to needs. The word stands squarely against injustice and oppression and is clearly on the side of salvation for the weak, the poor, and the disenfranchised.

Salvation is what God has been about throughout history, principally illustrated by the salvation of the Israelites from Egypt and our salvation through Jesus. Further, God's salvation is the principle sign of shalom justice. We usually think of salvation as God's divine rescue of sinners, of being saved in the afterlife from the consequences of our sins. But Yoder's extensive study of the words *hoshia*, *hassil*, and *sodzo*, each translated to refer to saving actions, suggests an additional, more earthly meaning. The terms are often used with a human as the subject, as in Exodus 2:16–17, where Moses came to the rescue of seven daughters of a priest. And in both the Old and New Testaments the term is most often used to refer to liberation of people from physical or political oppression or personal distresses. For example, the term *sodzo*, "to save," is used 111 times in the New Testament. Either God or Jesus is almost always the subject, but the term rarely refers to spiritual matters or sin. It refers mainly to dealing with physical or material problems, as in Mark 5:23 that deals with physical sickness, or Matthew 8:25 that deals with physical danger, or Mark 15:30 that deals with threat of physical death. Thus, while salvation has a spiritual component, the Bible usually talks of salvation as material, physical liberation or deliverance. As Yoder explains, "In the Bible, however, we have seen that God's salvation is not one which expresses concern only for people's suffering in the next world but does nothing about people's oppression and suffering in this world, their present hell. God's salvation is meant to be a present reality, aimed at liberation here and now. It is to liberate those presently being oppressed, to heal those presently ill! God's judgment . . . stands against all who would hold back this liberation."[1]

Thus, the biblical message of salvation applies to transformation of the present, and shalom is lacking without this transformation.

1. Yoder, *Shalom*, 50.

Shalom fosters present transformation through three basic dimensions of meaning found in the both the Old and New Testaments: living in right relationship with one another and with God; physical well-being, at a minimum a situation where things are all right; and a condition of honesty and moral integrity.

Importantly, each of these three elements does not stand alone. They are linked, and all three parts are necessary for shalom. They, individually and in combination, express the way things ought to be rather that how they are. This understanding of shalom transforms our understanding of peace and peacemaking. According to Yoder, "We are tempted at times to think of peacekeeping as maintaining the status quo without conflict. But our study of shalom shows us that *peacemaking is whitewashing when we think we can have peace in spite of oppression, exploitation, and unjust laws.* To maintain a situation of oppression, material want, and deceit about the way things are is not to keep peace, but is to do the opposite! Shalom making means transforming these situations into ones of fairness, equality, and justice. *Shalom demands transformation not façade*!"[2]

Thus, building shalom within the prison system requires a broad attack on all its injustices: the questionable aspects of our legal and judicial systems, the lock 'em up and throw away the key mentality of the war on crime, and the systemic exploitation and degradation of many inmates. Only a broad-based, structural attack can truly transform the system into what it ought to be. As discussed earlier, however, our objective is more modest. It is to work within the system, *mano a mano*, one day at a time, to improve the lives of people who are locked in cages. And prison ministry volunteers can do things to build shalom for each individual and lay the groundwork for a longer term transformation.

RELATIONSHIPS

The way that "shalom" is used that is closest to the way "peace" is usually used contemplates good, regulated, normal relationships between nations, groups, or individuals or between individuals and God. This meaning is demonstrated, if in its violation, by the words of Psalm 41:9: "Even my close friend, whom I trusted, he who shared my bread, has

2. Ibid., 18, emphasis in original.

lifted up his heel against me." And in Jeremiah 38:22, "All the women left in the palace of the king of Judah will be brought out to the officials of the king of Babylon. Those women will say to you: 'They misled you and overcame you—those trusted friends of yours. Your feet are sunk in the mud; your friends have deserted you.'" And the apostle Paul writes in Romans 12:18, "If it is possible, as far as it depends on you, live at peace with everyone" and in chapter 14, verse 19, "Let us therefore make every effort to do what leads to peace and to mutual edification."

Thus, shalom describes how things ought to be among individuals and between individuals and God. It describes relationships that are right, positive, and good—not just an absence of conflict or tolerating one another for the benefit of the kids. It describes relationships that transcend prison walls and are maintained in the face of physical separation and alienation.

Prisons breed the separation and alienation from friends and loved ones that shalom aims to overcome. James Samuel Logan, associate professor of religion and African American studies at Earlham College, has described alienation as "a basic and tragic human tendency: namely, to turn away from our mutual affections for one another, to participate in neglectful indifference toward—and even the most virulent oppression of—persons and groups other than the ones to which we believe ourselves to belong."[3] Logan suggests that our contemporary prison system, with its focus on vengeance and humiliation of individual inmates, along with its collateral social consequences, causes and reinforces corrosive alienation among inmates, family, friends, and the community. This alienation reinforces the very human conditions that contributed to the criminal acts in the first place.

Let's hear it from the horses' mouths. David, an inmate introduced earlier, put his take on prisoners and relationships: "Relationships, friendships, and love can be either active or inactive. The prisoner sits on one side of the walls and friends and families on another. As time stretches forward, the wall gets higher." After the years pass, "Friends have dissipated altogether while perhaps a select few family members remain a constant presence in life. These are active love, or the love that is. The ones who have lost contact with him—they are inactive, love that isn't."

3. Logan, *Good Punishment?*, 101.

David explained that his love of his mom is an active and flourishing relationship, if nevertheless crippled because of the physical limitations imposed by prison. But he hasn't seen or heard from his best, inseparable friend from before incarceration for six years. This has become a collection of past experiences, thoughts, emotions, memories, and recollections that represent an inactive love. David likens this to the love of God, because, whether active or inactive, it is infinite and never ending. And only by concentrating on his love of God do love of family and relationships fall into place.

Richard, also introduced earlier, says, "I can't stress too much how important relationships are to inmates. I mean, relationships are universally important, but for inmates, relationships connect us to the outside like nothing else. Relationships within prison are between an individual and correction officers and peers, and while there's constant interaction between them, there's always a boundary that keeps people from getting too close. Inmates must keep their guard up, because there's lots of manipulation involving and revolving around these relationships."

Richard explained the obvious—that when a person is incarcerated, all his former relationships change. Relationships with family, loved ones, and friends become distant, limited, and strained, and "99 percent of the time this is the most stressful factor of being in prison." He demonstrated the alienation by example: "Inmates stand in groups for mail call every evening, five days a week. Inmates are willing to pay $450.00 for an illegal cell phone, so they can call loved ones and friends unrestricted, and visits are the highlight of a week or even a month. All of these examples center around relationships."

Richard worries about his relationships after he gets out, and in particular what he is doing to his mother. He wrote, "I'm killing our mother. I've been to prison three times and each time seems worse than the last. My mother doesn't think she'll live to see me free and it's her fear."

~

A number of prison ministries aim to address inmates' personal alienation and help establish meaningful relationships. Paramount among these are various mentoring programs. Richard is involved in a mentoring program, which he explained this way: "The mentor program provides me with a good healthy relationship between myself and another Christian man. Gene comes to meet with me once a week, and he sets an example for me to follow by his service and the person that he is. The program is building me up to be a mentor, not just as a prison mentor, but a mentor to my nephew, my friends, and my family. When I get out my lifestyle will speak louder than words . . ." He continued, "I see Gene more times a month than my own family," and "we often get deep and discuss serious issues."

Gene is Gene Cantwell, a retired oilman who lives in a Houston suburb not far from several Texas prison units. He is usually in prison on a volunteer basis as many as four days a week. He has been working in prison ministries for more than thirty years and has mentored more than forty inmates—of all ages, incarcerated for a wide variety of offenses. I asked Gene why he devoted so much time to this effort. In our rather rambling conversation, he captured the essence of mentoring:

> It's fun. I can't not do it. The number one thing I take to them is God. When they come in, I just do a little prayer, and say, "Father, I don't know what they need, but help me be able to meet it." And it seems like that whatever they need, you can go to Scripture or go here or go there. A lot of it is talking about stories of other guys, and how they have been successful. And I even like to talk about other guys who have not been successful, because there is an important story there as well. I try to listen to them and respond to their needs rather than go in and overtly evangelize. Mentoring is very much an exercise in listening. The more you listen, the more stuff comes out. These guys have never had anybody to listen to them. You are someone to listen to them—to trust them—somebody who believes them—somebody who recognizes their worth. Many of these are talented, smart kids. And there's a lot of good guys in prison. You establish a bond between two human beings.

The bond is not always easy, often requiring an element of confrontation. M. Scott Peck has noted in *The Road Less Traveled*, "There is a traditional concept that friendship should be a conflict-free relationship, a 'you scratch my back, I'll scratch yours' arrangement, relying solely on a mutual exchange of favors and compliments as prescribed by good manners. Such relationships are superficial and intimacy-avoiding and do not deserve the name of friendship which is so commonly applied to them. Fortunately, there are signs that our concept of friendship is beginning to deepen. Mutual loving confrontation is a significant part of all successful and meaningful human relationships. Without it the relationship is either unsuccessful or shallow."[4]

Bridges To Life is a ministry helping to establish personal relationships through a type of confrontation that emphasizes responsibility and accountability. The program also involves segments on forgiveness and reconciliation. Each inmate participant is required to write a letter, which may or may not be actually sent, to a family member. The letters usually involve matters of forgiveness and attempts to re-establish relationships. Jack, an inmate in a large Texas prison, wrote a letter to his wife and decided to send it. Her response, a portion quoted below, tells us much about how forgiveness can foster shalom by improving relationships:

> Baby: First I want to say that I love you beyond words! Thank you for writing that letter to me. It was so weird but when I read it, I felt all the old hurt and anxiety flood out of my body. I felt such relief and I don't know why. I guess I just felt like verbalizing it washed it away. Thank you so much. You never needed my forgiveness, just your own and God's. You have His. I love you. As bad as the last 3 years have been without you, I guess God's purpose was to bring about the changes he was looking for in both of us. I believe he has succeeded. Thank you for your letter. It's the best one I've gotten from you. And I have a whole box of letters from you. We're gonna make it, Baby.

Many other prison ministries aim to improve relationships between inmates and God: preaching ministries, Bible studies, Bible study correspondence courses, and others. One of the biggest is The InnerChange Freedom Initiative (IFI), a faith-based pre-release program operated by Prison Fellowship Ministries in Minnesota, Missouri, Arkansas, Kansas, Iowa, and Texas—discussed in more detail in chapter 7. Volunteers from this organization work with inmates as mentors, serving as role models and friends, Bible instructors, chaplain's assistants offering counseling and spiritual guidance, and family support group leaders. All are seeking shalom through improved relationships among inmates, between inmates and people in the free, and between inmates and God.

4. Peck, *The Road Less Traveled*, 153.

MATERIAL WELL-BEING

Shalom also means material, physical well-being. Life is all right, okay. Sometimes even in abundance. In Genesis 43:27–28, when Joseph's brothers come to the palace to see him, he asks about them and their father: "He asked them how they were, and then he said, "How is your aged father you told me about? Is he still living?" They replied, "Your servant our father is still alive and well." And they bowed low to pay him honor. In 1 Samuel 17:17–18 it's clear that a father is concerned with the physical well-being of his sons: "Now Jesse said to his son David, 'Take this ephah of roasted grain and these ten loaves of bread for your brothers and hurry to their camp. Take along these ten cheeses to the commander of their unit. See how your brothers are and bring back some assurance from them.'" In Esther 2:11, Mordecai is concerned about Esther's physical well-being, as "Every day he walked back and forth near the courtyard of the harem to find out how Esther was and what was happening to her." And in Mark 5:25–33, a woman who had suffered from bleeding for twelve years is told by Jesus to "Go in peace and be freed from your suffering."

Thus, again, shalom is more than an absence of turmoil, conflict, or war. It is also the presence of well-being, health, or all-rightness. This means that if we are to build shalom, we must strive to bring physical or material well-being into the lives of those who do not now enjoy it.

Inmates have many physical and material needs in their current situations and for the future. As discussed in earlier chapters, people who are locked in cages were rarely physically and materially okay before they were locked up. By and large, they have never been okay. They are mainly the poor, the undereducated, the mentally challenged, the small-time drug dealers and thugs who live on the margins of society. While they are in prison they need protection from an often brutal environment, help in dealing with the incredible boredom of prison, assistance in overcoming addictions, money for their commissary account, and on and on.

Volunteer opportunities to improve the material well-being of inmates while they are locked up are limited. Volunteers don't run prisons, and they face significant restrictions on giving inmates things or doing things for them in a material sense. They mainly can help inmates deal with the hand they are dealt, by listening to them and encouraging them to take the initiative to improve their own lives. Perhaps more important, volunteers can advise, teach, and otherwise help inmates prepare themselves to cope after their release. The Prison Entrepreneurship Program is an example of a program doing this. While not an explicitly faith-based program, it is committed to applying ten "driving values" derived from Judeo-Christian principles, and to fostering values-based personal transformation among inmates and those who are released. The crux of the program is a five-month in-prison entrepreneurship course taught by corporate executives and MBA students, followed by extensive post-release assistance in obtaining and retaining employment. Participants from various Texas prisons who are approaching their release dates and meet other requirements are invited to participate in a rigorous application process. Those selected for participation are transferred to the Cleveland facility, a privately-run pre-release prison operated by the GEO Group, Inc.

Once at the facility, a class of sixty to one hundred inmates participates in a comprehensive business and life-skills training program. The program is comprised of classroom instruction, computer training in the program's computer lab, and development of a business plan for post-release business activities. Special weekend events have corporate executives address topics such as venture capital, selling, business plan competition, etiquette, and employment.

I attended employment night. Approximately thirty volunteers, many from beyond the borders of Texas, gathered at the prison just before two in the afternoon. After an airport-like security check, we were escorted into the inner sanctums of the prison, where we were met by two young men: neat, well-groomed, very articulate graduates of an earlier PEP class. They opened the door, and we entered the meeting room in a way I had not expected—through a long tunnel of sixty smiling, hand-slapping inmates, to the tune of blaring hip-hop music, with colored lights flashing. It was like a combination high school pep rally/sales promotion extravaganza. The room was a large, carpeted (highly unusual in a prison) meeting room decorated with reminders of what is required for business success. Inmate participants were in charge of the session. After the cheering stopped, there was time for "mingling," intended to help inmates develop their networking skills. Many were already well-developed. After some time we were "prayed in" and entertained with groups of inmate hip-hop dancers. Then we got down to business.

The business of the day was training and instruction in job interviewing skills. Each participant had completed applications for three different hypothetical jobs. Volunteers acted as pretend hiring executives. Each participant engaged in four mock interviews and received feedback on his performance. They were without exception engaging, prepared, and enthusiastic. Most would have received job offers had the situation been real. And all, hopefully, moved incrementally toward shalom in their lives.

Volunteers can participate in many post-release, reintegration programs that aim to help released offenders reclaim their material well-being. The Annie E. Casey Foundation's Healing Communities program, discussed in more detail in the following chapter, is a good example. Its primary focus is addressing issues of release and reentry, such as housing, employment, peer support, church home, reconciliation, and restitution. Volunteers also assist families of defendants, prisoners, and released offenders through mentoring relationships and assistance with material needs, transportation, child care, and helping the families build relationships with offenders. Individual opportunities to enhance the well-being of released inmates are too numerous to detail: food pantries, churches, service centers, family assistance programs, residential facilities, and many others. They all aim to build shalom through improving material well-being. All combine to provide offenders with a substantial faith that their lives will be okay.

HONESTY AND INTEGRITY

The third meaning of shalom is honesty, integrity, and straightforwardness—the opposite of deceit, lies, evil, guilt, and hypocrisy. This is the moral element of shalom. Psalm 34:12–14 provides, "Whoever of you loves life and desires to see many good days, keep your tongue from evil and your lips from speaking lies. Turn from evil and do good; seek peace and pursue it." Zechariah 8:16 says, "'These are the things you are to do: Speak the truth to each other, and render true and sound judgment in your courts; do not plot evil against your neighbor, and do not love to swear falsely. I hate all this,' declares the Lord." And Galatians 5:22 provides, "But the fruit of the Spirit is love, joy, peace, patience, kindness, goodness, faithfulness, gentleness and self-control. Against such things there is no law."

Christian morality says that the best way to behave is to live in keeping with the teaching of Jesus. Within the prison setting morality involves a sense of behavior that distinguishes between right and wrong, good and bad, or even evil. It is a code to guide people's choices and direct them toward those that our culture, laws, and, for many, religion hold to be the good and right ones. The presence of morality is indicated by how inmates behave rather than by what they think or believe.

Personal morality comes from many sources: family, schools, the culture and society in which we have lived, religion and the teaching of religious leaders, the actions of role models, our experiences and what we have observed others experience, and on and on. From all this, we choose, either consciously or by default, the ones that apply to our lives. All such influences inform our personal morality and make us who we are.

Moral behavior requires that a person understand the difference between right and wrong and act on that understanding. Most of us know what is right and wrong in our culture, under our laws, and according to our religion. We've been taught since childhood. Our problem is in having the self-discipline and personal commitment to do what we know we ought to do. Sometimes we do what we know is wrong because it's easier, or more profitable, or just makes us feel better for a time.

The situation is often different for inmates. For many, right and wrong is not that clear. A while back I got an interesting take on morality from the point of view of many, perhaps most, people who are locked in prisons. While my story is an anecdotal experience that a statistician wouldn't bless, it is a true one that accurately represents the real world. I was working with several small groups of juvenile delinquents. These kids, age fourteen to seventeen, were in a secure lockup for offenses ranging from persistent truancy to aggravated burglary. All were poor and involved in drugs—using, delivering, selling, or all the above. Essentially none of them lived with their fathers, many had never met him, and some didn't know who he was. Most saw nothing wrong with their lives and lifestyle except that they had been caught. Without dramatic change, they were simply a farm team for the big house.

The program curriculum asked the groups to discuss moral codes, including some of the moral codes of the Bible. I expected that, by and large, their moral codes would be substantially different than mine. I was surprised to learn, not that their moral codes were different, but that, with essentially no exceptions, they had no comprehension of the basic concept of a moral code. I was met with blank stares when I asked them about their moral code.

These kids, prison inmates-in-training, told me they live by various codes: what they learned from an abusive drive-by father, the code of the street—you gotta do what you gotta do, the unspoken rules of the drug culture, the law of the gang. They were not without a moral code. They just didn't call it that, and it was a bad one. But in a few years they will comprise a significant portion of the prison population.

One can argue that kids like these, as well as the prison inmates they are becoming, know certain behavior is wrong, and that I was just being too easy on them. But let's look at it. All of them no doubt understand, for example, that stealing violates the law. If they didn't know when they did the act (highly unlikely), they learned it in the judicial process. But there is a difference between violating the law and doing an immoral act, particularly in the view of many offenders. For them, walking out of big, rich Walmart with something they need or selling a joint to someone who wants it violates a law passed by a bunch of old, rich, white men. But doing so is not really wrong for a desperately poor person. Especially one who has observed his parents and friends do the same thing since first memory.

How does one help a prison inmate adopt a morality that society endorses? Many, perhaps most, arrive behind bars with limited moral awareness, compounded by a low level of education, questionable reasoning skills, and little hope of a better future. In prison they are offered a PhD in immorality, with exposure to the violence and retaliation, the hustling, the con games, the sexual abuse, the gangs, the jailhouse conversions, and all the other elements of prison life that are so out of step with a moral society.

The intersection between the moral quagmire that is prison and the continuing struggle to develop programs that reduce recidivism, has given rise to a number of faith and character-based restorative justice programs in correctional systems. However, confirming a relationship between faith/character instruction and morality, and deciding what works to genuinely improve inmates' moral discernment, has been a challenge. Some people have concluded that nothing works. Others believe that crime is a moral issue, that religion plays a profound and necessary role in the creation and maintenance of a moral and law-abiding community, and that programs that support faith and religion also build morality. Warden Burl Cain, introduced earlier as warden of the infamous Angola prison, has the latter view. He believes that his main charge is moral rehabilitation of inmates under his supervision, and the quickest, best way to such rehabilitation is through spiritual change brought about by religion. The reported 74 percent reduction in violence at Angola since initiation of their inmate ministry program indicates he is on to something real.

Research generally supports the view that religion helps reduce criminal behavior. Byron R. Johnson, director of the Institute for Studies of Religion at Baylor University, analyzed 272 studies on religion and crime that were published between 1944 and 2010 and concluded that 90 percent of the studies reported "an inverse or beneficial relationship between religion and some measure of crime of delinquency."[5] However, religion and faith are complex issues, and the literature is fuzzy at best regarding whether programs that foster faith and religion really change inmate morality or long-term behavior. There is simply a scarcity of defensible research studying the impact that faith-based education has on the moral development of people who are locked up.

One study examined the faith and moral development of a small number of participants in the "Life Learning Program" developed and sponsored by the Good News Jail and Prison Ministry at a Midwestern men's maximum security division jail. The program is a faith-based correctional education program that involves Bible studies, lessons on life skills, exposure to positive role models, living in a separate unit from the general inmate population, more open and honest communication, treating others justly, and being held accountable in a loving way. Moral codes and moral reasoning based on biblical principles, as well as topics such as respect, values, conflict resolution, interpersonal communication, and care are part of the curriculum. Its purpose is to produce a measurable change in the lives of those incarcerated and return inmates to society as individuals who are prepared and willing to be productive

5. Johnson, *More God, Less Crime*, 78.

citizens and embrace a value system based on accountability and personal responsibility.

A follow-up study indicated that program participants increased their knowledge of faith beliefs and gained a more personal relationship with God through completing Bible studies and participating in classes that taught the tenets of the Christian faith. This created a more moral community characterized by an ethic of care. Community problems or issues were often discussed and resolved on the basis of biblical principles. Each of the participants claimed to have made a faith decision that involved repenting from their sins, placing their faith in Jesus Christ for salvation, and choosing to be committed to following him. Discipline inherent in the program structure, goal setting, and practicing spiritual disciplines provided direction and assisted participants in cultivating positive actions, habits, and attitudes. When participants developed a relationship with God and came to understand a biblical moral code, their conscience became more sensitive to moral and immoral behavior.

Participants were excited about their faith immediately following their release, but as the weeks and months went by, faith became a lower priority, biblical knowledge waned, and the desire to do what is moral declined. The transition out of incarceration into society, where inmates go from living in a highly controlled environment and making a minimal number of decisions to living in freedom, challenged participants' faith and moral practices. Those who had accepted the faith of chaplains and volunteers faced new freedoms and opportunities to develop their own faith identities and worldview, and claim their faith as their own outside of the prison faith community.

The temptations of the outside and the responsibilities of trying to get a job and pay bills often pulled them back into their previous lifestyle. Inmates who had developed their faith while incarcerated and learned to live it on the inside were not necessarily prepared to live their faith on the outside. They no longer had spiritual and moral accountability, except to their parole officer and society's laws—which perhaps is a great improvement.

The study concluded with the obvious, that the effects of faith-based moral correctional education programs are complex and not easily determined. Many factors influence an individual's faith and moral development. Measuring the "faith factor" is difficult and separating faith and moral components is not easy. However, peers, volunteers, and chaplains who embody their faith in words and actions provide a positive influence in the lives of the participants. And continued relationships with a mentor, membership in a faith community, and other transition services are critical to continuing success.[6]

~

Thus, many opportunities exist for volunteers to build shalom through participation in faith-based programs or merely demonstrating morality in their own lives. Building each of the aspects of shalom in a prison is not easy. Infusing morality in people raised and living largely in immorality is almost as tough as putting Humpty Dumpty back together again. Providing physical well-being while people are locked inside walls is nearly as difficult. Relationships between volunteers and inmates are really surrogates, rarely as meaningful as those with family and friends ought to be. But there is synergy, and the elements can work together to be more than the sum of their parts. Volunteers working on each of them provide, at a minimum, a ministry of presence that builds toward peace, even if limited in place and time. And peace, the more common definition of shalom, is certainly an important step toward the more comprehensive shalom that is desired.

6. Swanson, "Faith and Moral Development," para. 4.

10

Restoration

Biblical history is littered with people who saw failure, including Samson, Abraham, Solomon, Jonah, the Hebrews, the disciples of Jesus, and others. Even King David, a man after God's own heart, failed and displeased the Lord. They all pledged allegiance to God, but, like most prison inmates, committed willful, disobedient wrongs.

The good news is that the overarching theme of the Bible is restoration, or divine rescue. The word of God is an astonishing record of the Lord's effort to reclaim and to restore those who have gone astray. We are introduced to restoration in Genesis 20 when God orders Abimelech in a dream, "Now therefore, restore the man's wife, for he is a prophet, and he will pray for you and you will live. But if you do not restore her, know that you shall surely die, you and all who are yours." In the book of Psalms the concept of restoration is applied to the people of Israel's need to return to the God who made them. And in Galatians 6:1 we are told, "If a man be overtaken in a fault, ye which are spiritual, restore such a one in the spirit of meekness; considering thyself, lest thou also be tempted."

Most prison inmates are broken and in pain. Fostering their personal restoration is a critical aspect of prison ministry. Carol Vance, introduced in chapter 3, is the son and grandson of Methodist ministers. He was elected Harris County District Attorney at the age of thirty-two, and after nearly twenty-two years as DA and a stint in private law practice, was appointed to the Texas Board of Criminal Justice where he quickly became its chairman. Today he is retired, but teaches Bible lessons weekly in three prisons, preaches at the Harris County jail and a homeless facility, and is involved in numerous related activities. Vance's objective is to transform—to restore—the offenders with whom he works. When I interviewed him he said

> The basis for restoration really starts with a person's soul and their heart. Jesus spent his whole life dealing with the have-nots of society—people who were demonized, people who had strong mental illness, people who were crippled, people who were blind. He sat a real example as to how we are to minister to people. Matthew 25 centers around his command to visit people who are sick, or in prison, and take care of their basic needs. Jesus' entire ministry was built around restoration of individuals and making them whole again. He came to set the oppressed, the prisoners, free of the burden of their sins, whatever is consuming their lives. Part of the experience of being set free is to share the faith and try to make others whole—in God's eyes and also in society's eyes. Restore them. Everything Jesus did was reaching out to somebody who was hurting in some way—maybe physically, maybe mentally. He sat that example of love and unselfishly reaching out to others. The whole process brings about restoration to the person doing the ministry and the person receiving it. Restoration goes beyond living a normal, law-abiding life. God considers it much more broadly. We are restored in our relationship to God and are to do his will unselfishly for others to help them have a full and abundant life. This is the real restoration.

Howard Zehr considers the same issue in an explicitly restorative justice context, noting that "Offender advocacy, prisoner re-entry programs, or religious teaching in prison . . . play an important role in a restorative system, especially if they are reshaped to include a restorative framework."[1] He notes that a restorative framework for prison ministry recognizes that prisoners themselves have often been harmed, emphasizes their healing and integration into the community, treats them respectfully, and values personal change above compliant behavior. Programs that support restoration also encourage offenders to understand the harm they have caused, take appropriate responsibility, work to make things right, and be active participants in addressing their own needs.

We often think of restoration as returning to God, but, as Vance and Zehr have suggested, it is much more. Like repentance, restoration involves inmates turning from a life of crime and making a fundamental

1. Zehr, *Little Book of Restorative Justice*, 57.

change in who they are. But restoration goes further, is more active, and includes a sense of recovery, of return to the best that one has been, of beginning life anew, and of hope for the future. Restored inmates experience personal healing and become part of the Christian community, even in the midst of all the suffering so prevalent in prisons.

Restoration is not easy for anyone, much less people who are locked behind bars. Such a transformation requires moving out against the inertia of indolence fostered by prison life and deviating from the norm in a society where flying below the radar and looking out for number one is the safest way. It requires new and different thinking and action in a culture that rewards, or at least limits punishment for, compliance and conformity. Change and spiritual growth involve risks of failure, of ridicule, and perhaps of physical danger that may lead an inmate to refuse to try. So inmates need help, and volunteers can provide it. They can assist inmates in their restoration efforts by helping them recognize and exploit the freedom available to them, accept responsibility for what they have done, tear down walls and reconcile with others, and maintain hope.

FREEDOM

Luke 4:18–19 tells of Jesus teaching in the synagogue and reading from the prophet Isaiah, "The Spirit of the Lord is on me, because he has anointed me to preach good news to the poor. He has sent me to proclaim freedom for the prisoners and recovery of sight for the blind, to release the oppressed, to proclaim the year of the Lord's favor." To think about how the biblical charges to "proclaim freedom for the prisoners" and "release the oppressed" play out for ministry volunteers today, let's begin by comparing biblical prisons to current ones.

Many Bible characters were imprisoned at one time or another: Joseph, Samson, Jeremiah, Micaiah, Zedekiah, Daniel, John the Baptist, Peter, James, John, Silas, Paul, Epaphras, Aristarchus, and Junia. Even Jesus was held in custody between his arrest and execution and, in death, imprisoned in a guarded tomb. While the times, the culture, and the prisons were different, today's prisons are more like those of biblical times than we care to admit.

Prisons in biblical times were places of great suffering. The king gave orders to put Micaiah in prison and give him nothing but bread and water. The Psalmist talked of the groans of the prisoners, and of them sitting in darkness and the deepest gloom, suffering in iron chains. Jeremiah was put into a vaulted cell in a dungeon and when released for interrogation pleaded not to be sent back because he was afraid he would die there. But the officials wanted him to die, so they took him and put him into a cistern filled with mud. Matthew writes of a man being turned over to jailers to be tortured until he paid back all he owed. Herod gave orders to have John arrested, bound, put in prison, and then beheaded.

Today we don't speak of dungeons or cisterns, and torture is not condoned. Contemporary prisons are more humane than those of the past. But our prisons generally foment suffering, much as in biblical times. They are not country clubs as some people allege. A review of chapter 4 recalls the solitary confinement on one hand or the overcrowded cells or dormitories on the other, the excruciating boredom, the hustling, and sometimes the violence, rape, abuse, and gang fights. There is the extreme loneliness in the face of no privacy, the continuing inmate counts, the humiliating strip searches, and the essential absence of a first name. Yes, our prisons are different from what they were in biblical times. But, like the prisons of old, they are places of great suffering.

The second similarity—prison as an instrument of oppression rather than an instrument of justice—is less clear, more controversial. Biblical law favored restitution over retribution as a way of dealing with wrongdoers, and imprisonment generally was not used as a form of criminal punishment as it is today. Prisons were used mainly for military and political ends—as instruments of oppression more than instruments of justice. The king of Judah imprisoned Jeremiah because of the way he prophesied. Micaiah was imprisoned and given only bread and water because the king of Israel didn't like his prophesy. Joseph's brothers threw him into a cistern before selling him into slavery. The Sadducees arrested the apostles and put them in jail because they were healing the sick and preaching the gospel. Paul and Silas were beaten, flogged, and thrown into prison because they were Jews and were advocating unlawful customs. And Jesus was held in custody and then hung on the cross for his beliefs and teachings, including participation in a protest directed at some of the commercial practices associated with the temple.

In the U.S. today, prisons are used to get offenders off the street, to punish, and, some argue, to deter criminal offending rather than to oppress political or religious opponents. Of the approximately 2.3 million prisoners in over five thousand prisons and jails, all are no doubt charged with or convicted of some type of criminal activity. They are not locked up because of their views or for religious or political purposes. But, like the meaning of "is," whether contemporary prisons are used as a means of unfair oppression depends on the meaning of the word. If "oppress" means to "keep down by the cruel or unjust use of power or authority," as Webster says it does, then Christians are compelled to conclude that, like those of biblical times, our prisons are instruments of oppression. If there is doubt, review chapters 3 and 4. Bernie Madoffs, Jeff Skillings, and Lindsay Lohans in prisons are as rare as teeth on a hen. People are in prison because they chose to commit crimes, and they need to be held accountable. But it is naïve, perhaps dishonest, to claim that no oppression of one group of people by another is involved. Mainly, poor people and minorities go to prison. Many are drug users, addicts, or mentally ill and not a real threat to anyone. But they have violated laws that largely reflect the worldview of the white, the rich, and the powerful. Prisoners are confined to institutions that are similar in spirit to the violence and mayhem that they claim to combat. And when offenders are released, they are held down socially and economically by continuing discrimination and laws that prohibit employment for reasons that often are questionable, to say the least. Thus, while prisons seem necessary to help protect society from those who prey on other human beings, they also tend to oppress and abuse many others in the name of law and order. Under these circumstances, people hold conflicting views as to what it means to restore prisoners to freedom.

~

Lee Griffith, in *The Fall of the Prison*, maintains, "It would be a mistake to assume that the words of Luke 4 can be limited to the pronouncement of a psychological or soteriological liberation for those who are 'imprisoned by sin.'" Instead, "The powers may pretend that captivity is based on justice, but Jesus declares that henceforth all prisoners have a right to liberty . . ."[2] Thus, Griffith suggests that Jesus' statement concerning freedom for the prisoners and release of the oppressed is a charge to open prison doors.

2. Griffith, *The Fall of the Prison*, 108–9.

But there is 1 Peter 2:13–16: "Submit yourselves for the Lord's sake to every human authority: whether to the emperor, as the supreme authority, or to governors, who are sent by him to punish those who do wrong and to commend those who do right. For it is God's will that by doing good you should silence the ignorant talk of foolish people. Live as free people, but do not use your freedom as a cover-up for evil; live as God's slaves. Show proper respect to everyone, love the family of believers, fear God, honor the emperor."

In *Beyond Retribution: A New Testament Vision for Justice, Crime, and Punishment*, Christopher D. Marshall argues that this reference, as well as the similar charge in Romans 13:1–5, suggests that "The role of governing authorities in punishing crime is referred to with obvious approval," and "There can be no doubt that it refers at the very least to punitive or disciplinary action by those in political authority to control and requite criminal activity."[3]

I do not argue that prison doors should be thrown open and all prisoners sent into the free world. While I believe too many people are imprisoned, that is a bone to be picked another day. The case to be made here is that prisoners can be set free and released from their oppression while still behind brick or barbed wire. They may not be freed from prison, but prison can be freed from them.

Theologian Karl Barth has stated, "Unfree man is a creature of chaos, a monster begotten by his own pride, his own laziness, his own lies . . . Sinful man is not free, he is a captive, a slave."[4] Sounds a lot like a prison inmate. Barth also teaches that human freedom is a gift of God, and "The event of man's freedom is the event of his thankfulness for the gift, of his sense of responsibility as a receiver, of his loving care for what is given him."[5] Freedom awakens one to true selfhood and new life. "Each individual is called by his own name as a member of the people of God. Each one is responsible for his relationship with God and his fellow men. He is free because he chooses, decides, and determines himself to be this person. His freedom is the joy of that obedience which is given to him."[6]

3. Marshall, *Beyond Retribution*, 147.
4. Barth, *The Humanity of God*, 76.
5. Ibid.
6. Ibid., 79.

Freedom is not the right to do as we please. It is the power and capacity to decide what we ought to do and to do it. Freedom is not avoiding responsibility, but is taking responsibility for the right choices. Freedom is an inner contentment with who we are and with what we have, and the ability to allow God to be in control of our life. It is particularly concerned with human relationships that flow from right relationship with God through faith in Jesus Christ, as illustrated in Galatians 5:13–15: "You, my brothers and sisters, were called to be free. But do not use your freedom to indulge the flesh; rather, serve one another humbly in love. For the entire law is fulfilled in keeping this one command: 'Love your neighbor as yourself.' If you bite and devour each other, watch out or you will be destroyed by each other."

Thus, true Christian freedom is not the license to do what one wants or to be released from a properly assigned criminal justice penalty but to be free to serve God and one another in love. In fact, the New Testament often defines freedom in terms of relief from spiritual, rather than physical, oppression, as in John 8:31–36: "To the Jews who had believed him, Jesus said, 'If you hold to my teaching, you are really my disciples. Then you will know the truth, and the truth will set you free.' They answered him, 'We are Abraham's descendants and have never been slaves of anyone. How can you say that we shall be set free?' Jesus replied, 'Very truly I tell you, everyone who sins is a slave to sin. Now a slave has no permanent place in the family, but a son belongs to it forever. So if the Son sets you free, you will be free indeed.'"

Paul used the same image of slavery to sin and freedom in Christ in the sixth through eighth chapters of Romans. In the first and second chapter of James the writer calls the gospel the "law of liberty," which may mean the law which sets men free from sin. Even an inmate in the deepest bowels of the deepest prison, locked up for life, can be free through faith in and obedience to Christ.

~

Unfortunately, inmates frequently define freedom behind bars in the immortal words of Janis Joplin: "Freedom's just another word for nothin left to lose." Cal Ray Biggins, locked up for two life sentences for double murder, helps us understand the prison meaning of Joplin's words. He told me, "I was afraid at first, but then I realized I got two life sentences and I'm not gonna never get out. So I developed an attitude, 'You can just take my life right here.' This kinda gave me an edge. My fear went away and I was on a suicide mission. I didn't care, and I guess that kept me alive and kept me going."

Victor Frankl had another description for freedom while locked up. Frankl, a Jewish psychiatrist and Holocaust survivor spent from September 1942 to April 1945 in a series of concentration camps: Theresienstadt, Auschwitz , and Türkheim, a Nazi concentration camp affiliated with Dachau. While imprisoned, he was assigned to work as a general practitioner, in a psychiatric care ward, and as a slave-laborer. Without in any way implying a similarity between Nazi concentration camps and U.S. prisons, Frankl's description of freedom behind bars nevertheless has impressive parallels.

> Most important, do the prisoners' reactions to the singular world of the concentration camp prove that man cannot escape the influences of his surroundings? Does man have no choice of action in the face of such circumstances?
>
> We can answer these questions from experience as well as on principle. The experiences of camp life show that man does have a choice of action. There were enough examples, often of a heroic nature, which proved that apathy could be overcome, irritability suppressed. Man *can* preserve a vestige of spiritual freedom, of independence of mind, even in such terrible conditions of psychic and physical stress.
>
> We who lived in concentration camps can remember the men who walked through the huts comforting others, giving away their last piece of bread. They may have been few in number, but they offer sufficient proof that everything can be taken from a man but one thing: the last of the human freedoms—to choose one's attitude in any given set of circumstances, to choose one's own way.[7]

Similarly, while prison inmates have many constraints on their physical freedom, God created them with free will. They have the freedom to choose between right and wrong and to choose what attitude will govern their lives. They can choose the attitude of a victim, of their prior history, or of the prison system. Or the attitude of a hustler, continuing to battle the system. Or the attitude of a beaten person. Or, hopefully, the attitude of a survivor, a winner (even in prison), an important child of God who is not one smidgeon less divine than anyone

7. Frankl, *Man's Search for Meaning*, 74.

else and who has accepted God's gift of freedom. Taking this attitude can set inmates on a journey that has the potential to heal rather than to harden if they take their guilt and misery by the hand and walk by faith from their damaged past, through their present struggles, into a better, if scary, future.

~

Prisoners have many choices. First and foremost, they have the freedom to practice their faith and religion as they choose and grow in their relationship with God. Courts have long ruled that the U.S. Constitution protects religious freedom in prison. While prison officials are normally granted a good deal of discretion in determining how this protection is administered, they cannot restrict inmates' freedom of religion unless the restriction is reasonably related to security and safety concerns. All inmates, even those in solitary confinement, can read the Bible or other religious books, pray to their God, and witness to their faith. And most inmates can attend religious services and participate in other religious practices.

Inmates also have the freedom to minister to others behind bars and in so doing help to set them free. Cal Ray Biggins also explained how the ministry of another worked to set him free:

> But my turning point didn't really come 'til I got to the Central unit and met Richard Callahan, another inmate, about thirty years old, who had a very strong faith and would do anything to help another person. Nothing negative comes out of his mouth and he never gets upset. He showed me that I could be a better person, and he accepted me for who I was at the time and helped me see that just because I was in prison my life wasn't over. He showed me things about myself I wasn't able to see and introduced me to—I say God, my spiritual side. He taught me that I could be a better person if I wanted to and made me want to keep on going. He was so young, about twenty-five years younger than me, and he spoke the truth and just gave me hope. Just listening to what he was saying made a lot of sense. That was the first time I really listened to somebody. He told me about Christ and that he was saved and how it felt to be living in the spirit. He showed me the value in myself and that I could get out of this place and see my kids again. He cared about me as a person, not just to get something. I had never had that before. Anyone who said he cared wanted something. He was someone

> I could talk to, share things with. He taught me that no matter what I did, don't let it get me down. There is a power higher than all of us. I thought I had all the answers. Come to find out I didn't have any answers at all. He gave me the spiritual food I needed. I can now lay down and talk to God. Feel comfortable with who I am. Can look my crime straight in the eye and own up to it. I didn't feel like that before Richard.

At a minimum, inmates are free to reflect and live Christian lives. They can do things Christian people do together over time in response to the life and teachings of Jesus Christ. They can do things through explicit human acts of hospitality and compassion that address the fundamental human needs of their fellow inmates. They can express a kind word, offer a listening ear, share a treat from the commissary, or do any of a million acts of kindness that are available between human beings who care.

And people behind bars can restore their relationships with people on the outside. Bars don't prevent one from forgiving and accepting forgiveness, living a life of repentance, and rebuilding relationships. Inmates can write letters confessing of their past wrongs, asking for forgiveness, and seeking reconciliation. At a minimum, they can release their anger and choose to love their enemies and those who have hurt them.

On another level, people in prison are free to set personal goals and do things to move toward them. They can break drug and other bad habits, take advantage of self-improvement activities such as school or other classes—even do exercises to restore their physical well-being. All are freedoms, choices that help restore people who are locked in cages to the life of a full human being.

RESPONSIBILITY

Weldon Long, who spent more than a decade in prisons, jails, and halfway houses before becoming the CEO of a multimillion dollar business, has written, "The key to turning around a less than fulfilling life is to accept complete responsibility for one's current circumstances and quality of life. Until a person accepts responsibility for where he is, he has little hope of taking responsibility for where he is going."[8]

8. Long, *The Upside of Fear*, 157.

Responsibility is often confused with accountability, and the two concepts are so similar and closely related that a note of explanation is in order. Chapter 8 discussed accountability as an important aspect of forgiveness. Accountability was defined as being answerable, implying a legal, moral, or other obligation to someone as though they are sitting in judgment and can in some way call you to account. One needs to be accountable—answerable—to the person from whom he is asking forgiveness. Responsibility, on the other hand, has to do with fulfilling one's obligations, being trustworthy, and acknowledging the consequences of one's actions. Restoration requires people to behave responsibly by fulfilling their obligations to self and to society. Those to whom they are accountable can decide if they met their responsibility.

Responsibility involves questions of cause and effect. We often think of cause and effect (or consequence) as a very simple process, where "x" causes "y," which in turn causes "z," and so on. But life is not so simple. Cause-effect relationships are usually messy, circular, and often not at all clear. Many influences cause us to do what we do. Our actions cause many consequences, some we can see and others we cannot see, and typically affect many people. Consequences are often bigger than we think they should be, and several causes usually exist for any problem.

A person is responsible for something if he was one of the causes. Think about Dennis's story. He is locked up for aggravated burglary. As we think about his learning problems as a kid, the abuse in his family, his alcoholic father, his father's abuse of him, his life of poverty, and his lack of support from his mother, the question of responsibility becomes messy. Dennis's criminal behavior might be blamed on bad parenting, societal neglect, or social conditioning. Perhaps his father, his mother, a deficient school system, or a justice system that did not rehabilitate him could be blamed. And he can be blamed. Like tributaries in a river, several upstream causes came together to influence him to behave as he did. Like the many channels in a river delta, his behavior went in many directions and caused downstream consequences to several people in addition to his specific victims: the higher insurance rates, increased taxes for more policemen, fearful people, drug addiction, and other negative effects of his life that he is unable or unwilling to see.

A legal concept, called joint and several liability, that allows a plaintiff to recover all his damages from any of several defendants, regardless of their individual share of the liability, helps us think about this situation.

Similarly, all those who contributed to a situation are in some sense a cause. And each is responsible. Other people and institutions were part of the river that helped make Dennis who he is. But Dennis is responsible for all of who he is and for all the consequences of his actions.

~

Inmates who want to change who they are and restore an acceptable life have to change their behavior: what they say and do, and not just how they think or feel. They have to create a better future. It does no good to hope for a better past, but the essential first step in their healing journey is to take responsibility for their past as it was. They need to acknowledge their past behavior and its consequences, including a life in the misery of prison. They can then use this acknowledgment—this accepting of responsibility—as a springboard toward moving to the future.

Accepting responsibility is not easy. Prisons encourage hurtful, conflict-ridden lives where the incentive is to avoid rather than to accept responsibility. Incarcerated offenders, their criminal thinking covering them like a heavy wool blanket, are masters of avoiding responsibility for their behavior. They can, and often do, deny that their actions caused their incarceration. They hide from themselves, repress their actions in their unconscious, pretend things didn't happen, or convince themselves that bad consequences did not result. They may rationalize away the consequences, allow their mind to construct false explanations, or minimize the effects of their past actions. Or they may blame others, trying to shift responsibility to someone else by claiming that it is their fault. If a person uses any of these thought patterns to deal with his past, he is not facing up to his responsibility.

Alex, for example, claimed that he did not commit murder and that shooting a woman in the head was an accident, even though a unanimous jury said he murdered her. Sometimes juries are wrong, but often people deny the truth, as Alex did. Sally convinced herself that her addiction hurt only herself and that her drug sales were justified by her need for money. She was rationalizing. Jed said he drove while drunk because his father was a drunk who frequently beat him. Jed was blaming. Alex, Sally, and Jed need to learn from history. They all need help in accepting responsibility. Volunteers often face a real challenge in helping inmates take this difficult step. Two approaches, each involving a few simple questions, can be helpful.

First, volunteers can help offenders determine their responsibility by having them consider a series of "why" questions. "Why" questions will help an offender look beneath the obvious and see who or what contributed to an event or its consequences. Why did someone get hurt? Why did certain things happen as a result of certain actions? Why did I do what I did? Honestly answering such questions will help an offender discover both the direct and indirect causes of his criminal actions and hurt or broken relationships, and provide a starting point for correcting his behavior.

A second approach is to help an offender ask himself a series of "if only" questions and honestly answer them. He can ask, "If only I had (done or not done something), would the consequence have happened?" Think of Dennis and the "if only" questions that could be asked in his situation. "If only Dennis' father had not abused him, and instead had been a good father, would Dennis be in prison?" Possibly not, so the father probably holds some responsibility. "If only Dennis had not committed burglary, would he be in prison?" Probably not, so Dennis is responsible for being in prison.

The key to success in both exercises is in making sure an offender asks himself the tough questions and responds honestly. Easy, irrelevant "why" or "if only" questions with answers that shade the truth only support criminal thinking and serve to let an offender off the hook. Thus, volunteers need to ask questions and insist on answers that create a tension, and push inmates to get beyond their criminal thinking and tell the truth about what they have done and the consequences of their actions.

Inmates can move toward freeing themselves of their troubled past by acknowledging their crimes and accepting responsibility for them. They can accept that their hope for the future is in their hands and God's. They can accept responsibility for forging their new lives, and not depend on family, friends or others to do so for them. Only the inmate himself can establish a relationship with God, control his anger, refrain from drugs, find a job, and do many other things for which he, and he alone, is responsible.

A final thought on the extent of responsibility. All of us need to assume responsibility for ourselves, but in doing so we must be able and willing to reject responsibility that is not truly ours. This balancing act can be difficult for inmates. They have done things—bad things—for which they need to accept responsibility. But inmates also need to reject responsibility that is not theirs. They need to feel guilt for what they have done, but stop short of shame for who they are. Although they are responsible for the effects of their actions, they also are valued human beings made in God's image. Many have dysfunctional family and friends in the free world, and taking the blame or feeling badly for what these others have done, or being defined by the relationship with them, is too much. It can only lead to further shame. In these situations, inmates need to move beyond the narrow frame of reference of their past lives and childhood experiences, and understand, often with the help of a free-world volunteer, that another, better world is available. They need to accept the limits of what they can control, and not worry too much about the spilt milk resulting from things they have done in the past that they can no longer control.

RECONCILIATION

We typically associate prisons with walls. Our thoughts range from musty medieval dungeons to modern concrete cellblocks. We focus on physical walls—brick, barbed wire, or otherwise—that control and contain those who transgress society's boundaries. Often, however, inmates are oppressed more by spiritual, psychological, or emotional barriers that are greater constraints than the physical ones. Inmates are at war with themselves, or have turned their backs on God and built walls of mistrust. Their families and loved ones are alienated by disappointment, embarrassment, or shame, and relationships are shattered. Friends are cut off by walls of inconvenience and ambivalence. Inmates are separated from civil society by fear, discrimination, or overreaching laws. Their essential powerlessness takes away their hope. All the walls isolate inmates in loneliness, doubt, and shame. The lyrics of "Prison Walls," by Angry Johnny and The Killbillies tells the tale:

> These prison walls are built of sorrow.
> These prison bars are built of pain.
> My prison cell is always with me.
> I live in hell, I've gone insane.
> This prison is my very own invention.

> Nobody sees the barbed wire but me.
> I think that they're just not paying attention.[9]

Restoration requires inmates to tear down the spiritual, psychological, and emotional walls that stand between a life of misery in prison and a life that is what it can be. It requires reconciliation. We most often think of reconciliation as the coming together of two people, perhaps two who have been estranged. But reconciliation means more. It can address all sorts of differences within one's self, between a person and God, and among people.

~

It is difficult, perhaps impossible, for a person to reconcile with another until he reconciles with himself. Doing so can mean various things, but above all it means being at peace with self. To gain this internal peace, one needs to recognize and acknowledge the conflict within his own being: confusion about who he really is, failure to acknowledge responsibility for his behavior, resentment or hatred toward others, guilt or shame for what he has done, emptiness or other destructive feelings and emotions.

Sandra is a good example of serious internal conflict and the need for reconciling with one's self that is present in so many inmates. She is forty-two years old with small, dull eyes, crooked teeth, and a blank stare in her eyes. She appears very frumpy in her loose hanging prison whites, which occasionally reveal the multicolored tattoo on her right forearm. Sandra has a history of drug abuse, selling drugs, and forgery. Shortly before her current incarceration, she was raped by two stoned drug dealers while she was buying drugs for her abusive boyfriend. She says her only mistake was having a coke pipe in her purse when the police arrested her for loitering at a bus stop, and that's why she is behind bars. Sandra cannot see herself as anything other than a victim of rape and unfortunate timing.

Without in any way minimizing the magnitude or consequence of the rape, it is accurate to say that she is an offender as well as a victim. She has never recognized the conflict between her life as a drug dealer and her life as a rape victim because she is denying so much of both. She

9. Online at: www.elyrics.net/read/a/angry-johnny-&-the-killbillies-lyrics/prison-walls-lyrics.html.

cannot resolve this internal conflict and reconcile with herself until she is honest about her whole life.

At other times internal conflict has to do with circumstances such as inmates' beliefs, the worldview that directs their life, or their priorities. They may be unclear as to right and wrong, or feel undervalued because their parents said they were no good, or feel hatred toward their parents, or otherwise fail to focus on what is really important. In summary, there is a side of themselves that they like and also a side that they don't like. To be a whole person, they need to reconcile the two sides.

Sometimes breaking down the walls of internal conflict is a long and difficult journey, and one needs help from a friend, spiritual advisor, or professional counselor. This is where a prison ministry volunteer can play an important role. Volunteers can remind inmates that God loves them, will help them, and that through him there is hope. Volunteers can help prisoners clarify who they are by asking them to discuss what they like and don't like about themselves. They can help inmates be honest with themselves, look deeply within themselves, face up to issues they have previously avoided, and be confronted by others and their own conscience. Volunteers can just listen with empathy when an inmate tells her story. They can also help inmates set goals, including goals relating to the type of relationship they want with God and with fellow human beings, and the type of persons they need to be to bring peace and reconciliation into their lives.

~

We also need to be reconciled with God. The apostle Paul, in Romans 5:6–11, provides an example of how God reconciles himself to us and how we can be reconciled with him by being his friend:

> You see, at just the right time, when we were still powerless, Christ died for the ungodly. Very rarely will anyone die for a righteous person, though for a good person someone might possibly dare to die. But God demonstrates his own love for us in this: While we were still sinners, Christ died for us.
>
> Since we have now been justified by his blood, how much more shall we be saved from God's wrath through him! For if, while we were God's enemies, we were reconciled to him through the death of his Son, how much more, having been reconciled, shall we be saved through his life! Not only is this so, but we also boast in God through our Lord Jesus Christ, through whom we have now received reconciliation.

Volunteers can help inmates be a friend of God by conveying a few simple points: that we are all his children, he has an unconditional love for us, and he has made clear his willingness to forgive us for our offenses. That friends are not here today and gone tomorrow. They stick it out through thick and thin, and the same is true if one is God's friend. Volunteers can help inmates communicate with him by encouraging them to read and study his word, and talk to him in prayer. This, hopefully, will lead them to surrender to his will and please him by living for his purpose, abiding by his commandments, and giving him the glory.

Reconciliation with others involves establishing relationships of mutual acceptance based on strength, love, and understanding. It requires a journey, often of many years, that focuses on win-win solutions that tear down the walls of alienation and distrust—a little like tearing down a brick wall by hand. Think of two people separated by a brick wall. They cannot get over it, go around it, or blast their way through it. The only thing they can do is to slowly, gradually break the mortar and remove one brick at a time. They must keep removing one brick at a time until the wall is low enough that they can get to the other side. Reconciliation that moves toward restoration is a similar process, where people remove the things that are hurting their relationship, one step at a time. It can mean a range of changes, including settling a quarrel or difference, reaching an agreement, changing conflict into peace, winning over to friendliness, or reestablishing a loving, intimate relationship.

Reconciling with another is rarely easy and is not always possible or advisable. Those involved are imperfect humans, and sometimes human frailties will prevent meaningful reconciliation. Sometimes grievances are difficult enough, or the relationship unimportant enough, that the parties will choose to let sleeping dogs lie. They may terminate the relationship or simply hope the conflict will melt away over time. Often, however, too much is at stake to defer the matter or walk away, and the people involved will conclude that they should try to reconcile. Each inmate has to decide whether reconciliation should be attempted, and if the answer is yes, decide on the type that makes sense.

Inmates need to remember that they can only control themselves. Trying to force their desires on another person most often leads, not to reconciliation, but to even further conflict, estrangement, and anger.

All they can do is control their own behavior and try to create an environment where the other person will want to reconcile. Inmates interested in reconciling with another should be encouraged to pray, seek forgiveness, build trust, and be humble.

Inmates need to pray for those with whom they wish to reconcile and for the success of their efforts. Prayer brings others into their hearts, helps them empathize, and helps break down the hostility and distinction between the parties. Praying for God's help in reconciliation will also help give inmates the courage to attempt what can be a difficult, risky endeavor. If they pray about reconciliation, God will make it easier for them.

Forgiving and asking for forgiveness are closely related to reconciliation. The risks and rewards were discussed in chapter 8 and will not be repeated here. However, without forgiveness the parties are not likely to trust one another, and lack of trust is probably the biggest problem in reconciliation. If trust doesn't exist the people involved are usually defensive and wary of one another, and build even bigger walls of suspicion.

Trust is the unwritten and usually unspoken contract that allows people to believe in the honesty, integrity, reliability, and justice of one another. Trust has many dimensions, none more important than honesty. The most important thing inmates can do to foster mutual trust is to be honest. This is true whether that term means being truthful in a general sense, doing what they say they will do, calling a spade a spade, being willing to confess and admit failure, being honest with self, or any of many other possibilities.

Finally, inmates need to demonstrate humility rather than false pride or arrogance. Humility requires inmates to see themselves as they are, warts and all, without self-recrimination, blaming, or feeling sorry for one's self. Laura Davis has noted in *I Thought We'd Never Speak Again*, "When we grow large enough to embrace our own faults and to honor the flawed humanity of another human being, we open the door to connection, integration, and love."[10] To reconcile, inmates need to be humble, not just in the sense of being gentle or meek, but also in the sense of being vulnerable and willing to be hurt. They have to be willing to go unnoticed, to be last, to receive the least.

10. Davis, *I Thought We'd Never Speak Again*, 27.

Trying to reconcile with another may not tear down an entire wall or bring closure in many situations. It can, however, bring people more peace and start a better chapter in their relationship. That makes it worth the effort. It creates a legitimate hope for the future.

HOPE

Hope is our quiet, never ending dream for the future. When our present situation is not enough to satisfy our souls completely, no matter how good or bad, we hunger for more. And our unsatisfied search for more is the basis of biblical hope. Hope is not just a wish or want, but is real faith regarding the future, a passion for what is possible. Our faith helps us see God working in our past, see our life as it is, and know that he will work in our lives in the future. Hope is the opposite of despair and gloom.

Basing hope for the future on their experiences of the past seems silly for many inmates. It's a big order for them to use their abuse or crimes of the past, or the misery and isolation of their present, to hope for restoration to a better life in the future. But 2 Corinthians 1: 9–10 tells the story of how Paul handled a similar situation. Paul wrote to the church at Corinth and told the people about his hard times when he went through Asia: crushed, overwhelmed, and fearful that he would never live through it. He wrote, "We felt we were doomed to die and saw how powerless we were to help ourselves; but that was good, for then we put everything into the hands of God, who alone could save us, for he can even raise the dead. And he did help us, and saved us from a terrible death; yes, and we expect Him to do it again and again."

Similarly, prison inmates often feel doomed, whether they will admit it or not. They see no way to restore their lives to what they should be. Volunteers need to help them understand that there is hope of restoration through God, and their broken, crime-ridden past does not confine them to a similar future if they refuse to be constrained by any phony "realism" as to what is possible and impossible. Even though their options are limited while they are locked behind bars, inmates can maintain a legitimate hope of restoration to a better life if they put their lives in God's hands.

Praying to God will open inmates' minds to him. Asking for his help with difficult problems acknowledges their belief that anything is possible—the essence of hope—and allows them to construct a vision of what their hope can attain. Asking God for help also provides an early success in the healing process, because all that is necessary to heal their relationship with God is to ask. When they do so and work their God problems out, an important goal has been attained and they have a success.

Restoring a relationship with God can set the stage for addressing the many problems facing inmates who have accepted responsibility for their past mistakes. Whether inmates are dealing with addiction, looking to improve their education and training, seeking reconciliation with important people in their lives, or addressing any of a myriad of other issues necessary for a restored life, they need a real faith that they can succeed. The words of Edwin provide a perspective. When he was eighteen, Edwin was involved in a burglary—and to his surprise, an accomplice murdered a person. Although Edwin didn't do the killing, he was convicted of the offense. He has now served twenty-four years in the Texas prison system. Edwin is a muscular, six foot-three inch former athlete. Even today, at age forty-two, he looks like he could play tight end for the Green Bay Packers. Edwin explains biblical hope this way: "When I first got here, I believed in God but I had no connection with Him. Prison was vicious—a scary and rough situation—and I didn't understand how He would carry me. I saw no light at the end of the tunnel. Over time, I read the Bible and prayed for a real connection with God. Gradually, I calmed down, more honestly assessed my life, and learned to not worry about what I could not control. God carried me through, and this has given me hope."

Sometimes God uses Christian ministries as an instrument of hope. The Annie E. Casey Foundation's Healing Communities program and their Stations of Hope are wonderful examples of the Christian community providing hope through comfort, healing, and restoration to persons involved in the criminal justice process and their families. To learn more about these efforts I visited with Dr. Dean Trulear and Reverend Gene Beerens. Dr. Trulear is associate professor of applied theology at Howard University School of Divinity and director of the Healing Communities Prison Ministry and Reentry Project in Philadelphia. Gene Beerens is a volunteer associate pastor at the Impact Wesleyan Church in Lowell, Michigan, founder of Exodus Correctional Ministries (a rehabilitation ministry that provides reentry services for ex-offenders), and a leading force in establishing Stations of Hope throughout churches in Michigan. Each of them greeted me with open arms and a wealth of information.

As we sat in his office on the beautiful Howard University campus in the center of Washington, D.C., amidst the jumble of papers, books, and numerous other trappings of a busy academic life, Dr. Trulear explained that Healing Communities are intended to exemplify the gospel of Matthew 25—the care for the hungry, the thirsty, the stranger, the sick, and the imprisoned—within church congregations. They do this, he believes, by transforming the values of those involved and building important relationships within the church community. The vision of Healing Communities is that Christians and their churches will "reach out and support individuals and families in their own congregations that are affected by the criminal justice system . . ." This includes offenders, victims, and the family members of each. The effort involves no outside organizations, 501(c)(3) corporations, or other external programs. It is, instead, church congregations doing what church congregations are supposed to do.

Gene Beerens explained the effort this way: Church groups take a one-year initial commitment to establish a Station of Hope, modeled on the Annie E. Casey Foundation Healing Community, in their congregation. Volunteers familiarize themselves with the criminal justice process and issues relating to crime, identify their resources, and get to work. Their aim is to guide and help persons among their church community who are arrested, incarcerated, or coming home from incarceration. They offer to help early and often: accompany offenders at the time of arrest, visit the person in jail or prison, listen, offer to help with court appearances, hold the person accountable, and help prepare for release and community supervision.

The story in Acts 12 of Peter's miraculous escape from prison provides a metaphor for restoration and for a healing community. Peter was in prison, but the church was earnestly praying to God for him. The night before he was to go to trial, an angel of the Lord appeared and escorted him out of the prison. Peter at first thought it was a vision, but when he realized it was for real he went to the house of Mary the mother of John, where people were gathered and were praying. The people were astonished, but they opened their door for him. Similarly, Healing Communities, Stations of Hope, and other similar ministries open their doors to offenders and others affected by crime, and give them hope.

Conclusion

What Can I Do?

CHRISTIANS ARE CHARGED TO be present and help their fellow human beings who are in prison. Ed Davis, former college professor, coordinator of Restorative Justice for the Episcopal Diocese of Texas, and an active, hands-on prison volunteer, talked about responding to that charge:

> Prison ministry is the easiest ministry in the world. You know the old pun—you've got the captive audience. And they are broken, and they know it. And they know they can only go up. So they are receptive, and they are also desperate for relationships because in prison there's danger in relationships. They are defensive and don't really reveal themselves. So we need to help them be able to say what they need to say in order to heal. The most powerful ministry that any of us really do is a ministry of presence. Simply going in and helping people have an interaction with those on the outside in a different culture helps them function when they get back in that culture. That itself is transformative. They have a relationship with someone who doesn't speak the prison lingo all the time. A ministry like Kairos, for example, is so powerful—not because they are any more talented than anyone else, but because they come back, and they come back, and they come back. When they keep coming back, this is saying I love you, I love you, I love you . . . and you have value.

Ed continued, "Nothing is more ecumenical than restorative justice or prison ministries. Nobody has enough resources to accomplish a great deal by themselves, so do like Henry Blackaby said in his famous comment, 'go where you see the Lord at work and join Him.' We don't need to have our name tag on it. Christ would say, 'forget your denomination, and do what I have called you to do.' So I will work with anybody."

It's easy to find a place and a way. You don't need an organized church, a 501(c)(3) organization, or a large scale effort. All you need is one person willing to help one human being. I am almost embarrassed to repeat "The Starfish Story," adapted from *The Star Thrower* by Loren Eiseley, because it seems so trite and universally familiar. But a few readers may not have heard it, others will enjoy it again, and the simple story wonderfully illustrates the essence of prison ministry.

> Once upon a time, there was a wise man who used to go to the ocean to do his writing. He had a habit of walking on the beach before he began his work.
>
> One day, as he was walking along the shore, he looked down the beach and saw a human figure moving like a dancer. He smiled to himself at the thought of someone who would dance to the day, and so, he walked faster to catch up.
>
> As he got closer, he noticed that the figure was that of a young man, and that what he was doing was not dancing at all. The young man was reaching down to the shore, picking up small objects, and throwing them into the ocean.
>
> He came closer still and called out "Good morning! May I ask what it is that you are doing?"
>
> The young man paused, looked up, and replied "Throwing starfish into the ocean."
>
> "I must ask, then, why are you throwing starfish into the ocean?" asked the somewhat startled wise man.
>
> To this, the young man replied, "The sun is up and the tide is going out. If I don't throw them in, they'll die."
>
> Upon hearing this, the wise man commented, "But, young man, do you not realize that there are miles and miles of beach and there are starfish all along every mile? You can't possibly make a difference!"
>
> At this, the young man bent down, picked up yet another starfish, and threw it into the ocean. As it met the water, he said, "I made a difference to that one!"[1]

Like the starfish thrower, each of us can help one person. Perhaps that's the best way. I asked Davis what he believed was the greatest need for prison ministries. He answered,

1. Eiseley, "The Starfish Thrower."

> Mentoring. There are not enough one-on-one mentors. In an ideal world, you'd have somebody to mentor all those who have a date specific to get out. Stay with them on the outside. Mentoring someone means they are important. It means I care, and you have value. Mentoring says everyone in society is not against me. And it helps them understand what society on the outside is like—the social mores and customs of the day. They have been in a sub-culture—and the only place they'll find that sub-culture in the free world is with ex-offenders or criminals. So mentors need to present a paradigm that is a different way to live than in prison—not the criminal world from which they came.

Who is the person that a prison minister really helps? Davis says,

> Brings meaning to their life, and to mine. God didn't create us to waste us. A guy who says he is a Christian and means it, he's got a command—Matthew 25, starting with verse 23. When I was asked to go into prison for the first time, I said no. And I said no by saying I've got an obligation on that day. Now unfortunately the guy that asked me went to my church and I saw him every Sunday. I should have changed churches right then. But Doug Duncan would ask me every month on the second Sunday. He asked me for seventeen consecutive months to go into prison and do Kairos for two hours. Seventeen times I gave him a reason why I couldn't do it. Now, it eventually occurred to me that I was lying. For seventeen consecutive second Sundays, I probably really wasn't obligated to do something. Looking in the rear-view mirror, I had caught the vision from the ten o'clock news or whatever I had been exposed to, that I did not want to be with these people. I actually think I was afraid of them, because they are so demonized. And I bought into that demonization. The eighteenth time, I said yes. I had been out of excuses for a long time. I didn't want to get out of my comfort zone. I don't know why, but I believe I was physically afraid. Being a man, I'm not supposed to say that. But I've been going in ever since.
>
> Course when I got there—I went thinking I was going to minister, and came home realizing I had been ministered to so thoroughly that I wondered why I had been such a fool.

Bibliography

Addiction Treatment Magazine. "Effective Drug and Alcohol Counseling Programs in Prison Could Save Nation Money." March 8, 2010. Online: http://www.addictiontreatmentmagazine.com/addiction-treatment/effective-drug-and-alcohol-counseling-programs-in-prison-could-save-nation-money/.

Alexander, Elizabeth. "Michigan Breaks the Political Logjam: A New Model for Reducing Prison Populations." American Civil Liberties Union, November 2009. Online: http://www.aclu.org/files/assets/2009-12-18-MichiganReport.pdf.

Alexander, Michelle. *The New Jim Crow: Mass Incarceration in the Age of Colorblindness*. New York: New Press, 2012.

American Baptist Churches USA. "American Baptist Resolution on Restorative Justice." Policy statement 8212:11/01. November 2001. Online: http://abc-usa.org/LinkClick.aspx?fileticket=dgaJRknmWzg%3d&tabid=199.

The Annie E. Casey Foundation. "Partnerships Between Corrections and Child Welfare." 2007. Online: http://www.aecf.org/MajorInitiatives/Family%20to%20Family/Resources/Partnerships.aspx.

Associated Press. "After 40 years, $1 trillion, US War on Drugs has Failed to Meet Any of Its Goals." May 13, 2010. Online: http://www.foxnews.com/world/2010/05/13/ap-impact-years-trillion-war-drugs-failed-meet-goals/#ixzz1zWOpqW7N.

Barba, Alisa. "America's Forgotten War: A Series Overview." NPR, April 2, 2007. Online: http://www.npr.org/templates/story/story.php?storyId=9286922.

Barth, Karl. *The Humanity of God*. Translated by John Newton Thomas. Louisville: John Knox, 1960.

Bowen v. Kendrick, 487 U.S. 589 (1988).

Bureau of Justice Statistics. "Correctional Populations in the United States, 2009." February 16, 2011. Online:. bjs.ojp.usdoj.gov/index.cfm?ty=pbdetail&iid=2316.

———. "Direct Expenditures by Criminal Justice Function, 1982–2007." June 2012. Online: http://bjs.ojp.usdoj.gov/content/glance/tables/exptyptab.cfm.

———. "Drug Use and Dependence, State and Federal Prisoners, 2004." October 2006. Online: http://bjs.ojp.usdoj.gov/index.cfm?ty=pbdetail&iid=778.

———. "Parents in Prison and Their Minor Children." January 2009. Online: http://www.ojp.usdoj.gov/bjs/pub/pdf/pptmc.pdf.

———. "Profile of Nonviolent Offenders Exiting State Prisons." October 2004. Online: http://bjs.ojp.usdoj.gov/content/pubpdf/ppnoesp.pdf.

———. "Survey of State Prison Inmates, 1991." March 1993. Online: bjs.ojp.usdoj.gov/index.cfm?ty=tp&tid=13.

Bureau of Labor Statistics. "Occupational Employment and Wages, May 2009." May 2010. Online: http://www.bls.gov/oes/2009/may/oes_nat.htm.

Byrne, James. "Commission on Safety and Abuse in America's Prisons: Summary of Testimony." Online: http://faculty.uml.edu/jbyrne/byrne_james_m.pdf.

Califa, Katy. "Prisoners as Parents: The Importance of Strong Parent-Child Relationships During Parental Incarceration." January 27, 2006. Online: http://papers.ssrn.com/sol3/papers.cfm?abstract_id=977050.

Califano, Joseph A., Jr. "Criminally Unjust: Why America's Prison Policy Needs Repair." *America: The National Catholic Weekly*, May 24, 2010. Online: http://www.americamagazine.org/content/article.cfm?article_id=12311.

California Department of Corrections and Rehabilitation. "California Department of Corrections and Rehabilitation Salaries." Online: http://www.glassdoor.com/Salary/California-Department-of-Corrections-and-Rehabilitation-Salaries-E41905.htm.

Casey, Rick. "A Predicted and Vicious Political Lie." *Houston Chronicle*, February 26, 2010. Online: www.chron.com/news/casey/article/Rick-Casey-A-predicted-and-vicious-political-lie-1605526.php

Caulkins, Johathan P., et al. "How Goes the 'War on Drugs'? An Assessment of U.S. Drug Problems and Policy." January 2005. Online: http://www.rand.org/pubs/occasional_papers/OP121.html.

Colorado Criminal Justice Reform Coalition. "Private Prisons and Public Money: Hidden Costs Borne by Colorado's Taxpayers." September 2002. Online: http://www.ccjrc.org/pdf/CostDataReport2002.pdf.

Conklin, John E. *Why Crime Rates Fell*. New York: Pearson, 2003.

Coppolo, George, et al. "Consequences of a Felony Conviction Regarding Employment." April 5, 2005. N.p. Online: http://www.cga.ct.gov/2005/rpt/2005-r-0311.htm.

Corrections Corporation of America. "Corrections Corporation of America Form 10-K: For the Fiscal Year Ended December 31, 2010." December 31, 2010. Online: phx.corporate-ir.net/External.File?item= UGFyZW50SUQ9NDE5MTEwfENoaWxkSUQ9NDMyMjg1fFR5cGU9MQ==&t=1.

———. "Weathering the Economic Downturn in Corrections." April 2010. Online: http://www.cca.com/static/assets/Weather-the-Economic-downturn-2010.pdf.

Crary, David. "Faith-Based Prisons Multiply." *USA Today*, October 2007. Online: http://www.usatoday.com/news/religion/2007-10-13-prisons_N.htm.

Crosswalk Ministries USA, *Newsletter*, "Under the Influence," (September 8, 2010). No Pages. Online: www.crosswalkusa.org/newsletters.html.

Damrosch, Leo. *Tocqueville's Discovery of America*. New York: Farrar, Straus and Giroux, 2010.

Davis, Laura. *I Thought We'd Never Speak Again*. New York: HarperCollins, 2002.

De La Cruz, Ralph. "Closure Only Part of Needed Prison Reform." Florida Center for Investigative Reporting, January 2012. Online: http://fcir.org/2012/01/16/closures-only-part-of-needed-prison-reform/.

Demos, John. *The Enemy Within: 2,000 Years of Witch-Hunting in the Western World*. New York: Viking, 2008.

The Disaster Center. "United States Crime Index Rates Per 100,000 Inhabitants." 2010. Online: http://www.disastercenter.com/crime/uscrime.htm.

Dutton, Charles V., Jr. "Every Felon Gets a Life of Trouble." *Houston Chronicle*, May 17, 2010. Online: www.chron.com/opinion/outlook/article/Every-felon-gets-a-life-of-trouble-1615476.php.

The Economist. "Rough Justice." July 22, 2010. Online: http://www.economist.com/node/16640389.

Eisley, Loren. "The Starfish Thrower," adapted from *The Star Thrower*. Online: http://bellaonline.com/articles/art8236asp.

Federal Bureau of Investigation. "Crime in the United States 2009." September 2010. Online: http://www2.fbi.gov/ucr/cius2009/data/table_01.html.

———. "Crimes and Crime Rates by Type of offense: 1960 to 2009." November 2010. Online: www.fbi.gov/stats-services/crimestats/.

Fellner, Jamie. "Ill-Equipped: U.S. Prisons and Offenders with Mental Illness." Human Rights Watch, 2003. Online: http://www.soros.org/reports/ill-equipped-us-prisons-and-offenders-mental-illness.

Fletcher, Michael A. "High Incarceration Rate May Fuel Community Crime." *Washington Post*, July 12, 1999. Online: www.washingtonpost.com/wp-srv/national/daily/july99/prisons12.htm.

Florida Department of Corrections. "Faith- and Character-Based Correctional Initiative." December 2011. N.p. Online: http://www.dc.state.fl.us/oth/faith/index.html.

Frankl, Viktor E. *Man's Search for Meaning: An Introduction to Logotherapy*. New York: Simon and Schuster, 1984.

Fudge, Edward. "God's Embedded Agents." *New Wineskins* (October 31, 2010): n.p. Online: http://www.wineskins.org/filter.asp?SID=2&fi_key=314&co_key=2306.

General Board of Global Ministry of the United Methodist Church. "Restorative Justice Mission Study." 2011. Online: http://new.gbgm-umc.org/missionstudies/restorativejustice/.

GEO Group, Inc. "2010 Annual Report." December 31, 2010. Online: phx.corporate-ir.net/phoenix.zhtml?c=91331&p=irol-reportsAnnual.

Gershon, Stuart. "Life Is Too Short To Be Unforgiving or Unforgiven." September 19, 2009. Online: http://www.templesinainj.org/content/sermons/pdf/2009-09-19-HHDSermon.pdf.

Gibbons, John J., and Nicholas de B. Katzenbach. "Confronting Confinement: A Report of the Commission on Safety and Abuse in America's Prisons." June 2006. Online: http://www.vera.org/download?file=2845/Confronting_Confinement.pdf.

Global Commission on Drug Policy, "Report of the Global Commission on Drug Policy." June 2011. Online: http://www.globalcommissionondrugs.org/wp-content/themes/gcdp_v1/pdf/Global_Commission_Report_English.pdf.

Gonnerman, Jennifer. *Life on the Outside: The Prison Odyssey of Elaine Bartlett*. New York: Farrar, Straus and Giroux, 2004.

Graczyk, Michael. "Day After Cellmate's Execution, Killer in '98 Robbery Put to Death." *Houston Chronicle*, May 13, 2010. Online: http://www.chron.com/default/article/Day-after-cellmate-s-execution-killer-in-98-1716105.php.

Griffith, Lee. *The Fall of the Prison: Biblical Perspectives on Prison Abolition*. Grand Rapids: Eerdmans, 1993.

Grits for Breakfast. "Private Prison Bubble Bursting? Empty, Speculative Jails in Texas." March 10, 2011. Online: http://gritsforbreakfast.blogspot.com/2011/03/private-prison-bubble-bursting-empty.html.

Harrop, Froma. "Waging War Against War on Drugs." *Houston Chronicle*, January 4, 2011. Online: www.chron.com/opinion/outlook/article/Froma-Harrop-Waging-war-against-war-on-drugs-1555691.php.

Hillenbrand, Laura. *Unbroken: A World War II Story of Survival, Resilience, and Redemption*. New York: Random House, 2010.

Houston Chronicle. "Texas Has Worst Record of Sex Abuse in Prisons." September 20, 2010.

Hudson, Nick. "For-Profit Lock-up Leaves Littlefield Taxpayers with Texas-sized Headache." Burnt Orange Report, February 8, 2010. Online: http://www.burntorangereport.com/diary/11840/forprofit-lockup-leaves-littlefield-taxpayers-with-a-texassized-headache.

Hughes, Robert. *The Fatal Shore: The Epic of Australia's Founding*. New York: Knopf, 1987.

Human Rights Watch. "Old Behind Bars: The Aging Prison Population in the United States." January 2012. Online: http://www.hrw.org/sites/default/files/reports/usprisons0112webwcover_0.pdf.

Human Rights Watch. "Punishment and Prejudice: Racial Disparities in the War on Drugs." May 2000. Online: http://www.hrw.org/legacy/reports/2000/usa/.

Hunsinger, George. *How to Read Karl Barth*. Oxford: Oxford University Press, 1991.

Institute on Women and Criminal Justice. "Quick Facts: Women and Criminal Justice—2009." Women's Prison Association, 2009. Online: http://www.wpaonline.org/pdf/Quick%20Facts%20Women%20and%20CJ%202009.pdf.

Johnson, Byron R. *More God, Less Crime: Why Faith Matters and How It Could Matter More*. West Conshohocken, PA: Templeton, 2011.

Jones, L. Gregory. *Embodying Forgiveness: A Theological Analysis*. Grand Rapids: Eerdmans, 1995.

Jones, Peter Rhea. *Studying the Parables of Jesus*. Macon, GA: Smyth and Helwys, 1999.

Joseph, Deanna. "The Starfish Story." (Adapted from "The Star Thrower" by Loren Eiseley.) BellaOnline: The Voice of Women. Online: http://bellaonline.com/articles/art8236.asp.

Justice Policy Institute. "Pruning Prisons: How Cutting Corrections Can Save Money and Protect Public Safety." May 2009. Online: http://www.justicepolicy.org/images/upload/09_05_REP_PruningPrisons_AC_PS.pdf.

Kairos Prison Ministry International. "Kairos Prison Ministry." Online: http://www.kairosprisonministry.org/.

Kanapaux, William. "Guilty of Mental Illness." *Psychiatric Times* 21/1 (January 1, 2004): n.p. Online: http://www.psychiatrictimes.com/forensic-psych/content/article/10168/47631.

Karpowitz, Daniel, and Max Kenner. "Education as Crime Prevention: The Case for Rein-stating Pell Grant Eligibility for the Incarcerated." 1995. Online: https://www.stcloudstate.edu/continuingstudies/distance/documents/EducationasCrimePreventionTheCaseForReinstatingthePellGrantforOffendersKarpowitzandKenner.pdf.

Keller, Timothy. *Generous Justice: How God's Grace Makes Us Just*. London: Dutton, 2010.

Kimbrough v. United States, 552 U.S. 85 (2007).

King, Ryan S., Marc Mauer, and Tracy Huling. "Big Prisons, Small Towns: Prison Economics in Rural America." The Sentencing Project, February 2003. Online: prison.ppjr.org/files/tracy huling prisons economy study.pdf.

Kirchhoff, Suzanne M. "Economic Impacts of Prison Growth." Congressional Research Service, April 13, 2010. Online: http://www.fas.org/sgp/crs/misc/R41177.pdf.

Lanagan, Patrick A., and David J. Levin. "Recidivism of Prisoners Released in 1994." Bureau of Justice Statistics Special Report. June 2002. Online: http://bjs.ojp.usdoj.gov/content/pub/pdf/rpr94.pdf.

Lausanne Congress on World Evangelization. "The Lausanne Covenant." July 1974. Online: http://www.emeu.net/pdf/lausanne_covenant.pdf.

Law Library—American Law and Legal Information. "Incapacitation—The Scholarly Literature On Incapacitation and the Measurement of Incapacitative Effects." January 2002. No pages. Online: http://law.jrank.org/pages/1358/Incapacitation.html.

Lawrence, Sarah and Jeremy Travis. "The New Landscape of Imprisonment: Mapping America's Prison Expansion," Urban Institute, April 2004. Online: http://www.urban.org/UploadedPDF/410994_mapping_prisons.pdf.

Lee, David S., and Justin McCrary. "Crime, Punishment and Myopia." *The National Bureau of Economic Research*, NBER working paper 11491 (July 2005): 1–38. Online: http://emlab.berkeley.edu/~jmccrary/crime_myopia.pdf.

Levitt, Steven D., and Stephen J. Dubner. *Freakonomics: A Rogue Economist Explores the Hidden Side of Everything.* New York: Harper, 2005.

Logan, James Samuel. *Good Punishment? Christian Moral Practice and U.S. Imprisonment.* Grand Rapids: Eerdmans, 2008.

Long, Weldon. *The Upside of Fear: How One Man Broke the Cycle of Prison, Poverty, and Addiction.* Austin, TX: Greenleaf, 2009.

Males, Mike, et al. "Striking Out: The Failure of California's 'Three Strikes You're Out' Law." *Justice Policy Institute* (March 1999): 1–11. Online: http://www.cjcj.org/files/strikingout.pdf.

Marshall, Christopher D. *Beyond Retribution: A New Testament Vision for Justice, Crime, and Punishment.* Grand Rapids: Eerdmans, 2001.

National Gang Intelligence Center. "National Gang Threat Assessment 2009." January 2009. Online: http://www.fbi.gov/stats-services/publications/national-gang-threat-assessment-2009-pdf.

New York Times. "The Abuse of Solitary Confinement." June 20, 2012. Online: www.nytimes.com/2012/06/21/opinion/the-abuse-of-solitary-confinement.html.

Oliver, Willard M., and James F. Hilgenberg Jr. *A History of Crime and Criminal Justice in America.* Boston: Pearson, 2006.

Olsen, Lise. "Feds Are Slow to React to Rapid Rise in Texas Overdoses." *Houston Chronicle*, February 7, 2011. Online: www.chron.com/news/houston-texas/article/Feds-are-slow-to-react-to-rapid-rise-in-Texas-1691395.php.

Pastor, Ann L., and Kathleen Maguire, eds. *Sourcebook of Criminal Justice Statistics 2003.* Bureau of Justice Statistics, 2005. Online: www.ncjrs.gov/app/publications/abstract.aspx?ID=208756.

Peck, M. Scott. *The Road Less Traveled: A New Psychology of Love, Traditional Values, and Spiritual Growth.* New York: Simon and Schuster, 1978.

Perkinson, Robert. *Texas Tough: The Rise of America's Prison Empire.* New York: Henry Holt, 2010.

Pew Center on the States. "Prison Count 2010." April 2010. Online: www.pewtrusts.org/uploadedFiles/Prison_Count_2010.pdf.

———. "State of Recidivism: The Revolving Door of America's Prisons, 2011 Prison Population Count 2010." April 2011. Online: http://www.pewtrusts.org/uploadedFiles/wwwpewtrustsorg/Reports/sentencing_and_corrections/State_Recidivism_Revolving_Door_America_Prisons%20.pdf.

Pew Charitable Trusts. "Collateral Costs: Incarceration's Effect on Economic Mobility." September 2010. Online: http://www.pewtrusts.org/uploadedFiles

/wwwpewtrustsorg/Reports/Economic_Mobility/Collateral%20Costs%20FINAL.pdf?n=5996.

Political Research Associates. "Defending Justice: Poverty and the Criminal Justice System." May 2005. Online: http://www.publiceye.org/defendingjustice/pdfs/factsheets/11-Fact%20Sheet%20-%20Poverty.pdf.

The Released. Directed by Karen O'Connor and Miri Navasky. Frontline, April 2009. Online: http://www.pbs.org/wgbh/pages/frontline/released/view/.

Remen, Rachel Naomi. *Kitchen Table Wisdom: Stories That Heal.* New York: Riverhead, 1996.

Roberts, Richard Owen. *Repentance: The First Word of the Gospel.* Wheaton, IL: Crossway, 2002.

Romano, Andrew. "Jailbreak! The Odd Alliance Changing the Way We Think About Crime." *Newsweek* 159/17, 18 (April 23-30, 2012): 22.

Ruffin v. The Commonwealth, 62 Va. 790 (1871).

Sabol, William J., and Heather Couture. Heather. "Prison Inmates at Midyear 2007." Bureau of Justice Statistics Bulletin, June 2008. Online: http://bjs.ojp.usdoj.gov/content/pub/pdf/pim07.pdf.

Sacks, Ethan. "Mike Huckabee's Presidential Hopes Damaged by Suspected Cop Killer Maurice Clemmons' Clemency." *New York Daily News*, December 1, 2009. Online: http://articles.nydailynews.com/2009-12-01/news/17941858_1_maurice-clemmons-mike-huckabee-presidential-campaign.

Salary Expert. "Prison Warden Salaries." Online: http://www.salaryexpert.com/index.cfm?fuseaction=Browse.Prison-Warden-salary-data-details&PositionId=21175.

Santos, Fernanda. "Plan to Close Prisons Stirs Anxiety in Rural Towns." *New York Times*, January 27, 2008. Online: www.nytimes.com/2008/01/27/nyregion/27prison.html?pagewanted=all.

The Sentencing Project. "Incarceration and Crime: A Complex Relationship." January 2005. Online: http://www.sentencingproject.org/doc/publications/inc_iandc_complex.pdf.

Smith, Phillip. "Prohibition: Drug War is a Failure, Associated Press Reports." *Drug War Chronicle* 632 (May 14, 2010): N.p. Online: http://stopthedrugwar.org/chronicle/2010/may/14/prohibition_drug_war_failure_ass.

Snodgrass, Klyne R. *Stories With Intent: A Comprehensive Guide to the Parables of Jesus.* Grand Rapids: Eerdmans, 2008.

Soering, Jens. *The Church of the Second Chance: A Faith-Based Approach to Prison Reform.* New York: Lantern, 2008.

Stephan, James J. "Census of State and Federal Correctional Facilities, 2005." Bureau of Justice Statistics report. October 2008. Online: http://www.bjs.gov/content/pub/pdf/csfcf05.pdf.

Substance Abuse and Mental Health Services Administration. "Results from the 2008 National Survey on Drug Use and Health: National Findings." September 2009. Online: http://www.oas.samhsa.gov/nsduh/2k8nsduh/2k8Results.pdf.

Swanson, Karen. "Faith and Moral Development: A Case Study of a Jail Faith-Based Correctional Education Program." *Journal of Correctional Education* 60/4 (December 2009): 343–58. Online: http://www.thefreelibrary.com/Faith+and+moral+development%3A+a+case+study+of+a+jail+faith-based...-a0224912270.

Taleb, Nassim Nicholas. *The Black Swan: The Impact of the Highly Improbable.* New York: Random House, 2010.

Tarnoff, Ben. *Money-Makers: The Wicked Lives and Surprising Adventures of Three Notorious Counterfeiters.* New York: Penguin, 2011.

Texas Department of Criminal Justice, Volunteer Services. "Handbook for Volunteers." May 2010. Online: http://www.tdcj.state.tx.us/documents/Volunteer_Handbook.pdf.

Tootle, Deborah M. "The Role of Prisons In Rural Development: Do They Contribute to Local Economies?" April 2004. Online: www.realcostofprisons.org/materials/Prisons_as_Rural_Development.pdf.

United States v. Booker, 543 U.S. 220 (2005).

U.S. Department of Justice. "The Violent Crime Control and Law Enforcement Act of 1994." October 24, 1994. Online: https://www.ncjrs.gov/txtfiles/billfs.txt.

Van Ness, Daniel, and Karen Heetderks Strong. *Restoring Justice: An Introduction to Restorative Justice.* Southington, CT: Anderson, 2006.

Visher, Christy A. "Incapacitation and Crime Control: Does a 'Lock 'Em Up' Strategy Reduce Crime?" *Justice Quarterly* 4/4 (December 1987): 513–43. Online: http://www.tandfonline.com/doi/abs/10.1080/07418828700089511#preview.

Von Drehle, David. "What's Behind America's Falling Crime Rate." *Time*, February 22, 2010. Online: http://www.time.com/time/magazine/article/0,9171,1963761,00.html#ixzz1zWIPuU2O.

Waco Herald-Tribune. "A New Jail in McLennan County—But No Inmates to Fill It." April 23, 2010. Online: http://www.nonewjail.com/Home/Around_the_country.html.

Wagner, Peter. "Crime & Punishment in the U.S.: The Roots of Crime?" Prison Policy Initiative report, 2003. Online: http://www.prisonpolicy.org/prisonindex/rootsofcrime.html.

Walker, Samuel. *Popular Justice: A History of American Criminal Justice.* New York: Oxford University Press, 1998.

Walton, Reggie B. "The National Prison Rape Elimination Commission Report." June 2009. Online: http://cybercemetery.unt.edu/archive/nprec/20090820155502/http://nprec.us/files/pdfs/NPREC_FinalReport.PDF.

Weinstein, Corey, and Eric Cummins. "The Crime of Punishment: Pelican Bay Maximum Security Prison." ThirdWorldTraveler.com, 1996. Online: http://www.thirdworldtraveler.com/Prison_System/CrimePunish_Pelican.html.

Williams, Edward Huntington. "Negro Cocaine 'Fiends' New Southern Menace." *New York Times*, February 8, 1914. Online: http://www.druglibrary.org/schaffer/history/negro_cocaine_fiends.htm.

Windham School District. "2011–2012 Budget and Salary Schedule." Online: www.windhamschooldistrict.org/PDF/BB_2012.pdf.

Yoder, Perry B. *Shalom: The Bible's Word for Salvation, Justice, and Peace.* Nappanee, IN: Evangel, 1987.

Zehr, Howard. *The Little Book of Restorative Justice.* Intercourse, PA: Good Books, 2002.

Subject/Name Index